Second Cities

SECOND CITIES

Globalization and Local Politics in
Manchester and Philadelphia

JEROME I. HODOS

TEMPLE UNIVERSITY PRESS   PHILADELPHIA

TEMPLE UNIVERSITY PRESS
Philadelphia, Pennsylvania 19122
www.temple.edu/tempress

Library of Congress Cataloging-in-Publication Data

Hodos, Jerome I. (Jerome Isaac), 1967–
 Second cities : globalization and local politics in Manchester and Philadelphia /
Jerome I. Hodos.
   p. cm.
 Includes bibliographical references and index.
 ISBN 978-1-4399-0231-8 (cloth : alk. paper) — ISBN 978-1-4399-0233-2 (e-book)
 1. Cities and towns—England—Manchester—Case studies. 2. Urbanization—
England—Manchester—Case studies. 3. Globalization—England—Manchester—
Case studies. 4. Cities and towns—Pennsylvania—Philadelphia—Case studies.
5. Urbanization—Pennsylvania—Philadelphia—Case studies. 6. Globalization—
Pennsylvania—Philadelphia—Case studies. I. Title.
 HT133.H63 2011
 307.7609427'33—dc22

                                                                    2010042419

Printed in the United States of America

2 4 6 8 9 7 5 3 1

For my father,
who has had more influence on this book
than he knows

Contents

List of Tables and Figures

TABLES

FIGURES

Acknowledgments

As a child growing up in upstate New York in the 1970s, I remember watching the film version of the musical *Hair* with my family—it was one of my mother's favorites. Little did I know at the time that I would eventually travel "across the Atlantic Sea" to "Manchester, England, England," as the song goes. To make this book possible required the work and assistance of a cast of characters bigger even than that of *Hair*, and I am grateful to them all.

My first and most substantial debt is to my academic advisors—Ewa Morawska, Elijah Anderson, and Doug Massey—who (too long ago) nurtured this project and my intellectual development throughout graduate school. I am deeply grateful for the many conversations we have had, especially those that pushed my thoughts and my work in directions that I would not have pursued on my own. I am also grateful to Mick Gusinde-Duffy, my editor at Temple University Press, who guided this manuscript into its current, final form. These four people are responsible for much of whatever insight lies within these pages.

Second, I am indebted to the institutions that made this study and the research behind it possible. I have been the fortunate recipient of a grant from the School of Arts and Sciences at the University of Pennsylvania, an Otto and Gertrude K. Pollak Summer Research Scholarship from the University of Pennsylvania's Sociology Department (which funded one summer's research in Manchester), the Andrew W. Mellon Foundation's Sawyer Seminar on Globalization and Inequality at Penn in 1997–1998, a National Science Foundation Doctoral Dissertation Improvement Award (proposal number 9972075), and a U.S. Department of Housing and Urban Development Doctoral Dissertation Research Grant (number H-21185SG). I also received a much-needed semester's leave from my current institution, Franklin & Marshall College, to complete the book manuscript. It should be noted that the interpretations and conclusions presented in this study do not necessarily reflect the views of any of my funders (including the U.S. government). Moreover, responsibility for the accuracy of the information and arguments contained herein lies solely with me.

Several agencies provided other kinds of nonfinancial institutional support. The most important was an honorary visiting fellowship at the University of Manchester's Sociology Department, which afforded me an office and access to a computer and to the university's excellent library collections; without these privileges the research would not have been possible. I am extremely grateful to Mike Savage, then head of the department; to Steve Quilley for a consultation about sources; and to the late and much-missed Rosemary Mellor, who allowed me to use her office. In addition, of necessity, historical sociologists lean heavily on the librarians and archivists who devote their time and energy to helping us poor sods find our obscure materials. I received invaluable professional assistance from the staff at the University of Pennsylvania's libraries, the University of Manchester library and the Manchester Central Reference Library, the Franklin & Marshall College library, the Free Library of Philadelphia, Temple University's Urban Archives, and Philadelphia's excellent collection of independent, nonuniversity libraries and historical collections. I am grateful to John Svatek for his excellent work in turning the maps and other graphics into publication-ready art and to Marcy Dubroff for the author photo.

I am also grateful to the following organizations for their permission to reprint various materials: American Premier Underwriters, Inc., and Mr. Jay Gohman, for the map of the Pennsylvania Railroad system in Figure 6.1; Mr. Douglas Wornom, for the Pennsylvania Railroad advertisement in Figure 6.2; Temple University Press, for material in the Chapter 7 discussion of the history of the Centennial Exhibition and Philadelphia politics, from Jerome Hodos, "The 1876 Centennial in Philadelphia: Elite Networks and Political Culture," in *Social Capital in the City*, edited by Richardson Dilworth, 19–39 (Philadelphia: Temple University Press, 2006); and *City and Community* and the American Sociological Association for material in Chapters 1, 3, 4, and 7, from Jerome Hodos, "Globalization and the Concept of the Second City," *City and Community* 6, no. 4 (December 2007): 315–333.

Third, I am indebted to those colleagues and friends who, at various times, offered helpful comments on or questions about different parts of the work as it progressed. David Schuyler very kindly agreed to read the entire manuscript. The searching criticisms and comments from the anonymous reviewers for Temple University Press have made this a much better book. Among those who read chapters or sections are Michael Katz, Dave Grazian, Joel Eigen, Richard Dilworth, Elaine Simon, David A. Smith, Randall Collins, Harold Bershady, Tonya Taylor, Susan Watkins, Scott Frickel, Kristen Harol, Patricia Stern, Doug Anthony, and Scott Schaffer. I am also grateful for comments from colleagues and audience members at a range of venues where I presented early versions of some of the material, including the American Sociological Association's annual conferences, the Social Science History Association's conferences, the European Social Science History Conference, the International Conference on Globalization and Identities, the Manchester Metropolitan University, the Second Cities conference at the University of Glasgow, the Urban Studies Program and the Sociology Department at the University of Pennsylvania, and Franklin & Marshall College.

Finally, I have been blessed with communities of spirited but sympathetic intellectual companionship throughout my life. Above all, I could not wish for a better, smarter friend than Siddhartha Mitter. I am grateful to him for our wide-ranging conversations about almost everything, for discussions that helped clarify the differences between the planning efforts in Chapters 6 and 7, and for his excellent editing skills. I feel lucky to have found a congenial, supportive, collegial home in the Sociology Department at Franklin & Marshall College. I have benefited from the support—always critical but also always helpful—of colleagues in the United States, including Misty Bastian, Eliza Reilly, Greg Drevenstedt, Jon Mote, Elaine Simon, Laura Carpenter, and Ed Gallagher. Also deserving of recognition for their companionship and commentary are friends and colleagues from Manchester, including Talja Blokland, Will Gibson, Monica Tanaka, Darren O'Byrne, Joanne Britton, the late Derek Wynne, and Sandra Trienekens. For all involved, this book affords only a partial repayment of their investment of time, kindness, and mentoring, but I hope that they will lay responsibility for its weaknesses with me—where it belongs—and take credit for its strengths.

Second Cities

1

Introduction

Globalization, Urbanization, and the Second City

In 1946 the victorious powers of World War II deliberated over where to house the prospective United Nations. Philadelphia was one of the finalists for the permanent headquarters, together with San Francisco and New York. The city based its argument explicitly on global considerations, including international travel times and the city's historic role as a center of liberty. The Pennsylvania and Delaware governments offered official motions of support, and the Pennsylvania legislature authorized the federal government to take city land for the site. In early December, on the first vote, Philadelphia tied for first with San Francisco, winning support from the United Kingdom, the Soviet Union, and India, among others. On December 11, however, John D. Rockefeller announced his willingness to donate land in New York City, between Forty-second and Forty-eighth streets; this changed several delegates' minds, and the next day New York won the final vote, 33 to 7 with 6 abstentions. Philadelphia had once again lost a global city function to New York, repeating its earlier losses of the first half of the 1800s.[1]

The story of how the United Nations ended up in New York City instead of Philadelphia demonstrates many of the themes of this book and provides one answer to the question of why, in an era of globalization, one should study cities. The story suggests, first, that globalization as a process is older than we often think; it goes back decades, if not centuries. Second, it shows that cities like Philadelphia, which we do not ordinarily associate with globalization, can make credible claims to being globally engaged and integrated. Simultaneously, however, the story of how the United Nations was located in New York City suggests both that the number of global cities is limited and that moving up in the global urban system is a rare occurrence. Most cities might be better off trying to define an alternate pathway to global integration than striving to copy or dislodge a global city like New York or London. Third, it implies that cities and their residents can and do organize to pursue their own interests on a global scale. In the process they become agents of globalization, helping to further it. Fourth, and perhaps most important, it demonstrates the intimate connection between globalization and urbanization. Despite widespread claims that globalization liberates people from the chains of geography, globalization is a profoundly urban process.

These may seem like counterintuitive propositions. Skepticism about the relevance of urban studies and the future of cities is widespread. After all, many people maintain that globalization facilitates the abolition of space. The past forty years have witnessed dramatic changes in the world economy and in people's interconnectedness. Technologies like satellite communications, computer networking, and rapid air travel mean that any activity can be located anywhere. Electronic financial transactions circle the globe in the blink of an eye, jobs leave one country for another, workers move thousands of miles in search of employment, immigrants videoconference with distant family members, and the latest songs, films, and performances draw audiences perpetually in search of the next trend. This is what we call globalization: a process of increasing interconnectedness and increasing awareness of the world as a single place.[2] These developments pose challenges on multiple levels: for individuals, they bring threats to personal well-being and to one's sense of identity; for societies, they bring new risks to security and social cohesion; and for social science, they raises questions about the relevance of our ideas and theories. For all, globalization forces us to rethink how we understand the world and our place in it.

In fact, cities are not in any sense disappearing; rather, the world is urbanizing at an incredible pace. The global urban population is increasing at a rate of more than seventy million people per year, and in 2007, for the first time ever, more than 50 percent of the human race lived in cities. Not only can these changes be profoundly disorienting—the inflow or outflow of migrants, the flooding of a peaceful village with new consumer products or "dangerous" political and social ideas, the storms of both high-rise and informal construction in rapidly growing areas, the threat of layoffs from a new and distant company owner—but they also seem contradictory. How are we to make sense of this simultaneous rise of an ever more urbanized population together with space-demolishing technologies?

The answer, perhaps paradoxically, is that globalization actually makes cities more important. Globalization, in the simplest conceptualization, is a process with two main components. It frees people, goods, capital, and information to circulate around the world more easily and swiftly, especially across borders. Also, it increases people's consciousness of the world as a whole, demonstrating how distant factors shape and have ramifications for a person's own actions. But neither of these components implies that social life loses its grounding in space. The flows of goods, people, information, and capital that constitute globalization are all processes that happen in and through space; they must travel through some set of channels, between points or nodes, along trade routes, cables, and satellite networks.

Indeed, globalization is not so much an overcoming or abolition of space as it is a restructuring of how and where people, ideas, and things flow in space. Understood this way, globalization does not at all make space irrelevant. Instead, it reorganizes how places are connected to or disconnected from one another, and it changes the preexisting relationships between places and the channels that permit things to flow in space. What the social theorist Anthony Giddens calls the "disembedding" of things and relationships from immediate copresence is only half of the story. The other half is a process of "re-embedding," in which other social relations are pinned down to specific times and places. In other words, each time globalization pushes people or activities to disconnect from a place, it also pushes them to establish a connection to a different place—a new home, a school, the faraway factory where one's shoes or tools are now made.[3]

In response to these transformations, many people and places wish to "hold down the global"—to capture some of these worldwide flows for themselves. Devising effective strategies to do so is, of course, risky and often difficult, but it is important to recognize that globalization is about the establishment of new connections as much as it is about the disruption of old ones. The inherently spatial nature of these breaking and establishing processes helps us understand why cities are important. Cities are critical sites for holding down the global. They are central nodes in the economic, cultural, and political flows that constitute globalization.[4] As nodes, cities concentrate social interactions and are the sources of innovations, new ideas, culture, and power. In addition, cities act as transformers, increasing the density, speed, and reach of sociospatial networks. Thus, they are the most important places for organizing and producing globalization, and an adequate understanding of globalization makes cities more, not less, important.

But not all cities experience or participate in globalization in the same way. This book is about how two cities in particular—Philadelphia, Pennsylvania, and Manchester, England—have engaged with globalization. Philadelphia and Manchester are not necessarily the sorts of places that first come to mind when one thinks of vibrant, globally engaged metropolises, but they both have been deeply integrated in global systems of trade, migration, and cultural innovation for more than two centuries. Moreover, their patterns of global integration have been strikingly similar, and they have developed along comparable paths. In this book I analyze how Manchester and Philadelphia, in the early nineteenth century, came to be second cities (the particular pattern of global integration each adopted) and how each struggled to maintain that position across successive historical periods and against challenges from other cities. Understanding these events, however, requires situating the experiences of Manchester and Philadelphia within the main currents of thinking and writing about globalization and cities.

Second Cities, Global Cities, and the World City Hypothesis

A number of scholars have argued that cities are the key sites for globalization. In particular, these scholars have detailed the roles played by the largest, most economically central cities—*world*, or *global*, cities, like Paris and Tokyo. According to the "world city hypothesis" (WCH), global cities are principally defined as economic coordinating nodes in the world capitalist system—the nerve centers of global capitalism. Exactly which activities or sectors count as constitutive of the global city varies across accounts, but the crucial functions typically include some mix of corporate headquarters; finance, insurance, and real estate (FIRE); and advanced producer services, like law, accounting, advertising, and architecture. The sociologist Saskia Sassen has done the most to offer a comprehensive definition. She wrote about a "new strategic role for major cities" centered specifically on the producer services. The main versions of the WCH, however, have many features in common.[5] They typically stress the following:

- The spread of capitalism as the most important causal force for urban change
- Global cities as sites for leading economic functions (and therefore the exercise of economic power): corporate headquarters, finance, and other producer services
- The crystallization of a global urban hierarchy through the functional specialization and differentiation of cities, with the implication that inequalities between cities or regions grow
- The role of global cities as magnets for international migration
- An increase in inequality within global cities caused by the growth of global city functions (this inequality sometimes produces social or political conflict)

Analytically, there are two main principles for defining the set of global cities. The first principle is a functional one: there is a worldwide division of labor among cities, and global cities specialize in certain critical activities.

All definitions of the global city rely to some extent on this principle, whether they focus on corporate headquarters, producer services, or global finance as the key activity. The financial sector, however—the most internationalized industry of all—plays a particularly important role. In fact, the set of global cities is substantially similar to the sites of the world's major stock, commodities, and financial markets; the presence of an international capital market appears to be a sufficient if not always a necessary criterion for global city status.[6] The second principle is hierarchical: the distribution of power across cities is fundamentally unequal. Most analysts see the international urban system as explicitly hierarchical, with the global cities that concentrate and house the most important activities also exercising dominance over activities in other cities. In other words, the operation of the first principle produces the second principle as a consequence.

Because globalization concentrates economic power rather than disperses it, global cities are few in number; even in the broadest definitions, only a few dozen exist. In the United States, in addition to New York, there are Los Angeles and Chicago, with frequent mentions of Miami, San Francisco, and Washington, D.C., as well; in the United Kingdom, only London qualifies. The Globalization and World Cities project (GaWC) at Loughborough University in Leicestershire, England, for example, has used a network analysis of international linkages in the producer service industries (accounting, law, advertising, and finance) to identify a set of fifty-five world cities.[7]

This vision of concentrated power is consistent with most WCH writers' reliance on the world-systems theory of Immanuel Wallerstein—a theory of global-scale inequality—as their major intellectual frame.[8] World-systems theory takes the historical *longue durée* of capitalism—over a span of five centuries or more—as central, and explicitly argues that globalization is not a new phenomenon. The "modern world-system" originated in the "long sixteenth century" and involved the simultaneous formation of nation-states and global cities, the expansion of colonial rule, and the systematic institution of "core" and "periphery" economic roles. Cities like London, Paris, and New York have had global city roles (including in finance) for far longer than just a few decades, and most of the foundations of the current global urban system were laid in the nineteenth century, if not before. The global urban network per se is not a new development, although its shape and some of its dynamics may have changed.

But not all cities can be global cities; only a limited number can reach such an elevated position. I call Manchester and Philadelphia *second cities* precisely to point up the differences that separate them from the global cities. Second cities are the kinds of places people used to call provincial capitals. They have persistent, ongoing global interaction—they are globally integrated nodes—across several social spheres. They have significant relations with global and other cities all over the world, not just within their own countries. They differ sharply, however, from global cities. Their characteristic fields of global prominence include manufacturing and the economy in general, international migration, cultural innovation, and production, but not international finance; this lack of an international financial sector or market is one of the main factors that separates second cities from global cities. They also engage in repeated efforts to build transportation infrastructure to enhance their global connections, and, very importantly, gradually elaborate a specifically second city urban identity through giant cultural planning projects. Manchester and Philadelphia, therefore, are not just global cities in miniature, or global cities "lite"; they represent the second city as a historical alternative to the "global city" path.

I first encountered the phrase "second city" as a technical term in the economist Peter Karl Kresl's work on regional trade liberalization schemes. Kresl originally applied the term to Chicago and Toronto, and then he expanded it to include places such as Buffalo. His definitional criteria, however, were vague: second cities had some concentration of corporate headquarters but were economically subordinate to the first or global cities in their national economies. The regional economist Ann Markusen, with her collaborators, refined this idea into the concept of the "second-tier" city: medium-sized cities with vibrant economies that have grown rapidly in the past several decades.[9] In the chapters that follow, I join this notion of the second city explicitly to globalization theory and reframe the second city as an expansion and elaboration of the WCH; Philadelphia and Manchester are globally integrated even though they are not "global cities" per se. There is thus no single answer to the question of how cities "go global"; rather, there are multiple developmental pathways to global integration.

In addition to emphasizing the patterns of interconnection and exchange that characterize global integration, the WCH also stresses that globalization has characteristic effects on urban social life. In particular, the process of globalization significantly increases inequality and polarization, both between and within cities. In terms of polarization between cities, the clear assumption in much of the discussion about global cities (which we might call the "peripheralization hypothesis") is that as global cities enjoy a relative increase in their power, other places are progressively marginalized. Such cities therefore suffer declines in economic well-being and prestige as a result of globalization. Saskia Sassen makes this claim explicitly: "Alongside these new global and regional hierarchies of cities . . . [a] multiplicity of formerly important manufacturing centers and port cities have lost functions and are in decline." Another hypothesis suggests, however, that globalization entails new opportunities for nonglobal cities. The recent and increasing openness of national urban systems gives greater latitude for direct international linkages on the part of lesser cities. Donald Lyons and Scott Salmon, for example, argue that the erosion of nation-state borders brought on by globalization is dispersing "global control potential" to some cities lower down in the urban hierarchy. In other words, global flows may pass around global cities as well as through them.[10] The difficulty is that very little existing scholarship has actually examined "nonglobal" cities explicitly or analyzed what alternate pathways of globalization might exist. The notion of the second city is one way to fill that broad space between the global city and the hopelessly marginalized city, thereby extending the reach of global city theory to new places. It enables a more complex and fully elaborated understanding of the global urban system than we have so far been able to capture or describe.

Within cities, the WCH argues, the growth of globally active firms and industries produces inequality in two main ways. First, these firms and industries typically have a bifurcated wage structure, with lots of high-wage and low-wage jobs but few middle-income ones. Second, the combination of high-wage workers and immigration leads to a rapid growth in low-wage and informal-sector service work at the lower end of the labor market, as elite professionals increase the demand for restaurants, document delivery, doormen, dog walkers, and a whole range of personal services. Furthermore, in global cities one sees these extremes of wealth and poverty right next to each other, in glaring juxtaposition. This within-city inequality is also true of Philadelphia and Manchester, but with a twist: inequality in these cities is shaped by their distinctive migration patterns, so that inequality plays out at least as much on racial, ethnic, and religious dimensions as along class lines (I discuss class and ethnic/racial inequality in Chapters 3 and 4). These two kinds of inequality, between places and within places, are just as important in Manchester and Philadelphia as in global cities, but they manifest differently.

Manchester and Philadelphia

I chose Manchester and Philadelphia for two main reasons: I wanted American and British cases, in order to mirror the overwhelming focus on New York and London in the globalization and cities literature. I also deliberately chose the oldest, earliest second cities, in order to give the longest historical perspective possible. The two cities started out in the seventeenth century in very different places, and through the turn of the nineteenth century they seemed to be becoming increasingly different from each other. But by the early nineteenth century that pattern shifted, and they started becoming increasingly alike. This occurred during a widespread era of structural change that reconfigured the global urban hierarchy: Manchester's rise implied the decline of Dhaka, Bangladesh, and other older textile centers; Philadelphia switched positions with New York; and manufacturing cities in general displaced many commercial centers. This process of growing similarity, or convergence, has continued ever since. Manchester and Philadelphia have managed to maintain their positions as globally integrated second cities for nearly two hundred years. Indeed, globalization implies that cities come to resemble one another primarily because they fulfill similar global functions or roles, not because they are located in the same country. We should expect, therefore, that the global cities may have more in common with one another than with other cities in their respective countries, and the same goes for second cities.

This concern with longevity also helps answer a particular question: why not Chicago? Chicago for much of its history developed as one of the world's archetypal industrial cities, with an economic base in commerce and in transforming the raw materials of its extensive western hinterland. It was a transport and communications center, and it drew in both domestic and international migrants by the tens of thousands. Its role as the home of the Chicago School of Sociology and of modern architecture, particularly the invention of the skyscraper, made it a center for innovation in global culture. And it claimed the title "second city" for itself after the census of 1890, when it surpassed Philadelphia in the U.S. population rankings. But it is widely acknowledged that Chicago has in the past several decades ascended out of the ranks of second cities and become a global city. Not surprisingly, the key factor in the city's ascension is its international financial role as the center of the world commodities and futures markets, via the Chicago Mercantile Exchange. Significantly, Chicago first began losing its second city characteristics during the deindustrialization of the post–World War II era. Chicago's global reach was secured in recent decades with the emergence of the city's financial sector as a real driver of urban development. In other words, Chicago traded second city status for global city status, a transformation not unlike that of Toronto or Sydney at the same time. This transformation introduced several complications that made it difficult to focus on what was specific to second cities.[11]

Philadelphia was founded in 1682 by William Penn, the proprietor of colonial Pennsylvania. Manchester is much older but was only a minor market town with a small population before 1700. The two cities' historical trajectories have also been remarkably similar, as evidenced by their overall patterns of population change. Table 1.1 shows the history of population change in both cities and their surrounding regions. Manchester's population describes an arc, from about 300,000 in 1851, up to 714,000 in 1911, and down to almost 400,000 in 2001.[12] Philadelphia's population shows evidence of a similar arc, but over a longer timescale, and its population decline in recent decades has not been as marked. Both cities' peak growth rates had ended by 1850, and they had become very large cities. They started to empty out in the 1950s; Manchester has lost about one-third of its population since World War II, and Philadelphia has lost more than one-fourth.

The similarities between them extended to their economies and their status as regional centers. In the nineteenth century Philadelphia and Manchester were two of the world's most prominent industrial metropolises; in

TABLE 1.1   POPULATION CHANGE: SELECT YEARS, 1850–2001
(IN THOUSANDS)

		Manchester			
Year	City	GMC	City as %	Region	City as %
1851	303	574	52.8	1,655	18.3
1891	505	2,155	23.4	3,507	14.4
1911	714	2,638	27.1	4,281	16.7
1951	703	2,716	25.9	4,642	15.1
1971	544	2,729	19.9	4,940	11.0
1991	405	2,499	16.2	4,840	8.4
2001	393	2,482	15.8	4,762	8.3

	Philadelphia		
Year	City	PMSA	City as %
1850	409	703	58.2
1890	1,047	1,580	66.3
1910	1,549	2,268	68.3
1950	2,072	3,671	56.4
1970	1,950	4,818	40.5
1990	1,586	4,857	32.7
2000	1,518	5,101	29.8

Sources: Great Britain, *Census of Great Britain in 1851* (London: Longman, Brown, Green, and Longmans, 1854); Great Britain, Office of Population Censuses and Surveys, *Census of England and Wales* (London: HMSO, 1891, 1913, 1953, 1973, 1991); Great Britain, Office for National Statistics, *Census of England and Wales* (London: HMSO, 2001); U.S. Bureau of the Census, *Compendium of the Seventh Census* (Washington: AOP Nicholson, 1854); U.S. Census Office, *Ninth Census of the United States, 1870* (Washington, DC: GPO, 1872), and *Tenth Census of the United States, 1880* (Washington, DC: GPO, 1883); U.S. Department of Commerce, Bureau of the Census, *Census of Population and Housing* (Washington, DC: Government Printing Office, 1892, 1914, 1952, 1972, 1984a, 1992, 2001).

Note: In 1850 Philadelphia numbers are for Philadelphia County. The Philadelphia PMSA (primary metropolitan statistical area) includes Philadelphia plus the suburban counties of Bucks, Chester, Delaware, Montgomery, Burlington, Camden, and Gloucester. The GMC is the ten-municipality Greater Manchester Council, consisting of Manchester plus Bolton, Bury, Oldham, Rochdale, Salford, Stockport, Tameside, Trafford, and Wigan. In 1851 the GMC number includes only Bolton, Bury, Manchester, Oldham, Rochdale, Salford, and Wigan, and the regional number includes only Lancashire, minus Liverpool. The Manchester region includes the GMC plus Cheshire and Lancashire counties (but not Liverpool/Merseyside).

fact, each was second only to the global cities in their respective countries. Both were massive centers for the textile industry—Manchester in cotton yarn and cloth and Philadelphia in wool, carpets, lace, hats, and clothing. Manchester was the home of the Industrial Revolution, while Philadelphia was a center of advanced manufacturing, including machining, shipbuilding, and locomotive construction. Both suffered greatly, however, as their manufacturing strength eroded in the middle of the twentieth century. A slow industrial decay was temporarily masked by World War II, but it resumed after the war and reached crisis proportions between 1960 and 1980.

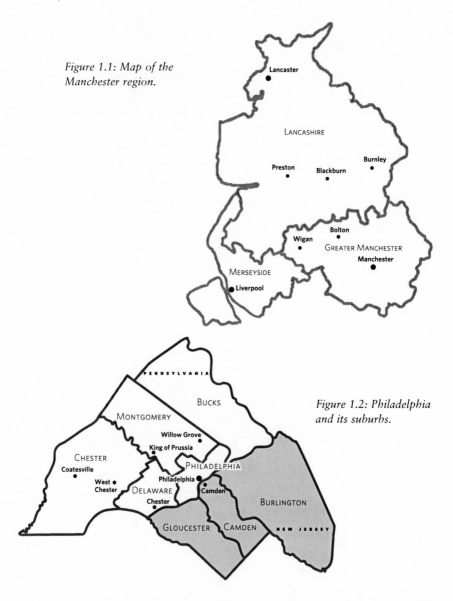

Figure 1.1: Map of the
Manchester region.

Figure 1.2: Philadelphia
and its suburbs.

The two cities have now lost approximately 90 percent of their former manufacturing employment. Starting in these same decades, however, both experienced a massive expansion of service industries, and attempts at rejuvenation by local politicians began only a few years apart in the 1980s.

Both cities have long served as regional hegemons, dominating large hinterlands. Figures 1.1 and 1.2 map the two study regions. One important difference between them is that Manchester has always constituted a minority of its regional population. Manchester's industrial economy, from the beginning, was a regional structure of firms arrayed in surrounding towns with Manchester as the coordinator; as a result, these towns became heavily populated with factories and workers. For two centuries, Manchester has dominated the economies of these surrounding mill towns and has also claimed to be the undisputed "capital of the North" of England. (My definition of the region, as is conventional, excludes Liverpool and its surrounding district of Merseyside.) Philadelphia, on the other hand, for a long time monopolized regional nonagricultural activity, and it was vastly larger and more powerful than any other city in the region. The city lies near the confluence of the Delaware and Schuylkill rivers and historically has integrated nearly the entire watershed of these two rivers. It has also competed with Baltimore for the Susquehanna River watershed in central Pennsylvania. The city sent tentacles of control out to Trenton, New Jersey; Wilmington, Delaware; and the Pennsylvania towns of Bethlehem, Reading, and Lancaster, as well as to the southern New Jersey shore. The fact that the city's hinterland lies in three states—New Jersey, Delaware, and Pennsylvania—but fully encompasses none, has complicated issues of politics and governance.

In both cities an existing literature, extending back to the nineteenth century, analyzes their economies, histories, and political cultures. Manchester's political and economic success—and more particularly, its triumphalist arrogance regarding its own virtues—spawned a substantial tradition of critical analysis. J. P. Kay, who studied the city after the cholera epidemic of 1832, was Manchester's first social critic and investigator. He pointed out the importance of poverty and neighborhood environmental conditions for public health. And of course, in *Hard Times* there was Dickens's thinly veiled Coketown, the city whose bricks "would have been red if the smoke and ashes had allowed it," with its portrait of Josiah Bounderby, the new middle-class man who would have everyone "discard the word Fancy altogether" in favor of "nothing but fact." But the city's most famous critic is undoubtedly Friedrich Engels, who lambasted the smoke, noise, and foul rivers; the deplorable living conditions of workers in general and the Irish in particular; and the habits of greed and willful neglect practiced by the wealthy.[13]

In the modern era the local interpretation of deindustrialization and postindustrialism has focused on the nearly two-centuries-long hegemony of free-market liberalism. These writers are critical of the ideologies of liberalism and neoliberalism, but they see liberal ideas ascendant everywhere in local politics. Despite a strong local union movement stretching back at least to the 1820s, labor's interests rarely carried the day or drove local politics and policy. Instead, liberalism fostered a disregard for poverty and inhuman living conditions in the mid-nineteenth century, and it encouraged the export of capital overseas rather than reinvestment in modernizing domestic production in the late nineteenth century. Liberalism's ideological hegemony produced few benefits for the majority and gave too much priority to the market. More recently, a neoliberal rapprochement with capital by the Labour Party's political managers gutted social benefits in favor of a boosterist economic development policy that stressed interurban competition. Relatively autonomous local politicians have done capital's bidding because the old left-wing political coalition fell apart, and neoliberalism turned out to be a discursive and political project that could (at least weakly) unite a new set of constituencies.[14] In the end, however, most of these critics offer a grudging appreciation for what Manchester achieved in the 1990s, in the wake of its crisis of the 1970s and 1980s: "Manchester has at least been able to engender the trappings (if not the substance) of a postindustrial economic project: telematics, a significant international airport, a 'successful' Olympic bid, a degree of growth/agglomeration in the financial and advanced services."[15]

The Philadelphia school of interpretation has been concerned above all with the relationship between elite leadership (or its failure) and the functioning of the local state, conceived variously as corruption, privatism, elite withdrawal, or fragmentation.[16] It argues that the mechanisms of the local state and local politics have been enduringly dysfunctional and thus that even in times of one-party control (much of the city's history) there has been no effective ideology that could push either a class or a collective universal interest forward. For E. Digby Baltzell, the Quaker withdrawal from politics in the eighteenth century combined with Philadelphia's extraordinary early wealth to create an insular, aristocratic elite that persisted in enjoying its privileges even as it abdicated public leadership. The divide between the social elite and the economic leadership produced a dysfunctional polity in which the local state served no one's interests well. Sam Bass Warner Jr., by contrast, argued that members of Philadelphia's elite had the dominant political economic ideology they wanted—a capitalist, utilitarian, and profoundly instrumental ideology that he called "privatism." In practice, however, this ideology led to incompetent governance, in large part because it confined government to fostering wealth creation by individuals and to preventing infringement of property rights. "Such political failures would be repeated over and over again in Philadelphia's later history. . . . No urban, economic democracy emerged with time because the popular goal of Philadelphia was the individual race for wealth."[17]

More recently, Carolyn Adams and her coauthors have placed much of the responsibility for the city's late-twentieth-century difficulties on deindustrialization and the evaporation of the economic "glue" that formerly held the city together.[18] But they also have reinvigorated the older tradition of political critique, arguing that such economic difficulties require effective political responses and that the city's political leaders have squabbled among themselves instead of cooperating on workable solutions. On this interpretation the Philadelphia elite and city government generally have lacked the political will and leadership necessary to defend the city's collective best interests, and thus the city's success has come despite rather than because of their efforts.

These schools are not simply critiques, however; each school is intimately tied to the particular historical trajectories, in the eighteenth and early nineteenth centuries, by which Manchester and Philadelphia came to occupy second position. The belief in the political effectiveness of liberalism in Manchester, for example, even when that effectiveness is being criticized, once again represents "the triumph of liberalism" as the city's historic political culture. The same is true for Philadelphia: the analytical focus on elite withdrawal and state weakness does not stand apart from the city's political culture as an objective, outside assessment, but embodies and even reinscribes the city's declensionist self-understanding. The different contents of Philadelphia's and Manchester's identities as second cities thus are intimately connected to their different historical pathways. The ways in which Mancunians and Philadelphians found themselves embedded in global processes long ago, and the actions they took to leverage that embeddedness to their own advantage, profoundly shaped the course of their development.

The Argument of the Book

The chapters that follow are divided into two overarching themes. Chapters 2 through 5 show how both cities came to occupy second position in the early nineteenth century and how they have been situated in global flows of capital, goods, people, and ideas ever since. These chapters detail the connections Philadelphia and Manchester have had to other cities and countries around the globe, both in terms of flows and organizational ties. The dominant theme is that these cities, rather than being marginalized or excluded, have long been fully active participants in global society across a range of dimensions. These chapters also compare and contrast Manchester's and Philadelphia's patterns of global integration with the global city pattern, to demonstrate the distinctiveness of the second city's role.

Chapter 2 analyzes each city's pathway or entry into second city status, between 1770 and 1840, when a structural shift in the international urban hierarchy led a new group of cities to emerge into "second" roles. Manchester and Philadelphia were two of the most important of this new crop, but they arrived at second position by different routes. Manchester rose into second city position from obscurity by means of industrial production and what we usually call the Industrial Revolution. Philadelphia became a second city industrial powerhouse following the loss of global city functions, particularly with the eclipse of the city's financial industry, and thus its entry into second city position was one of decline; it was during this period that New York replaced Philadelphia as America's global city.

Chapters 3 through 5 describe Manchester's and Philadelphia's positions in global flows and activities. Chapter 3 discusses economic patterns, including industrial concentrations, corporate headquarters, foreign direct investment (FDI), and international transportation links. Manchester and Philadelphia have continuously been active economic nodes in international networks of trade and industry, integrated as both locations for headquarters and sites for branch plants. The chapter makes use of a specially constructed database of international corporate hierarchies in order to demonstrate the two cities' global integration. Each city specialized in two or three of the leading industries of an era; historically, each city's economy was more focused on manufacturing than the global cities' economies were, and, significantly, each lacked an internationally oriented financial sector. Philadelphia and Manchester, over time, developed large firms and overall concentrations in selected advanced service industries, particularly in "meds and eds"—health care and higher education.[19] Figure 1.3, for example, shows the impact of Philadelphia's transition toward services on the city's skyline. The two cities have also faced recurring needs for restructuring, or economic diversification, and their failure or success at achieving such restructuring has been one of the main factors that determined whether they maintained their second city position over time.

Chapter 4 clarifies the distinctive migration patterns to these cities. Where global cities are correctly thought of as magnets for very large and diverse streams of international migration, Philadelphia and Manchester

Figure 1.3: The Philadelphia skyline.

have been migration centers in a distinctive way. First, sources for international migration concentrate in just a few countries (precisely which source countries they concentrate in varies by geography, historical precedent, and other factors). This pattern of selective international migration contrasts sharply with both popular and scholarly accounts of global cities. Second, internal migration is relatively more important for these two cities; as regional powerhouses and hegemons, they have large hinterlands and continuously draw a large stream of domestic migrants. Furthermore, this internal migration is often rural-to-urban migration by people from an ethnically distinct background, usually from rural or agricultural areas in decline. These communities of domestic or internal migrants persist for decades and bring more diversity to these cities than they would otherwise possess. The point is not that these cities lack immigrant populations altogether—a circumstance that would argue against the cities' involvement in global networks. The point is rather that the participation of Philadelphia and Manchester in global society is selective and specialized; they have many migrants but few migrant communities.

Chapter 5 shows how Manchester and Philadelphia have been crucial sites for innovation and production of global culture. Their contributions to global culture tend to occur in political ideologies, in the professions, and in claims to codify new knowledge or expertise—in fields such as medicine, theories of economic development, or management. By contrast, the "pull" of global cities as centers for pop culture production, and their essential role in high-culture production, creates real difficulties for places like Manchester and Philadelphia in terms of developing critical masses of cultural producers in these fields. It is almost as if they are cultural centers for the "middle class," including the cultural codes and practices that define and organize middle-class life. These cultural innovations and specializations tend to be notably pragmatic, utilitarian, or even self-serving. Precisely because they are "second," and in at least some measure self-conscious of this second position, people in Manchester and Philadelphia tend to focus more on cultural contributions to the world as a whole that assist them in competing with other cities. Residents' second city consciousness thus plays out not simply in the struggle for material or economic capital and position, but also in the struggle for symbolic capital and position.

The remaining chapters (Chapters 6 through 8) analyze how the two cities have tried to bolster or maintain their global positions through repeated efforts at transportation planning and creating cultural projects. Further, these chapters put the cities in motion by describing the political coalitions that engaged in these efforts. The key theme in this latter part of the book is what I call "municipal foreign policy" (MFP): the efforts of cities, particularly city governments or the local state, to take action on their own behalf in search of greater global integration and global prominence or recognition. They seek not only to foster increased global connectivity but also to shape the pattern of international flows to their own benefit—to be masters of their fate. These attempts to shape space are central to their continued prosperity, to the vibrancy of their politics and social life, and even to their self-understanding as cities, regions, and communities. Furthermore, this municipal foreign policy pushes globalization processes forward. By their own actions—especially those in pursuit of deeper global integration—cities make globalization happen.

Manchester and Philadelphia have each exhibited a striking continuity over time, but this continuity has been contingent rather than foreordained. They have periodically renewed or reinvigorated their historic niches and roles in world society. Each city continued to have similar migration patterns, similar responses to competitive threats from other cities, and similar sectoral patterns of economic integration. Both also elaborated over time an increasingly specific sense of themselves as occupying an intermediate or secondary position relative to other cities. Their persistence as second cities happened neither by chance nor by some inexorably structural logic of globalization, however. It required great effort; people in the cities at various points chose courses of action that reinforced or reinvigorated their structural positions. Their continuity thus resulted at least in part from active attempts by city governments and the city elite to pursue increasing global integration.

As a result, the argument here tilts more toward the agency of cities and their residents than is common in the WCH. This is the key causal proposition of the book, and it puts me at odds with more structurally oriented globalization scholars. For these structuralists, economic globalization is an intractable, macro-level force that cities can only adapt to and not shape or influence. Most are deeply critical of the global marketplace, viewing it as a site of coercion and inequality that inevitably leaves large numbers of people—and places—behind. These concerns about the power of globalization to compel adaptation by cities often come paired with a critical attitude toward the economic and political restructuring of the past three decades and the neoliberal ideology that lies behind it. For example, Ash Amin and Nigel Thrift argue that globalization combined with economic restructuring results in the "disorganization of local government" and is "not likely to promise self-reproducing growth at the local level."[20]

I see things differently. My interest here is not so much in deciding whether globalization is good or bad as it is in determining whether our theoretical accounts of it are sufficiently comprehensive. It is not that there is no structure to globalization—indeed, I assume throughout this book that there is an urban hierarchy, and in Chapters 3 to 5 I detail Philadelphia's and Manchester's places in it. But focusing only on the structure and its power over cities is incomplete. Causality in analyses of globalization must be conceptualized as running in both directions. Globalization is not simply a cold, unforgiving structure, and cities are not simply component parts slotted into a global system. Instead, globalization is a process actively pursued (or, as many critics of globalization have pointed out, resisted) by groups of people who consciously attempt to restructure the world's economic and social space in order to bolster their own positions and who, through their actions, have the opportunity to alter where the nodes and flows are located.

Consideration of local state agency, therefore, has to be a part of the analytical and theoretical picture we paint of how globalization works; it is necessary for the purpose of closing the analytical circle.[21] Municipal foreign policy is perhaps the most important kind of local action that occurs at a global scale and has global consequences. Cities are states in their own right, even though they are subordinated to their national governments. As subordinated states, cities have partially autonomous relations with external actors: transnational corporations, social movements, nongovernmental organizations, other national cities, their own national governments, and other city governments around the world. Of course, we cannot treat city governments as undifferentiated unitary entities. We must pay attention to the shifting patterns of local politics—the conflicts and coalitions among politicians, the economic elite, immigrants, and other groups—that lie behind state actions. It makes sense, however, to treat local governments as collective actors, just as it makes sense to treat other corporations and government entities as actors, although we know their policy decisions were made by people within the groups and coalitions.

Chapter 6 focuses on attempts to improve the cities' *material* position in global flows by means of transportation infrastructure planning. Most major cities repeatedly design global transportation infrastructure projects—airports, railroads, water ports—to enable them to connect more easily with other cities around the world. These projects are the core of MFP and fulfill dual functions: they are explicitly designed to preserve or enhance a city's access to and participation in global flows, and they also, whether intentionally or not, contribute substantially to the city's economic diversification. Such infrastructure projects go far in determining how cities adjust and prosper over time; they are crucial economic development projects, the effects of which reverberate throughout the entire region. They are thus a key to the dynamics of the global urban system, to how cities rise and fall in position and status relative to one another, and to whether they can maintain a position across historical periods. Transport infrastructure also—and by design—reshapes the pattern of global flows and thereby helps constitute globalization. In addition, in Manchester and Philadelphia, transportation projects, although they may have originated with the local elite, were typically pursued or directed by the local state and endorsed by large, diverse political coalitions. The role of the local state repeatedly overshadowed that of private capital, constituting a kind of urban-based mercantilism.

Chapter 7 examines the two cities' efforts to improve their *symbolic* position in global society via the definition of a second city identity and via planning for cultural extravaganzas like world's fairs or the Olympics. Cultural plans of this magnitude entail a simultaneous triple reconstruction of the metropolis: physical (rebuilding sections of the city), political (rebuilding a workable political coalition or regime out of a situation of discord), and symbolic (renarrating a city's identity to emphasize its secondness). Figure 1.4, for example, shows the results of recent attempts to reimagine Manchester's docklands as a site of cultural consumption. It is in particular through these projects that concerns about the global position of the city relative to other cities consciously enter into urban life, and these concerns are the building blocks of a second city identity. The second city identity itself is constructed via several discursive and symbolic strategies: through claims of a glorious past, of superiority over lesser national cities, of equality with an international group of similar provincial capitals, of favorable comparisons with global cities, and sometimes explicitly of being "second." People compare their city with other cities and, through these comparisons, they develop a cultural sense of their own city. The chapter also analyzes the role that these efforts play in reconstructing and shaping urban politics and governance, thereby providing a direct connection between global concerns and local action. Those who engage in such

Figure 1.4: The L. S. Lowry Centre for the Performing Arts at Salford Quays, built on the site of the old Manchester Ship Canal docks.

comparisons are, in particular, civic and political leaders, the economic elite, planners, intellectuals, and the media, but they also crop up in everyday discourse and popular understandings among residents and travelers. Urbanites thus socially construct an image of themselves and their city's place in an urban system through observations of other cities.

In Chapter 8, I consider the broader, macro-level implications of Philadelphia's and Manchester's attempts to shape the course of globalization to their own benefit. Here I ask what other cities count as second cities, how cities rise and fall in position over time, and how the institutional role or significance of the city, relative to the nation-state in particular, is changing as a result of contemporary globalization. Manchester and Philadelphia, in their attempts to capture portions of the growing global traffic and to define their own positions in the global system, actively pursued the increase of cross-border relationships and flows. This fact by itself is not surprising. But the evidence in these two cases clearly points toward a conclusion that is both more incisive and more general: the local state is an actor, with its own interests, carrying out its own foreign relations—or MFP. Very often, this municipal foreign policy explicitly aims at increasing the extent of the city's global integration and thereby furthers the process of globalization in general. By their own actions and by the actions of people in them, therefore, cities are in fact creators, sustainers, and pursuers of globalization. They make globalization happen.

2
The Era of Second City Formation, 1770–1840

> *Our good city of Philadelphia—[i]n twenty years*
> *the Manchester and Lyons of America*
> —Peter Du Ponceau, president of the American
> Philosophical Society, toasting the city in 1829
> (quoted in Russell F. Weigley, ed., *Philadelphia:*
> *A 300-Year History*)

In March 1837 the financial condition of the United States was dangerously overextended. In the course of a real estate boom based on land speculation and westward expansion, loans and bank notes of, at best, dubious value had proliferated. Lured by the prospect of quick profits, many investors rapidly "flipped" properties and borrowed far beyond their capacity to repay, while bigger market participants established poorly capitalized banks that printed their own money and lent it out freely, with little assurance of a borrower's creditworthiness. As President Andrew Jackson left office and his successor Martin Van Buren was sworn in, the rapid cycle of borrowing, lending, and speculation collapsed. The Specie Circular—a federal measure against land speculation mandating that all sales of public lands be paid for in gold and silver rather than the often suspect paper money—together with the government's shifting of its own money out of some banks and into others, forced many lenders to call in their loans to Southern merchant houses. Simultaneously, a fall in the domestic demand for cotton meant that the merchants did not have the cash to cover these debts.

Within days of Van Buren's inauguration, trading houses in New Orleans started to fail. Their inability to pay their bills and debts led houses elsewhere, especially in New York City, to fail as well. Fear and distrust quickly spread to the population at large, and people began to demand the use of gold and silver rather than paper money in all kinds of transactions. As specie drained from bank vaults, and as they were increasingly unable to collect on their loans to merchants and other banks, the banks themselves were forced to suspend specie payments in May: banks in New York suspended specie payments on May 10, followed two days later by Philadelphia, Baltimore, New Haven, Albany, and New Orleans. Within two weeks, the suspension was enforced nationwide.[1]

The Panic of 1837 touched off a transatlantic financial meltdown. The drying up of credit inaugurated a six-year depression in both Britain and the United States, and hardship was widespread in both countries. *Niles' Register* reported that "by September, 1837, nine-tenths of the factories in the eastern states had closed. . . . One-half to two-thirds of the clerks and salesmen in large commercial houses in Philadelphia were without work by June, 1837." British merchants in Liverpool and London who traded with the United States for cotton, unable to receive cotton shipments from New Orleans and therefore unable to meet their own bills, also began to fail. The difficulty in the cotton market, of course, affected Manchester particularly badly. "At Manchester, during the summer of 1837, fifty thousand workers were said to be out of employment, and most of the large establishments were working only half-time." As late as July 1842, the Philadelphia diarist Sidney George Fisher recorded, "The streets seem deserted, the largest houses are shot up and to rent, there is no business, there is no money, no confidence & little hope, property is sold every day by the sheriff at a 4th of the estimated value of a few years ago, nobody can pay debts, the miseries of poverty are felt both by rich & poor, everyone you see looks careworn & haggard." By 1843, more than a third of the banks in the United States had closed, and many states, including Pennsylvania, had repudiated their bond obligations.[2] The economic crisis also stimulated a wave of social and political unrest; the strongest years of the Chartist movement in Lancashire were 1838–1842, and a series of anti-black and Protestant-versus-Catholic riots and disturbances that would last a dozen years in Philadelphia began in 1838.

The Panic of 1837 and the resulting depression both catalyzed and symbolized a deeper set of structural changes in the world economy that affected Manchester and Philadelphia as well. It was a time of upheaval related to the global expansion of European settlement and influence, a worldwide increase of trade and migration, and the rise of industrial capitalism and the transformation of production. It is during these first decades of the nineteenth century that a new division of labor across places emerged among the world's cities and regions. The network of financial, commercial, and production sites was reshuffled, and by the end of the reshuffling period—approximately 1840—the industrial city was a well-recognized category, the railroad had made its appearance, both capitalists and workers were making themselves felt as political forces, and debates over the cultural significance of the social changes wrought by industrialization were well under way. This new global division of labor would last for more than a century.

Manchester and Philadelphia emerged from this reshuffling period as massive industrial cities, specializing in manufacturing and production for world markets, with additional global niche roles in education and professional development. It was thus in these decades that Manchester and Philadelphia came to be second cities. They converged on a structural position in world affairs that was opened by industrialization, increasing trade, and cultural modernization. By the year 1840, both places had "settled" into second city positions, and they were beginning to consolidate their new roles.

They were arriving at the same destination from different starting points, however, and via distinct paths. Their convergence was thus contingent, not foreordained. Manchester's growth continued unabated through the first-third of the nineteenth century and beyond. These decades created in Manchester not only the city's industrial might but also a sense of political and ideological arrival on the part of the middle or bourgeois class. It became the "shock city" of the industrial revolution, and it would reach its years of peak wealth and power in the decades between 1840 and 1870.[3] Philadelphia's experience was more ambiguous. The city achieved its greatest prominence from the years of the American Revolution through approximately 1820. As the United States became more economically and functionally integrated, New York took over the role of international entrepôt, with primary responsibility for global communications and international finance. Philadelphia lost its earlier leadership in these functions. Yet throughout these decades and beyond, the city's population and economy grew at a tremendous rate as it transformed itself into America's first industrial and manufacturing center. Philadelphia's entry into second city status was thus characterized by the paradoxical combination of simultaneous growth and decline. It was precisely those elements of decline, moreover, that would have made Philadelphia into America's first global city.

Origins

Both cities rose to prominence in the eighteenth century from modest origins that gave little indication of the global roles they would later come to play. In the early 1600s Manchester was an unincorporated settlement of three thousand people. Located in the northwest of England, the city lay downstream from the Pennines and other surrounding hills, between the Irk, Irwell, and Medlock rivers, and nearly at the bottom of the large bowl that is Lancashire. Its climate was notoriously wet and rainy, and the region was full of streams and rivers—a nearly ideal location for spinning and weaving fragile cotton threads, although certainly not for growing it. Just below the city, the Irwell flowed into the Mersey, and thence to Liverpool; Manchester's position forty miles inland meant that it had to rely on Liverpool to serve as its main port.[4]

Philadelphia was founded in 1682 as the center of William Penn's Quaker colony of Pennsylvania. Penn's original plans envisioned a "greene country towne" of 10- to 100-acre plots, each with a house built at its center. Thomas Holme, his surveyor, laid out the pattern of five squares that still defines the central area of the city. He platted large, regular blocks extending between the Schuylkill and Delaware rivers, with boundaries at Vine and South (Cedar) streets. In its early decades, however, the city hugged the Delaware River. People of all backgrounds clustered together in a riparian strip only a few blocks deep and extending north and south along the river for a mile in each direction. Southwark, along the city's southern border, became an independent district in 1762, and Northern Liberties in 1771.[5]

By 1720, each town had grown to approximately 10,000 inhabitants and double that number by the 1750s. The two cities also shared a number of additional characteristics—English, Protestant, and mercantile, they partook of what the Quaker historian Frederick Tolles called "the cultural unity of the North Atlantic littoral." One crucial feature of that cultural unity was the catalyzing role played by radical, Dissenting Protestants, who were unhappy with the established Anglican Church. In Lancashire a variety of Dissenting sects took root, including Quakerism and most particularly Unitarianism. Pennsylvania was explicitly designed as a Quaker colony, even though other English, Swedes, and Germans had already settled on farmland in the area.[6]

The radical Protestant milieu in both locations emphasized a set of cultural values that fostered the two cities' later development and that contributed essential elements to their civic cultures. Chief among these values were industriousness, a preference for practicality or utility over idle philosophizing, and the desire for tolerance and openness; each promoted economic success and contributed to a rich civic life. Quakerism stimulated the establishment of an extremely full associational life, in particular of scientific and medical societies (exemplified by Ben Franklin's role as a convener), while Manchester's Liberals made their homes in voluntary clubs and Dissenting churches. Out of such soil would grow the American Philosophical Society and the Manchester Literary and Philosophical Society. In these associations the cities' distinctive cultural values were nurtured and ultimately transformed into globally significant cultural endeavors—science and the professions—merging claims of utility, special knowledge or expertise, and middle-class social status.

Despite their shared status as new and open cities, however, both places remained for a long time politically underdeveloped. Rather than being a chartered or incorporated city, Manchester was a manorial demesne—part of a feudal possession held for centuries by the aristocratic Mosley family. To the extent that it was ruled at all, it was governed by a few police and constables appointed by the lord, a Court-Leet that met several times a year to try cases and resolve disputes, and a magistracy tied both to the lord and to the Collegiate Church (the local Anglican seat). This political structure (or lack of one) distinguished Manchester from other, older English towns, like London and Liverpool, and also from continental centers.[7] The city remained unincorporated until 1838.

Philadelphia's Quakerism proved tolerant and welcoming of outsiders but was profoundly ambivalent about the practice of politics to define any common or collective good. The Society of Friends was pacifist, and strict believers preferred to keep their hands clean of any dealings with the machinery of governance. Still, Pennsylvania was a "Holy Experiment" in Quaker government that lasted for seventy-five years. Most Philadelphia mayors were wealthy Friends, and the Quaker elite served in leading positions on the city council and in the colonial Assembly. But the Quakers abdicated colonial government in 1756 over London's demands for military action and financial support during the French and Indian War. The story of the Quakers is thus partly about the tension between their religious and their social commitments; they bequeathed their ambivalence about governing to the city's political culture.[8]

The energy that town residents failed to put into politics they put into commerce instead. As Max Weber suggested, ascetic religion and commerce went hand in hand. The merchants and craftsmen became increasingly wealthy, however, not simply because of their own cultural and economic preferences and interests, but also because a series of profound economic shifts transformed the world economy. The global "opportunity structure" for urban places was in flux as the world economy expanded because of increased trade, colonialism, the faster and farther movement of people and goods, and European expansion. These shifts opened up opportunities for new centers of economic activity, and by their actions, merchants in both cities pushed Manchester and Philadelphia to occupy these new roles.

When Manchester entered into cotton textile manufacture, the industry was dispersed widely across Europe. Italy, Spain, Southern Germany, Switzerland, Flanders, and France, including the cities of Lyon, Montpellier, Nimes, Rouen, and Troyes, all had cotton clothing industries. Indeed, cotton weaving was most likely imported into England in the 1560s by Dutch and Walloon migrants. During more than a century, the primary cotton market shifted northwest, from Venice to Marseilles, Amsterdam, Hamburg, and then London, concomitant with the general trend in the European world economy. And as the market shifted, the main production sites moved as well; as some rose, others, especially in southern Europe, fell.[9]

Manchester took advantage of these changes with help from English mercantilism. Aggressive protectionist measures allowed city merchants first to take over the domestic market and later to expand into export markets in Europe and across the Atlantic. In 1700 import of calicoes from India and China was prohibited, and in 1721 all import of Indian cottons was banned, promoting English imitations despite their clear inferiority. Then imperial preferences restricted manufacturing in England's colonies and kept other countries from trading with the colonies. These events affected other centers of clothing production adversely. The French industry at Rouen, for example, burdened by taxation, corporate regulations, and limited access to growing American markets, increasingly proved unable to compete with Lancashire.[10]

As the older industries of wool and linen shrank, cotton took over nearly the entire region. Manchester dealers began buying yarn and raw materials from London and increasingly Liverpool, advancing it to spinners and weavers who worked in their own homes. This "putting-out" system, in which dealers extended materials on credit to producers, lasted in some places well into the nineteenth century. Manchester achieved hegemony over the other industrial towns of Lancashire and northern Cheshire because of its control over cotton dealing, and its prominence began to reshape its region. Cotton spinning, weaving, and dyeing spread up the rivers and streams into the surrounding towns of Ashton-under-Lyne, Bolton, Oldham, and Rochdale.[11] Entrepreneurs began a series of infrastructure improvements, such as the Bridgewater Canal, to facilitate the transport of coal for fuel, raw cotton, and finished goods. A new economic geography took shape.

By the 1770s, Manchester's advantages in cotton production had become seemingly unassailable. The long years of protectionist and mercantilist policies paid off. Lancashire's productivity had outstripped that of other centers, and the cotton trade became increasingly export-oriented, developing markets in West Africa, the Americas, and increasingly Europe as well. United Kingdom cotton imports—of which Manchester took three-fourths—more than doubled between 1750 and 1790, rising from £2.3 million to £5.9 million. By 1770, exports of cotton textiles exceeded 200,000 square yards (and this does not include yarn). It was at this time that the remarkable series of technical and mechanical improvements we associate with the Industrial Revolution began to appear. Trade expansion fully enmeshed Manchester and Lancashire in the world economy as the central production site of one of the world's most important goods.[12]

Philadelphia, as the most sophisticated mercantile center of the American colonies, was a beneficiary of the same global increase in trade as Manchester. The natural endowments of the Americas promised wealth and prestige to any individual or community that could harness them to its own benefit, and Philadelphia in the 1700s outstripped both Boston and New York. It became the raw materials processing center for the entire region, specializing in the craft-based production of flour, leather, sugar, shipbuilding, textiles, and iron. Philadelphia consolidated a commercial hold over the Pennsylvania colony's rapidly expanding hinterland (much as Manchester did over its region), including much of West Jersey.[13]

While Philadelphia's colonists were free to engage in manufacture, they could not export or trade these manufactures with other countries. Philadelphia's merchants plied their trade on both sides of the legal line, openly pursuing legal trade while finding ways to evade imperial restrictions on trade with other countries or their colonies, and turning the city into an entrepôt. They used their burgeoning shipbuilding industry to trade widely with the British West Indies and other Caribbean ports, as well as the Mediterranean. They exported their iron, lumber, flour and other grains, meat, and produce in exchange for rum, molasses, England's manufactures, and other goods. Colonialism thus ensured that Philadelphia's early economic development occurred in a global context, through trade, mercantilism, and migration. By 1770, Philadelphia was the largest and wealthiest city in the American colonies and it had become the second largest city in the British Empire, after London.[14]

The Rise of Industrial Economies

By the 1770s, then, both cities were bustling provincial centers. Deeply implicated in growing circuits of world trade, they dominated their regional hinterlands and were becoming increasingly aware of their own importance. Over the ensuing decades, each city would arrive at second city status via a distinct pathway. Manchester's development took the form of a continuous rise into a preeminent second city position in England, achieving worldwide renown—it became *the* industrial city par excellence, recognized the world over as the herald of the new economic and social order of the nineteenth century. Philadelphia's pathway in these years was more curvilinear. It tried to consolidate a position as America's global city in a competition with other seaboard cities (especially New York) but ultimately failed to do so. In the first half of the period it rose, becoming richer and grander, but in the second half it lost its way and shed a series of global city–making functions. Philadelphia—slowly, reluctantly—groped for an alternative place in global and American affairs, and it eventually found one as the first industrial metropolis in the United States.

Manchester famously consolidated an industrial position by becoming Cottonopolis, the center of the Industrial Revolution's technological and organizational transformation through textile production. Based in cotton spinning, weaving, and dyeing, the city's industrial economy also came to encompass engineering, chemicals, and other fields over time. The city itself underwent a tremendous process of growth; its population multiplied tenfold between 1770 and 1840, from 22,000 to more than 240,000. Nearby satellite towns like Bolton and Salford also grew tremendously as their economies industrialized and "cottonized." Between 1800 and 1840 Manchester's consumption of cotton multiplied tenfold; the United Kingdom's imports of cotton grew from 56 million pounds to 592 million pounds. By 1838, the Lancashire cotton industry employed more than 152,000 workers. Cotton industry output expanded by more than 7 percent per year and accounted for nearly half of British export earnings.[15]

The conventional story is that late-eighteenth-century inventions made Manchester's success possible. The list is familiar: Dutch looms in the 1720s, John Kay's flying shuttle in 1738, James Hargreaves's spinning jenny in 1767, and Richard Arkwright's water-driven spinning machine in 1771. The spinning mule of 1787 further sped up the spinning process, and Edmund Cartwright's power loom was first introduced that year as well, although it did not become popular until after the turn of the century. The city also developed new goods, such as cotton velvets, which quickly became popular throughout Europe. Progress in matching the bright dyes of India in the 1760s meant that Lancashire cottons were now as attractive as imports.[16]

These new machines and production techniques did indeed make Lancashire more productive than other industrial centers. But they were only part of the story. The technological breakthroughs also coincided with the forceful intrusion of merchants directly into the production process through the rise of the factory system, which enabled even more spectacular gains in productive capacity. During the course of the eighteenth century, the cotton merchants and some of the more successful weavers began buying multiple looms and employing larger numbers of workers in lofts and sheds. As the scale of enterprise grew larger, the factory started replacing the putting-out system, although the pace of factory development was quicker in spinning than weaving. As production capacity grew, therefore, it also became more concentrated in the hands of smaller numbers of larger producers, who became the cotton masters, or factory owners; by 1833, three spinning factories in Manchester proper employed more than one thousand workers apiece.[17]

Manchester primarily served as the industry's trading and mercantile center, although it increasingly engaged in production activities as well. The Manchester cotton exchange, which opened in 1729, centralized the region's market functions there; for the following century and a half, "high 'change" on Tuesdays would be one of the city's defining public spectacles. From the 1810s forward, the city added bleaching, dyeing, and finishing industries. And from the 1820s, this growth spilled over into related fields, like engineering, concentrated at first in textile machinery but diversifying over time into locomotives and other capital equipment. The built area of the city expanded rapidly, particularly to the south and east. Industry concentrated mostly along the southern edge of downtown and warehousing expanded along the western end. Salford, across the Irwell River to the west, also grew. In the early 1830s wealthy people began moving out of their central-city townhouses to new neighborhoods, replacing their old homes with warehouses, and a central business district proper emerged, spreading slowly outward from the exchange.[18]

The city's status as a growing commercial center, however, did not result in the formation of a local financial industry. There were no local banks until 1771, when Byrom, Sedgwick, Allen and Place formed in Manchester.

Before that time, short-term credit was provided directly by the dealers and traders. Even afterward, most financial activity gravitated toward London. Nathan Mayer Rothschild, for example, arrived from Frankfurt in 1800 with instructions from his father, a textile merchant, to cut out middlemen and buy textiles more cheaply. Between 1805 and 1809, as he moved into banking, Rothschild's activities shifted to London, and the Manchester office was shut for good in 1811.[19] Manchester thus developed from the start as an archetypal second city economy: industry and trade focused on serving world markets, but little by way of a local financial market, not to mention an international one, came to fruition.

Furthermore, a favorable geopolitical environment gave Manchester access to new markets as its production capacity rose. The spatial distribution of the world's cotton textile production collapsed on or imploded in Manchester, and Manchester's goods exploded out into world trade. British economic policy shifted to prevent competitors from arising; in the 1780s England began to prohibit the export of textile machinery and the emigration of skilled artisans. The combination of British policies on colonial manufacturing plus Manchester's technical improvements in productivity delayed the rise of American cotton weaving until well after independence; fully three-fourths of the American South's cotton crop went not to New England but to Lancashire. Manchester's success also ruined Ireland's hand-loom weavers and destroyed Dhaka's industry, giving Manchester access to India, the world's largest market for cotton goods. As textile factories in South Asia were replaced by textile factories in England, the global flow of textiles reversed and became West to East. These factors also hindered the ability of European weaving centers to compete. German merchants, for example, increasingly located themselves in the city for trade rather than trying to build up their own weaving capacity.[20] Manchester consolidated its position as a global industrial center, one of the pivots upon which the world economy turned.

In the late eighteenth century, by nearly any measure, "Philadelphia was a cosmopolitan city." It was the largest and most sophisticated urban center in the young United States, and its upper class was a national elite that exerted enormous political and ideological influence. It was the prime commercial, financial, and communications nerve center, with a larger newspaper and publishing industry than Baltimore, Boston, or New York City. Philadelphians built the original China traders and conducted a substantial portion of American trade with China and India, especially for reexport to Europe.[21] It was rich, diverse, and possessed of a remarkable collection of civic institutions that surpassed those of many European capitals.

Philadelphia's concentration of wealth, talent, and political significance made it the first American city to adopt characteristic global city roles. The most critical of global city functions involve a city's role as the filter and transfer point between the domestic and the international economy, including communications, trade, and financial intermediation. In the 1790s Philadelphia was a North American center in all these ways and was poised to become America's first full-fledged global city. But during the next four decades, it would cede its lead in each area. Philadelphia would turn to manufacturing and to the role of second city in effect as a consolation for losing global city status to New York.

Through its merchant riches and its role in arranging financing for the revolutionary struggle, Philadelphia became the financial capital of the new republic. The Pennsylvania Bank, the first bank in the United States, was established in 1780 in Philadelphia by private merchants to help fund the Revolution; the Bank of North America was a second Philadelphia-based Revolution-era bank. The Philadelphia Stock Exchange was established in 1790 at Merchant's Coffee House, and the city was also home to the U.S. Mint. The country's most powerful, wealthiest financiers—Stephen Girard and Nicholas Biddle—lived in Philadelphia and ran its financial institutions. Perhaps most notably, the country's early central banks, the First and Second banks of the United States, were headquartered in Philadelphia as well. To an early American, the name "Chestnut Street" meant everything that "Wall Street" does today.[22]

The city's defeats began simultaneously with the new century, however. Philadelphia had been the first center of national political life; the Declaration of Independence was signed there, and the Constitutional Convention of 1787 was held in the city as well. It was the national capital from 1777 to 1788, and again from 1790 to 1800. But republican fear of concentrated power and the need to provide a political balance between slave and free and commercial and agricultural interests led the Congress to put the American political capital at Washington, D.C., from 1800 forward.[23] Then, in the 1820s, New York beat out other seaboard cities in the race to cross the Appalachian Mountains by building the Erie Canal, becoming one of the country's top export centers. But neither of these events by itself was sufficient to topple Philadelphia from its incipient global position, nor to make the winning city a global city. More important, leadership in the two critical domains of international communications and finance also slipped from Philadelphia's grasp.

In 1818, New York succeeded in establishing the first packet shipping service to Liverpool, making it the preferred port for traffic with the old mother country and giving it a lead in international communications that grew over time. Packet services were desirable not because they were especially fast, but because they ran on regular, predictable timetables. They gave businessmen a strong incentive to route their transactions through New York. The Black Ball Line began operations in January, sending one packet ship in each direction across the Atlantic every month. By 1822, the Black Ball had doubled its service, and other lines had started running from the city not only to Liverpool but to London and Le Havre as well. Thomas Cope of Philadelphia established the Liverpool Packet Line in 1821, and another called the New Line started operations in 1822, but the advantage had already shifted decisively in New York's favor.[24]

Philadelphia's most important loss, however, was undoubtedly its surrender of national financial hegemony in the 1830s. The city was home to both national banks, the Bank of the United States (closed in 1811), and the Second Bank of the United States (chartered by Congress in 1816). In both cases, the bank presidency was generally held by a Philadelphian, as were many of the seats on the board. The Second Bank was gigantic for its time—$35 million in capital, 20 percent of which was owned by the government; Figure 2.1 shows its imposing neoclassical building on Chestnut Street. It quickly exercised a force over the American economy entirely unprecedented in the history of finance: "The primary purpose, real and avowed, of the federal Bank was regulatory. It was that of central banking." Nicholas Biddle, president of the Second Bank from 1823 to 1839, was skillful in regulating the flow of credit across the country's different regions. As the federal government's bank, it often received the notes issued by state banks; when Biddle pressed these banks to redeem their notes, they were forced to restrict the credit they granted to borrowers.[25]

Biddle's bank also served as the main financial intermediary between the U.S. and European credit markets, access to which was increasingly

Figure 2.1: The Second Bank of the United States.

important for the capital-starved, rapidly expanding United States (eventually more than half of its shares came to be owned abroad, mostly in Britain). The bank was the main U.S. dealer in foreign exchange. It monitored the balance of payments to protect the country against currency movements, negotiating short-term loans in Amsterdam, London, and Paris when necessary. Increasingly, the Second Bank also served as an agent for placing U.S. stocks and bonds abroad. The bank would buy bonds issued by state governments to fund infrastructure improvements like canals; it would then resell these bonds on European markets to raise foreign exchange or acquire bullion. As the main conduit between European capital seeking investment and American entrepreneurs seeking capital, the bank not only helped create a truly national economy in the United States, but it also more deeply intertwined the American economy with the global economy and magnified Philadelphia's global economic importance.

Biddle believed in the Second Bank's independence from politics, and his attempts to preserve that independence proved troublesome. When he refused President Andrew Jackson's requests to control appointments to the bank's board for the Democratic Party, Jackson started to attack the bank openly. Jackson vetoed extension of the Bank's charter, which was due to expire in 1836, and in late 1833 the federal government started shifting its deposits toward the state banks. Biddle's bank was rechartered as a Pennsylvania state bank in 1836, but without any central banking function.[26] The bank's relatively conservative policies had held speculation and the issue of dubious bank notes in check; as its official role declined, it was less and less able to restrain the issue of credit and notes by state banks around the country. It was only a matter of time before the reckoning came.

When the nation's banks suspended specie payments in 1837, Biddle realized that this was perhaps his last chance to restore the bank's former prominence. He engineered a great scheme to buy up as much of the cotton crop as he could to force a rise in its price in Liverpool, and so to rescue Southern farmers and merchant houses who depended on cotton's income. In effect, he provided the financing that would enable the crop to move from harvest to market, but at the same time he became a speculator and tried to corner the market in the most important transatlantic commodity of the day. In London and Paris, Biddle furiously tried to sell cotton and state bonds. He also attempted to raise loans in order to acquire foreign exchange and bullion, but he extended the bank too far for its own good. Eventually, Europe's bankers—the Bank of England, the Rothschilds, Baring Brothers, and others—grew skeptical, and they refused to grant the Second Bank further credit. In the fall of 1839, Biddle's bank was forced to suspend specie payments again, and in 1841 it failed for good.

This was the final blow to Philadelphia's colonial-era preeminence. The Bank's failure "shifted the money center of the country from Chestnut

Street to Wall Street" and symbolized the eclipse not just of Philadelphia's mercantile economy, but of the society that had prospered along with it as well. "Philadelphia closed its doors against the nation as a whole. The nation had rejected the leadership of Old Philadelphia; very well, Old Philadelphia rejected the nation. . . . Henceforth let vulgar Washington take over politics and vulgar New York take over finance."[27] The Panic of 1837 served as the switchman that made New York into the nation's global city and shifted Philadelphia's course from one track to another.

For even as Philadelphia was losing this crucial global city function, it was developing the basis for another sort of global role—a focus on industry and manufacturing. The city was home to thousands of skilled craftsmen and was from 1775 on the country's largest producer of textiles. Between 1800 and 1840 the city increasingly developed an industrial base in chemicals, shoes, machine tools, locomotives, and ships. Perhaps most emblematic was the rise of Matthias Baldwin, who got his start in the 1820s by building textile machinery and engraving equipment. In 1831 he was commissioned to build his first railroad locomotive, and he decided to make a business of it. "By 1837 Baldwin employed three hundred men in a $200,000 factory"; the firm eventually grew to become the largest capital goods concern in the United States, with more than 15,000 employees. By the end of the Panic-induced depression in the mid-1840s, the Second Bank had disappeared, and the industrialists—Frederick Fraley (coal), Nicholas Lennig (chemicals), Matthias Baldwin (locomotives), William Sellers (machine tools), Henry Disston (saws), and William and Richard Norris (locomotives), among others—were the city's new leaders.[28]

Industrial might entailed regional hegemony. Indeed, both cities became regional powerhouses—the centers of increasingly integrated regional economies and increasingly elaborated regional divisions of labor. The economic historian Diane Lindstrom explains that Philadelphia's industrial development restructured the whole of the Delaware and Susquehanna River valleys, as agricultural areas began increasingly to specialize in export commodities that could be traded for Philadelphia's manufactured goods. The city's influence also spread to the rich coal mining lands to the north and northwest. Manchester was the core commercial and trading center for the surrounding manufacturing and industrial towns, which lay in a ring to the north, east, and south, extending about twelve miles out from the central city. By 1838, the cotton industry employed more than 15,000 in Oldham, nearly 14,000 in Bury, 10,000 apiece in Blackburn, Rochdale, and Bolton, and thousands more in other Lancashire towns. Towns were beginning to specialize as well—Oldham in spinning, for example, and Bolton in weaving and dyeing.[29]

Transportation infrastructure facilitated the dominance of the two cities. Each secured a regional hinterland through transportation networks such as Lancashire's Bridgewater Canal and the Philadelphia-Lancaster Turnpike. The world's first passenger railway, the Manchester-Liverpool line, opened in 1830; it reduced travel time to hours instead of a day and a half, and it carried 300,000 people each year.[30] Also, each developed a substantial extra-regional hinterland and an economic clout that could justly be called global. Manchester achieved this through the growth of the export market for its cotton textiles. Philadelphia, however, stumbled badly; the city's international trade actually declined in this period. In part, the decline in the city's international trade was driven by its reorientation away from commerce and into industry and manufacturing for the domestic market, and by the worsening position of its major trading partners—the Caribbean and southern Europe. But the biggest reason Philadelphia lost its world mercantile position was that it lost out in its intercity rivalry with New York and Baltimore for the opening of a trade route to the West. In particular, New York's Erie Canal, begun in 1817 and completed in 1825, connected New York with the West and ensured that it would be the main U.S. port.

Philadelphia was squeezed both geographically and politically. It was difficult to engineer a mountain crossing in Pennsylvania, and the city also needed state authority to charter any large transportation projects. What is more, state unity was hard to come by: Pittsburgh had a more natural connection down the Ohio and Mississippi Rivers to New Orleans, and the farmers of southern Pennsylvania wanted to float goods down the Susquehanna River to Baltimore. In 1824 the state of Pennsylvania authorized survey work for a mixed system of canals and railroads that became known as the Main Line. By 1834, a connection via canal, rail, inclined plane, and coach enabled travel from Philadelphia to Pittsburgh in four days. The absurdity of a multimodal line that required transferring goods from rail to barge and back again soon became evident, however. Delays and difficulties related to the mountain passage, and to the need to close the canals in winter, made the State Works unprofitable. It was already obsolete on the day it opened.[31] One of Philadelphia's greatest challenges would be to reinvigorate its trade and transport connections in the 1840s and 1850s, a story that is told in Chapter 6.

Migration

The growth of industry entailed a substantial demand for labor, which had to be met by outsiders who moved to each city in search of work. In the four decades after 1800, Manchester's population grew from 70,000 to 243,000, and Philadelphia's from 41,000 to almost 94,000 (or from 81,000 to 258,000 for Philadelphia County as a whole). Much of this migration was internal and short distance. Manchester became the epicenter of a large stream of short-distance labor migration from rural Lancashire and surrounding counties in the North of England. Many of these migrants were already accustomed to wage labor, and many also had experience working in textiles under the putting-out system. As the older economy that combined putting out with small farming went into decline, families either moved en masse or sent some members into the booming cotton towns for factory work. Similarly, Philadelphia's growing economy attracted thousands of migrants from the interior of Pennsylvania (particularly those of German descent) or from other colonies or, later, states. Benjamin Franklin, who was born in Boston and traveled to the city at age 17, was only the most famous of a steady stream of migrants looking for commercial opportunities in the burgeoning city.[32]

As the example of the Pennsylvania Germans suggests, a good deal of the migration to these cities was composed of internal migrants whose ethnic or religious background differed significantly from that of the native population. This prevalence of culturally distinct internal migrants became a characteristic feature of their migration patterns. Some migrants of this sort came to Manchester from Scotland, but the largest and most significant group came from Ireland. In particular, many Catholic Irish immigrated to Lancashire as the weaving industry in Ireland disintegrated. In Manchester they could continue to practice handloom weaving as native English workers left handloom weaving for the factories. The Irish, numbering 25,000 to 30,000, were 20 percent of Manchester's population in the 1830s. More Irish settled in Lancashire than in any other part of England except for London.[33]

International migration concentrated at first—in both cities—among people seeking mercantile opportunities and religious freedom. In the late eighteenth and early nineteenth centuries, immigration to Manchester was small and composed primarily of successful European merchants who set up branches of their firms in the city. Good business sense came to dictate a location in Manchester; cheaper and less risky deals could be concluded there, ensuring a more regular supply to the merchants' home markets. They sent their brothers, nephews, and sons; this was how both Friedrich Engels and, before him, Nathan Mayer Rothschild came to the city. Germans in particular, many of them Jewish, dominated this movement. Jewish merchants first appear in Manchester in the 1780s, and in 1795 a group of Liverpool-based Jewish merchants and traders chose to settle in the area. The amateur historian John Scholes compiled a list of foreign merchants in the city from the 1780s forward. While undoubtedly incomplete, the list contains sixty-four German names in 1831 and eighty-nine in 1841, together with a smattering of French, Italian, and Greek traders. This core group of relatively well-off immigrants was the nucleus of later immigration to Manchester, which would be dominated by Germans and eastern European Jews.[34]

Pennsylvania was reputed far and wide for its devotion to religious tolerance; combined with its rapidly growing economy, this made Philadelphia "all but classless, but already polyglot" in the 1700s. Large numbers of German-speaking Protestants crossed the sea to build homesteads on

Pennsylvania's rich farmland, settling Philadelphia's Germantown suburb in 1683. Many Scotch-Irish also journeyed to the colony, and later to the new state, along with English and Welsh Quakers and smaller numbers of Dutch, Swedish, and Jewish traders and farmers. Philadelphia had from colonial times the largest free African American population in the North. This native population was supplemented by refugees from the slave South and by Caribbean populations arriving either free or as slaves from Haiti and Santo Domingo. These migrant groups quickly made homes for themselves and promoted the first stirrings of collective life. The first Catholic church, St. Mary's, was built in 1763, and Mikveh Israel was founded in 1782. Mother Bethel, founded in 1791, was the first African Methodist Episcopal church, and by 1838, African Americans had established about one hundred mutual-aid societies, with almost 7,500 members.[35] The result was the most vibrant local civil society in the hemisphere. This diversity of immigrant groups began to shrink after 1810, however, as the city's international trade stagnated and as New York City became the young country's dominant port.

Culture

The extent of its civil society made Philadelphia distinctive, but there was an underlying set of cultural values and attitudes that both Manchester and Philadelphia shared. These values—openness or tolerance, a commitment to practicality and utility, and a self-consciously bourgeois or middle-class self-understanding—shaped local politics and civic life. The tolerance and openness stemmed in large part from their religious heritages. In addition, both cities had in the eighteenth century a well-deserved reputation for being open economically to tradesmen and entrepreneurs. People were judged more by their achievements than their parentage. Both cities extended this respect for achievement into a religiously derived emphasis on practicality and utility.

The Quaker religious doctrine, common in both cities and dominant in Philadelphia, stressed pragmatism and commitment over the intellectual pursuits of leisure—"things over words." "Practical, methodical activity in the world was considered an evidence that one was indeed living 'in the Light'; the expenditure of physical energy and the handling of material objects was identified with industry, whereas abstract speculation and contemplation, when not directed towards purely religious ends, was equated with idleness." Benjamin Franklin and his alter ego Poor Richard are justly famous for promoting the utilitarian spirit of the age: "the Scriptures assure me that at the last day we shall not be examined what we *thought*, but what we *did*; and our recommendation will be that we did good to our fellow creatures."[36] This utilitarian bent implied an affinity between religion and scientific investigation, although the commitment to practicality would become increasingly secular and class-based with time.

These common values, and the influence they came to have on each city's activities and reputation, are perhaps best exemplified by two extraordinary individuals, John Dalton and Benjamin Franklin. Each was a migrant who came as a young adult looking for work, and each developed a reputation during his lifetime as a scientific investigator and civic hero of the first rank. Benjamin Franklin, of course, stands by consensus as the chief embodiment of Philadelphia's golden era. In his extraordinary career, he played a key role in national Constitutional debates, served as ambassador to France, and had a hand in establishing almost every civic enterprise in the city. He organized the Pennsylvania Hospital, the first firefighting company, and the first insurance society in the colonies. Also, he was a founder of the school that would become the University of Pennsylvania. In 1727 he established a debating society called the Junto, for artisans, merchants, and young members of the professions. The Junto eventually spun off the Library Company of Philadelphia and the American Philosophical Society. Via this group of knowledge-producing and scientific organizations, Franklin helped to institutionalize a network of like-minded people who could sponsor, collaborate, and further his own interests in meteorology, electricity, and "all philosophical experiments that let light into the nature of things, tend to increase the power of man over matter, and multiply the conveniences of pleasures of life." Franklin carried on a prodigious correspondence with prominent European scientists; he eventually held memberships in scientific societies in England, France, Germany, Holland, Italy, Russia, and Spain.[37]

John Dalton, "the founder of modern chemistry," was the central figure in establishing Manchester's scientific reputation. A Quaker from Cumberland, he was lured to Manchester in 1792 to teach at Manchester New College. In the 1790s and early 1800s he made his signal contributions to physics and chemistry, proposing the first hypotheses on color blindness (from which he suffered), keeping detailed meteorological records, and doing research on the diffusion of gases. His major achievement was the development of chemical atomic theory, which analyzed how elements combined in definite proportions to form compounds. He was elected to the city's main scientific body, the Manchester Literary and Philosophical Society (Lit&Phil), in 1794, and he would serve as its president for twenty-seven years, from 1817 to 1844.[38]

Established in 1781, the Lit&Phil was the first and most important provincial scientific society in England. Composed primarily of amateur naturalists, entrepreneurs, middle-class Unitarian Dissenters, and a group of doctors affiliated with the Manchester Infirmary, the Lit&Phil's members believed that scientific knowledge could offer practical benefits to human society. They devoted themselves to the investigation of the natural world—medicine, meteorology, chemistry, botany, and physics—and the society's meetings and its published *Transactions* formed a crucial gathering space that promoted intellectual ferment. Lit&Phil members would go on during the next century to play an important role in nearly every civic and scientific development in the city—the founding of the mechanics' institutes, the Manchester Statistical Society (which pioneered social scientific approaches to urban social and public health problems), Owens College, and more.[39]

Physicians played important roles in the establishment of vibrant local civil societies in both cities. The Manchester Infirmary (1752) had been founded almost simultaneously with the Pennsylvania Hospital (1751), the first hospital in the English colonies. The two most eminent physicians in the cities—Thomas Percival in Manchester and Benjamin Rush in Philadelphia—had both graduated from the University of Edinburgh Medical School, probably the most acclaimed medical school of the day, and both devised early codes of medical ethics.[40] Philadelphia served for more than a century as the center of medicine in the Americas; the College of Physicians was organized in 1786, and a host of other schools and organizations followed in the early to mid-nineteenth century. Classes in surgery were established at the College of Physicians in 1805, ahead even of Edinburgh.

So although Dalton and Franklin were leading lights, they were by no means alone. Their most frequent compatriots were men of industry, commerce, and medicine. They believed in trade, in working for a living, and above all in making oneself useful. They found in science a cultural claim to knowledge that could bolster their status claims as representatives of a new social order—an order not simply rational and utilitarian, but also bourgeois, liberal, and capitalist. This era, perhaps more than any other, witnessed the growth of an intellectual and professional elite that was not only international and cosmopolitan but also profoundly urban. Cultural production in Philadelphia and Manchester therefore did not chiefly reside in the activities we commonly think of as "culture"—art, music, or literature. Instead, the cities turned primarily to science and medicine, and their focus on these endeavors, along with the innovation inherent in them, eventually resulted in the development of their own civic identities as well. Both places were self-conscious of their distance and isolation from London, and they turned their isolation into a virtue against the old, stifling order of feudal and churchly privileges.[41] Their civic identities became explicit as well; each city began proclaiming a "second city" reputation in contradistinction to that of London or New York.

Politics and Identity

Even though Philadelphia and Manchester were arriving at the same place—an ensemble of second city characteristics—they were arriving from different directions, and that difference in pathway or trajectory would contribute distinctive elements to each city's political culture. Thus, their trajectories had not only economic aspects, as discussed previously, but political dynamics as well. Each political culture was defined by its competition and struggle with other cities, and each measured its own city's status as "second" in various ways relative to those competitors. While Philadelphia had possessed some measure of autonomy and national prestige from its founding, the repeated withdrawal and ineffectiveness of its political leaders made for a weak local state. Manchester's polity was forged in a protracted struggle by the city's rising bourgeoisie to win political representation in Parliament, as well to establish and control an effective local state, which did not exist in the eighteenth century. These contrasting trajectories produced contrasting political cultures by the 1830s: one of disfranchisement and indifference in Philadelphia and of can-do boosterism and elite hubris in Manchester.

The astounding political fact about Philadelphia is that the city allowed its early advantages to slip away, although it should have been in a good position to press its interests. Much of the responsibility for these losses must be put down to politics: Philadelphia proved unable to press its interests successfully in the state legislature or in Congress, and as a result lost ground in the intercity competition of the early nineteenth century. The city's political weakness had several sources. First, the city held within its physical boundaries a decreasing proportion of the local population and business activity; immigrants, the textile industry, shipbuilding, and other concerns were located largely outside the city limits and established their own city governments—Kensington, Southwark, Manayunk, and more—just steps away. This political fragmentation would become an increasing source of concern in the 1830s and 1840s. Second, there was substantial regional rivalry and antagonism among the different parts of Pennsylvania, dating back to ethnic, religious, and political differences in the colonial era among the urban and proprietary Quakers, the farming Germans, and the frontier Scots-Irish. Thus, it was often difficult for the city to win legislative approval for its proposals, such as for transportation infrastructure, without tacking on expensive and (from Philadelphia's point of view) troublesome additions to satisfy outlying constituencies.[42] Finally, the city's leaders themselves proved out of touch with popular sentiment in an increasingly democratic and populist era. These multiple political failures were most visible in Nicholas Biddle's unsuccessful battle against the Jacksonians in the 1830s over the national bank and in the city's inability to get the state to charter an effective passage over the Allegheny Mountains to the West until the mid-1840s. Thus, Philadelphia acquired its second city characteristics through the loss of a competition for global city status, a loss that was as much political as it was economic.

The city's impoverished governance and political culture of mediocrity stemmed largely from the most important political legacy of the colonial Quakers—quietism, or withdrawal from the political field. The Society of Friends was ambivalent or worse regarding governance and the exercise of political power, preferring private success to public authority. Quaker withdrawal from politics set a precedent. The Quakers failed to rise to the political demands of the day, and their renunciation of public life had a more lasting impact on Philadelphia's political culture than did their idealism:

> Most of the birthright Friends who took the lead in Philadelphia's Golden Age in the eighteenth century were read out of meeting. This Quaker policy of disownment eventually became a proper Philadelphia habit, highly visible in the class habit of disparaging exceptional achievement. . . . [There] was not only an unusual lack of drive toward leadership and accomplishment in their city but also a deeply ingrained class tradition that inhibited those who tried to do anything out of the ordinary.[43]

What E. Digby Baltzell described as a habit of the city's elite eventually became a part of the larger civic culture in Philadelphia, which since the 1830s has been legendary for its pessimism, withdrawal, and disfranchisement. This ambivalent attitude toward leadership served the city particularly badly in the early decades of the nineteenth century. The Philadelphia elite and city government lacked the political will and leadership necessary to protect their own advantages and position, and as a result the city was vulnerable to the efforts of competitors in other cities. Philadelphia effectively gave up in the race to be first or global, and looked instead, as the epigraph that begins this chapter shows, to Manchester and to Lyon, France, as its peers. That precedent has been periodically reenacted in the city's history.

Manchester's political development also lagged far behind its economic growth. On the one hand, there was no elected local government in the eighteenth and early nineteenth centuries. There was little in the way of local administration or public services; the lord and the Anglican Church chose magistrates and the wardens of the poor from among those who met the relatively high property qualifications and were also in good social and party standing. On the other hand, the merchants lacked representation in Parliament to press their interests. Manchester itself had no seats and neither did smaller cotton towns like Bolton. What Lancashire seats did exist—for the countryside and for old corporate towns like Preston—were generally Tory-held. Thus, manorial rule lasted far past the time when a new group—bourgeois, with money derived from trade and industry rather than land—came to desire political voice. The lack of incorporation, and consequent freedom for commerce and industry, that had originally made Manchester such a propitious place for the industrial implosion, in its own turn became an obstacle to the realization of the goals and ideas of the new capitalist class that industry had created.[44]

The struggle for political reform and for cotton manufacturers' eventual political hegemony took place in alternating cycles of agitation and repression during half a century. Liberal Quaker merchants in Manchester, Rochdale, and other nearby towns, and the Unitarians and Congregationalists of the Mosley Street, Cross Street, and Lloyd Street chapels, turned their exclusion from the Tory, Anglican, aristocratic elite into the fire that drove them to political power. Politics in Manchester was thus not about the class divide between owners and workers; rather, it was a struggle by the rising bourgeoisie to overthrow the political structures of feudalism, many of which remained in force, and achieve their own hegemony. The first round of Liberal pressure for political reform and Conservative backlash occurred in the 1790s, spurred by commercial and industrial resistance to William Pitt the Younger's tax measures and by frustration with exclusion from public life on religious grounds. The Tories prosecuted their opponents, and even though they won few convictions, the reform movement was broken; the era from 1792 until 1820 was one of reactionary conservatism and repression. A new cycle of agitation began in the wake of the local magistrates' massacre of demonstrating workers at Peterloo. Reformers focused first on creating institutions of middle-class interest formation, such as the *Manchester Guardian* newspaper, founded in 1821, and the Manchester Chamber of Commerce in 1820. These paradigmatically bourgeois institutions helped both to solidify middle-class opinion and to broadcast that opinion widely; they would play crucial roles in the ensuing decades. Activists pushed the ever greater number of people who made the property qualification to register as police commissioners, until they overloaded the commission with more than 1,800 members. And a small but increasing number of manufacturers and members of the middle class, like the newspaper publisher Archibald Prentice and the Rochdale mill owner John Bright, became more radical, espousing larger grants of suffrage and reforms more sympathetic to workers.[45]

The Reform Act of 1832 simultaneously granted political representation in Parliament to areas like Manchester and expanded the franchise to the "shopocracy and artisanate" by lowering property qualifications to £10. Lancashire's representation in Parliament increased from fourteen seats to twenty-six, and several of the textile cities, including Bolton, Manchester, and Oldham, won formal representation for the first time. Predictably, Liberals were elected to both of Manchester's new seats in the Commons and to most of the other new seats as well; they consolidated the Liberal Party as the party of the manufacturing interest.[46] From this time forward, political agitation for free trade replaced mercantilism, and pressure for changes in national and imperial policy and in foreign relations took off. But although the reformers had won a voice and a seat at the table, they had not yet won effective power.

For that, they needed control of an autonomous local government to show that their ideas could translate into a workable polity. "Incorporation was necessary if Manchester was to present a plausibly 'Liberal' face to the nation at large; it was also necessary as a means of attaching critically important groups in the electorate to the Liberal interest." They pursued a city charter, newly enabled by an 1835 act of Parliament, as a way to break the Tory stranglehold over the municipality. Cotton merchant and calico printer Richard Cobden, who wrote and published the pamphlet *Incorporate Your Borough*, was the chief militant in the movement. At a public meeting on the issue of incorporation in February 1838, Cobden declaimed, "The old state of the government of Manchester is so decrepit and worn out, that it has actually fallen to pieces, and gone to the death. . . . [W]hatever change you intend, a change you must have; for the old state of things cannot exist any longer."[47]

Tory partisans of the old regime put up protracted resistance, however. In the summer of 1838 there were opposing petitions in favor of and against incorporation presented to Parliament; a three-week investigation declared most signatures on both petitions to be fraudulent and left pro-incorporators with a seven-hundred-signature deficit. In August the Privy Council and the queen granted incorporation anyway. After further investigation, which opponents of incorporation boycotted, Parliament's vote for incorporation followed in October. Cobden wrote of his opponents, "By dint of hard work and some expense, we got at the filth in their Augean stable, and laid their dirty doings before the public eye. . . . [I]t will be a new era for Manchester when it shakes off the feudal livery of Sir Oswald Mosley, to put on the democratic garb of the Municipal Reform Act." The first elections were held in December. Liberal manufacturers and sympathizers predictably dominated the returns; among the first aldermen were Cobden, William Neild, J. E. Taylor (proprietor of the *Manchester Guardian*), Henry Tootal, Elkanah Armitage, William Callender, and Thomas Potter, who became the first mayor. The police commissioners of the old regime denied the new council entrance to the Town Hall, however, and refused to give up their policing powers and functions. This forced Parliament to pass a special bill in 1839 giving the central government direct control over all policing for two years, and Manchester's elected leaders did not assume full control of city government until 1841.[48]

Incorporation should be understood as the arrival of the "Manchester men," the Liberal manufacturing bourgeoisie, on the world political stage. Their achievement of political power left a dual legacy. One legacy was the rise of Manchester into a full-fledged second city—the home of a wealthy manufacturing class, the soapbox upon which those men could proclaim the worth of a capitalist social order in opposition to rural landlords and London's courtly aristocracy, the outstanding bourgeois metropolis of its day and undisputed leader of the provinces. "Incorporation achieved everything which Cobden and his associates had hoped for in 1838 short of a full democracy. . . . [T]he effacement of a manorial structure of local government was an appropriate if largely symbolic overture to a full scale battle with hereditary privilege."[49] And indeed, Cobden and the other manufacturers did not delay in turning their attention to new tasks: the organizing meetings for free trade and the Anti–Corn Law League were held during the first weeks of December 1838, at the same time as the city's first municipal elections.

The second legacy was the birth of Manchester's particular political culture. The manufacturers came to believe quite firmly in their own effectiveness and organizational strength as a specifically urban elite, possessed of a confidence in the social power of capital that was at least boosterist, if not hubristic. In turn, this liberal, boosterist ideology became the city's civic identity. For the next several decades, what Manchester politicians and businessmen said and did reverberated around the world. From being the manufacturing nexus that connected some of the world's most far-flung regions, Lancashire grew to become the nineteenth-century pulpit for the utopian free trade ideology preached at other times by Adam Smith, Friedrich Hayek, and Milton Friedman. The political culture generated during and "organic" to this period took over local politics and persisted long after the disappearance of its economic base. In Manchester an energetic can-do pragmatism has been periodically reinvigorated by political coalitions ever since the 1830s.

Thus, Manchester and Philadelphia, each in its own way, faced the transition into second city position as a political and status challenge at least as much as an economic one. It is important to remember, however, that the contrasts between them—in trajectory (rise versus decline), in local state autonomy and capacity (growing power and independence versus elite withdrawal), and in identity (can-do boosterism versus downcast pessimism)—fit within an overall frame of similarity. Though they gave it different spins, the two cities occupied fundamentally similar structural positions. In future decades each would continue to combine second city patterns of global integration with a local political culture that retained markers from its entry path. The political dynamics of each city's passage into second city position forged legacies that would animate their urban identities in the decades to come.

Conclusion: The Making of the Second City

By 1840, both places had developed most of the characteristics of a second city. First, they found economic specializations separate from finance. Manchester was almost wholly organized around cotton-clothing production for the world market, with a growing engineering industry centered on textile machinery, dyes and chemicals, and locomotives. Philadelphia was the biggest textile production agglomeration in the United States, with growing engineering, chemical, locomotive, and ship industries as well. Second, they possessed migration patterns similar to each other but increasingly distinct from global city patterns: a predominance of internal and short-distance migration, with significant international streams from just one or two places. Third, each city was becoming a center of cultural innovation in the production of knowledge, both scientific and ideological. Manchester was already witnessing the heated oratory of free trade advocates that would become louder and louder in the next decade as well as the rise of an important scientific community. Philadelphia had become one of the most developed and diversified medical centers in the world, and it was adopting one of the loudest protectionist voices. Fourth, each city's identity was being shaped by the twin influences of competition with other large cities and of a great regional hegemony either complete or in the making. Their experiences of interurban competition were just beginning to push them onto a common path or sequence of political and economic transformation, which would unfold in the ensuing decades.

The histories of these cities, therefore, were never restricted to a merely national frame; they were characterized by a total and thoroughgoing involvement in global patterns of trade, migration, and culture. Both cities moved into a newly opened structural position in world affairs—economic, cultural, and political—as apostles of industrialization and modernization. They combined manufacturing production, cultural innovation, and political striving to secure a global position and reputation for themselves. These achievements were not necessarily planned or fully intentional, although they were more obviously so in Manchester than in Philadelphia. But the two cities increasingly came to define themselves and their activities *by contrast with* New York and London—as places of industry, work, and practicality, rather than places of finance or of speculation (in the monetary or the intellectual sense). The goal for Manchester and Philadelphia would be to retain and revitalize their portions of this structural position over time, and this entailed a kind of convergence on the role of the second city.

Still, each city developed and retained a distinctive political culture. In later decades Manchester's experience of precocious growth would continue to color its self-image, producing a can-do political culture that many observers tagged as hubris. Philadelphia's political culture, after the city was stung by a series of defeats, has for nearly two centuries been characterized by withdrawal, disfranchisement, and the abdication of leadership. Their respective political identities derived in part from the different trajectories they followed into second city position and in part from their political responses to that trajectory. These identities and political cultures, in turn, would shape future city planning and future responses to global challenges; they provided enduring historical legacies that influenced the subsequent social structure, global connectedness, and self-perception of each city. Although these trajectories were distinct from one another, the urban identities they fostered would come to share an explicitly "second" character in later decades.

3

Second City Economies

In the 1850s more than three-fourths of Lancashire's raw cotton supply came from the American slave South. Worried "that some dire calamity must inevitably, sooner or later, overtake the cotton manufacture," especially given the growing tensions between North and South in the United States, Manchester merchants decided to stimulate cotton cultivation in other parts of the world. They formed the Cotton Supply Association (CSA) in 1857, with the blessing of the Manchester Chamber of Commerce. Prominent supporters included the MPs John Cheetham, Thomas Bazley, and John Bright. The CSA's primary focus was India; it sent shipments of cotton seed there, and also to Algeria, Egypt, and Turkey. The CSA conferred with British ambassadors and with representatives of foreign governments, and it supported "corresponding agencies" in Australia, Brazil, Italy, Paraguay, Portugal, and Spain. By 1865, the CSA had "distributed ten thousand hundred weights of cotton seed; sent out one thousand two hundred gins, for cleaning the cotton from the seed, prior to its being packed for shipment, and, besides, a great number of fly-wheels, to be used where steam power is not available."[1]

The merchants' fears were realized with the start of the Civil War and the North's blockade of Southern ports. The "Cotton Famine," as it became known in Britain, saw cotton prices rise to stratospheric heights and imports drop by nearly 60 percent between 1861 and 1862. By November 1862, applications for welfare relief exceeded 450,000, and tens of thousands of laid-off workers emigrated. Although imports from alternate suppliers—particularly India and Egypt—jumped, they did not make up for the American losses, and cotton manufacturers scrambled to increase cotton growing elsewhere. The Manchester Cotton Company, formed late in 1860, began cultivation in India but never raised enough capital to support its efforts and never imported any cotton. A similar fate befell fifteen other companies formed in England between 1858 and 1864. Ultimately, no British company that grew cotton in India for export was ever successful. By the end of the 1860s, the United States resumed its dominant position in the British cotton market, and production for export in other locales dwindled. The Cotton Supply Association itself fell apart in 1872.[2]

Although the push for cotton failed, attempts to expand its cultivation show how deeply Manchester's capitalists were engaged with the global economy in an era before the multinational corporation. The city's merchants and manufacturers openly tried to pursue their economic interests on a global scale. Opening up new lands for cotton supply was an attempt to ensure the industry's and the region's continued prosperity. It was also an attempt at vertical integration in an industry that was known for hundreds of small- to medium-sized disaggregated firms. Despite living in an era of family partnerships and bills of exchange rather than one of transnational corporations (TNCs) and telecommunications, Manchester's capitalists and workers were no less—and perhaps more—enmeshed in global webs of trade, labor, and resource exploitation than people and firms are today.

In this chapter I analyze how economic globalization has played out in Philadelphia and Manchester. The global economic prominence of these two cities was based first in manufacturing, in what were at the time the leading economic sectors, particularly textiles, chemicals, and capital goods. As manufacturing declined, they switched to particular service sectors—some of the "producer services" identified by Saskia Sassen and others, to be sure, but even more substantially to higher education and the medical sector. As their populations and firms suburbanized, Manchester and Philadelphia became the centers of vast, far-flung regions. Also, they retained small, select manufacturing concentrations, typically in advanced areas, like pharmaceuticals in the Philadelphia region or electronics in Greater Manchester. But the financial sector has not been particularly important—it is neither the largest nor the fastest growing. This pattern appears to represent a marked departure from the world city hypothesis (WCH), which defines finance and the advanced producer services as the paradigmatic urban pathway to global economic integration.

During the past thirty years, the economic geography of the global urban system has shifted significantly, not unlike the period of the early nineteenth century, when Manchester and Philadelphia became second cities. Deindustrialization and restructuring in the West, industrialization in the global South, especially Asia, and developments in finance and communications have combined to shuffle the deck of the world urban system. This transformation has posed a serious challenge to Manchester and Philadelphia, both in searching for new economic specializations and in combating the effects of economic dislocation. Success in maintaining second city position over time depends in part upon generating shifts in industrial concentration as a response to crisis or decline in dominant industries—in other words, economic diversification. Diversification is not an economic panacea, to be sure, but continued overreliance on old economic specializations would have carried even larger risks. Philadelphia and Manchester have been successful during the past thirty years in developing new specializations to replace their old, decaying ones and in preserving and maintaining their second city positions in ways that Detroit, Liverpool, Saint Louis, and Sheffield have not.

The chapter is divided into four sections. The first section describes the most salient differences between the WCH model of the global city economy and the experiences of Manchester and Philadelphia. In addition to analyzing the patterns of global cities' integration into the world economy, the WCH predicts rising inequality both between and within cities. In this chapter I focus particularly on how Manchester and Philadelphia complicate the WCH's picture of inequality between cities; although I do give some attention to economic inequality within the two cities, this issue is treated more fully in Chapter 4. The second section describes the population and employment patterns in both cities, including the shifts over time in dominant economic sectors. The third and fourth sections examine the core features of Philadelphia's and Manchester's economic globalization: how they are connected to other cities around the world via corporate hierarchies and foreign direct investment (FDI), how prominent they are as headquarter locations for transnational corporations, whether they possess an international financial sector, and which specific industries (in both the manufacturing and service sectors) they tend to specialize in. The conclusion addresses Manchester's and Philadelphia's success or failure in confronting the challenges of economic restructuring during the late twentieth century.

The Globalization of Urban Economies

The existing literature on cities and economic globalization implies that globalization produces a serious and growing gap between places in terms of their economic success, ability to determine their own fate, and degree of economic integration. The WCH typically focuses on those cities at the very top, which have the leading or chief activities, especially the locations of the world financial markets. These places concentrate on the most important, dominant economic activities and exercise significant command and control functions. They house the overlords of the global economy, and so we might be tempted to term them "successful," but at the same time they also display the greatest internal divisions of wealth and poverty. The impact of economic globalization on other places is unclear. It is possible, as some argue, that all cities are becoming global to different degrees. Another prominent strain of thinking emphasizes chronicles of decline, suggesting that globalization encourages a race to the bottom among cities, or that it simply exploits most places, taking from them what it wants and then leaving them bereft. In fact, however, there is a vast array of places that fall into the gap between these two extremes, and there is little reason to believe that all of them behave in the same manner, whether as global cities "lite" or as wastelands of exploitation and dispossession. What if there is more than one route to economic integration for cities in the global economy? The second city pathway pursued by Manchester and Philadelphia constitutes one such alternative.

There are three main ways of thinking about these global pathways. According to the first approach—the new international division of labor (NIDL) theory—the global economy is really an international division of labor structured by the operations of TNCs with "global reach." The economist Stephen Hymer argued that positions in the urban hierarchy would increasingly correspond to the corporate functions that occurred in a place—headquarters, research, production, sales. In effect, the positions of cities in the international urban hierarchy were determined by the spatial distribution of large corporations' headquarters, plants, and subsidiaries. According to the economic geographer Christopher Ross, "It is the intra-organizational division of labor, and the influence linkages within these firms that actually comprise the set of intermetropolitan linkages." Cities with lots of headquarters were highly ranked because headquarters implied a city's ability to exercise command and control over economic decisions in other places.[3]

NIDL scholars illuminated the spatial distribution of economic activity in two main ways. First, they studied the locations of corporate headquarters and how the pattern of location changed over time to determine which cities had the most command and control power. Second, they examined the spatial distribution of FDI—the pattern of companies' overseas subsidiaries—to cast light on how cities were tied into a larger global urban network. By examining the patterns of FDI across particular places—the number of subsidiaries local companies controlled, for example, versus the number of local firms actually owned by companies elsewhere—NIDL scholars could begin to describe a richly variegated landscape of economic power and command. The original formulations of the WCH grew directly out of NIDL theory.

In the second approach, Saskia Sassen modified the NIDL argument to take account of the shift from manufacturing to services as the driver of urban economies. In particular, Sassen wrote about "a new strategic role for major cities," concentrated on advanced producer services like law, accounting, advertising, and architecture. Her argument was that spatially concentrated agglomerations of these industries were the critical drivers of global city formation, independent of TNC headquarter locations and regardless of whether the individual firms were large TNCs themselves. Some of the firms in these new industries in fact might be quite specialized and small and therefore lack extensive international operations. Dense complexes of these firms, across multiple, interlinked activities, constituted globalization's "leading industries."[4]

The third approach turned its attention to one specific leading industry or sector—finance, especially international finance and the locations of financial markets. Sometimes called FIRE (for finance, insurance, and real estate), this is the most internationalized of all sectors and is in fact the only permanent leading sector of the global economy. The literature on financial centers suggests that international, or haute, finance has been the crucial sector for the rise of global cities. International banking, foreign bond and securities transactions, and foreign offices of financial corporations all have clustered in global cities to a greater degree than any other industry. New York banks, for example, held 69 percent of all foreign deposits in the United States in 1986 and nearly 12 percent of all U.S. employment in the banking industry.[5]

Philadelphia and Manchester have displayed a distinctive, long-term pattern of integration into the global economy that has differed from the global city pattern in characteristic ways along each of these three dimensions. Historically, they arose as global manufacturing centers, not as financial centers—this is the crucial economic difference between them and global cities. (In Chapter 8 I ask whether the second city pattern visible in these two cities might be applicable to other cities as well.) Manchester and Philadelphia are globally prominent but in ways that contrast with global cities. Both cities

- Have prominent TNC headquarters
- Are important sites for both outward and inward FDI
- Focus historically on the leading industries of each era, particularly manufacturing; across eras they have switched their economies to new leading industries
- Maintain a specialized rather than a comprehensive global services complex (their global service economies focus on select industries and a few giant service firms)
- Possess little or no international financial industry

To demonstrate these characteristics, I employ a unique database of corporate hierarchies and FDI patterns, both inward and outward, for Manchester and Philadelphia. The database provides a comprehensive picture of Philadelphia's and Manchester's global economic roles and linkages, offering a more complete view of the two cities' international economic integration, I believe, than exists for any other city. The database is culled from two series of volumes, published annually, titled *Who Owns Whom* and the *Directory of Corporate Affiliations*, which include information about the headquarters and branch locations of most publicly traded corporations.[6] The database covers both inward and outward FDI for the Philadelphia and Manchester regions at four times between 1972 and 1998. Included are the locations of foreign parents and subsidiaries, whether the local office is a corporate or national headquarters, local addresses, employment, and industry. Such useful sources, unfortunately, scarcely exist at the urban level in the nineteenth or even the early twentieth century. Furthermore, in the nineteenth century, very few corporations were large enough to set up overseas subsidiaries. Instead, most firms and investors relied on three other kinds of international transactions: family partnerships, portfolio investment, and trade. Therefore, I also rely on company histories, census and employment data from government agencies, trade statistics, and local business directories. Because they provide an essential overview, we begin with employment numbers describing the size of various sectors over time for both cities.

Employment in Second Cities

Despite differences in the details, Philadelphia and Manchester display remarkably similar overall employment trends. Both cities grew into manufacturing powerhouses during the first half of the nineteenth century. Philadelphia's economic restructuring in the first decades of the nineteenth century, together with the building of a regional transport infrastructure, laid the groundwork for the city's emergence as an industrial metropolis; "in the two decades before the Civil War, Philadelphians discovered that they had anticipated the new directions of growth." In 1850 the city had almost 58,000 manufacturing jobs; by 1880, this number had almost tripled, to 162,000. Manchester had already entered its full industrial maturity in the 1840s. The textile industry had just completed the most rapid phase of its expansion but would still grow for another half century or more, and the city's diversification into other fields, especially chemicals and machining, was taking off.[7]

For a century and a half, from 1800 to the 1950s, the single most important industry in both cities was textiles. They were the largest textile producers in their respective countries and developed global reputations for their products. Manchester, of course, was the global center of cotton spinning and weaving for the entire nineteenth century. Cotton spindles in England grew from 9 million in 1832 to 37.5 million in 1875, and approximately 500,000 people were employed in the mills in the 1870s; from 1850 through 1900, textiles occupied more than 40 percent of Philadelphia's workforce. Both cities' textile industries were organized as dense, highly interconnected networks of small- to medium-sized family firms, which generally specialized in particular stages in the production process and eschewed vertical integration. Philadelphia specialized in the higher end of the industry and was also the country's largest producer of carpets. Kensington, the city's main textile-producing neighborhood, "was home for the world's largest lace factory and the world's largest hat factory." Manchester concentrated on the earlier stages of cotton textile manufacture—spinning yarn and weaving cloth, plus bleaching and dyeing—rather than on making clothes. In and around Manchester, by the 1860s, there even arose a geographic division of labor, with spinning concentrated to the near north, particularly in Oldham and Bolton, and weaving concentrated in the southern parts, including Stockport, and the far north.[8]

This vast swarm of regional activity was coordinated via the Manchester Cotton Exchange (officially known as the Manchester Royal Exchange). Originally built in 1729, the exchange was the vibrant heart not just of the regional economy, but also of the entire global market for cotton textiles. Raw cotton, yarn, and woven goods were bought and sold there and production contracts negotiated. By the 1860s, more than 5,500 merchants were members, and every Tuesday thousands of "Manchester men," large and small, would descend on the city for "high 'change." Philadelphia and Manchester therefore also served as central places for their regions, providing essential services, warehousing and trade, newspapers and information, and entertainment. Downtown Manchester was the commercial and business service center for Lancashire mill towns, offering work to thousands of dealers, brokers, lawyers, and merchants and their clerks. Philadelphia was one of the country's major ports and transportation centers, home to both the Reading and Pennsylvania railroads, and Manchester was a railway center as well, with five stations ringing the city's downtown. Philadelphia's old financial district near Third and Chestnut streets still served as the city's commercial heart into the 1870s.[9]

The textile industry was not the only prominent industry in each city, however; both places experienced substantial economic diversification, particularly into machinery and other capital goods and chemicals. In Lancashire, the Platt Brothers' textile machinery company, Beyer Peacock's locomotive works, and Joseph Whitworth's armaments factory became crucial additions to the regional economy. By the 1860s, Manchester firms and chemists started patenting new artificial dyes, leading to the formation of such firms as the Clayton Aniline Dye Company. After the opening of the Manchester Ship Canal in 1894, economic diversification in Lancashire focused on the huge industrial complex at Trafford Park, just west of the city, which had almost no connection with Lancashire's traditional cotton industry. By 1907, the Trafford estate housed engineering firms, building contractors, timber merchants and sawmills, flour mills, and railway works, plus glass, lead-pipe, food-processing, and metal-refining facilities. And it had sixty-five million gallons of oil-storage capacity.[10]

Philadelphia, meanwhile, enriched by its role as a main supply point during the American Civil War, developed one of the most diversified manufacturing economies of any city in any country, and had tens of thousands of highly skilled workers turning out custom and quality goods. The Pennsylvania Railroad—the largest corporation in the world—stimulated demand for a whole range of industrial products and contributed as well to the processes of distribution and wholesaling and the development of the Philadelphia port. Matthias Baldwin's locomotive firm employed thousands of craftsmen and machinists, making three times as many locomotives as any other company in the world. Baldwin was joined by William Cramp's shipyard, William Sellers's tool works (see Figure 3.1), Samuel Merrick's Southwark Foundry, and Henry Disston's saw manufactory. The city had a large chemicals and pharmaceuticals industry as well, with nearly a dozen important family concerns and partnerships that provided the foundation for what has been, together with medicine, the city's most enduring sector.[11]

Table 3.1 gives employment in selected industries for both cities at their industrial maturity, in 1910 and 1911. Nearly half their workforces were employed in manufacturing, focused in particular on textiles, clothing and dyeing, which together employed more than 100,000 people in Philadelphia and almost 70,000 people in Manchester. Metals and machinery industries were also important, employing nearly 10 percent of each city's workforce, as were transportation and distribution. The clerical category was already large and growing; finance, however, was small, accounting for only about 1 percent of total employment, as were professional services (the core of Saskia Sassen's explanation of global city economies).[12] The overall picture, then, is of two heavily industrial cities focused overwhelmingly on the production and distribution of goods, with a small but important set of office and clerical occupations representing the industries that would later become "business" or "producer" services.

This period, on the eve of World War I, would prove to be the high point of the two cities' manufacturing economies. Textile production, for example, peaked in Manchester in 1913 and Philadelphia in the 1920s. Their diverse economic bases offered them some protection from the worst dislocations of the Great Depression, but even so they suffered. Textile factories and jobs began moving out of Philadelphia and heading particularly for the American South. Lancashire's export trade in cotton suffered heavily as Indian, Chinese, and Japanese production boomed and as synthetic fibers encroached on the market (nylon was invented in 1927). "British exports of cotton cloth fell by 80 per cent between 1913 and 1938. Output fell by 45 per cent over the same period, profits collapsed, and for the vast majority of firms re-equipment was completely out of the question."[13]

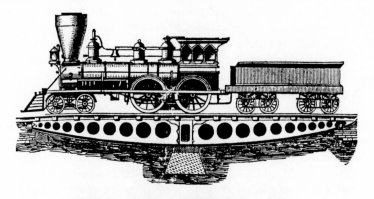

WM. SELLERS & CO.,
NO. 1600 HAMILTON ST.,
PHILADELPHIA.

MACHINISTS', FOUNDERS', SMITHS' & BOILER MAKERS'

TOOLS,
SHAFTING,

With Ball and Socket Bearings, and Double Cane Vice-couplings, admitting of the easiest possible adjustment.

A COMPLETE ASSORTMENT OF

PULLEY & WHEEL PATTERNS,

From which Castings or Finished Work will be furnished.

RAILWAY EQUIPMENTS,

TURNING AND TRANSFER TABLES,

AND PIVOT BRIDGES.

Sole Manufacturers and Licensees of

GIFFARD'S INJECTOR

FOR FEEDING BOILERS.

WILLIAM SELLERS.   JOHN SELLERS, JR

Figure 3.1: Advertisement for William Sellers and Company, 1867. (*Source: Edwin T. Freedley*, Philadelphia and Its Manufactures *[Philadelphia: Edward Young, 1867], 365.*)

TABLE 3.1   EMPLOYMENT IN SELECT INDUSTRIES IN PHILADELPHIA
AND MANCHESTER, 1910–1911 (IN THOUSANDS)

Industry	Philadelphia	%	Manchester	%
Total all industries	711.2		347.8	
Transportation	53.0	7.5	38.1	11.0
Total manufacturing	339.9	47.8	175.1	50.4
Construction	41.1	5.8	19.0	5.5
General labor	13.1	1.8	7.6	2.2
Food	10.9	1.5	21.9	6.3
Shoes	5.9	0.8	2.2	0.6
Textiles	49.7	7.0	20.1	5.8
Clothing and hats	54.9	7.7	41.8	12.0
Bleaching/dyeing	2.2	0.3	6.8	2.0
Iron and steel	30.2	4.2	0.7	0.2
Machining	27.7	3.9	27.0	7.8
Tool and die	1.7	0.2	6.8	2.0
Other metals	6.0	0.8		
Furniture	4.5	0.6	8.3	2.4
Chemicals	3.6	0.5	9.2	2.6
Paper and printing	12.1	1.7	11.7	3.4
Total services and trade	298.0	41.9	114.2	32.8
Merchants and clerks			22.9	6.6
Cotton dealers			12.2	3.5
Retail/wholesale	85.4	12.0	23.7	6.8
Clerical/office	62.5	8.8		
Professional services	34.8	4.9	13.1	3.8
Domestic services	43.2	6.1	19.8	5.7
Finance, insurance, and real estate (FIRE)	7.8	1.1	3.8	1.1
Hospitality	24.2	3.4	11.9	3.4

Sources: Great Britain, *Census of England and Wales* (London: HMSO, 1913), table 13;
U.S. Department of Commerce, Bureau of the Census, *Census of Population and Housing*
(Washington, DC: Government Printing Office, 1914), vol. 4, Occupation Statistics.

Note: Industries are not strictly comparable across cities because of differences in definition. Construction and general labor are counted under manufacturing because this is how
they were classified in the Philadelphia census. Because these data are based on occupational
classifications, manufacturing numbers in particular represent workers and exclude owners/
executives.

The 1930s Depression proved to be an extraordinary time of unemployment and suffering, although depressive economies had existed during
the preceding century, with poverty and recurring economic crises significantly affecting tens if not hundreds of thousands of people. The periodic
economic swings that greater global integration brought about led to trade
depressions in both cities not only during the 1930s but also from 1837 to
1845, 1873 to 1880, and 1893 to 1897. Deprivation was also intimately
associated with early industrialization in general. In addition to the foul

living and working conditions detailed for Manchester by observers like Friedrich Engels, the historian Walter Licht has shown that job insecurity was rampant in industrial Philadelphia. From the 1850s through the 1920s, the median job tenure at many firms, even successful ones, was only six months. Layoffs were frequent, and business in many industries was heavily seasonal. Along with poverty and low wages, people faced income instability. The historian Michael Haines estimated that annual wages for 1880 in Philadelphia varied from $978 for clerks and $1,188 for foremen to $472 for weavers and $336 for laborers. There is widespread evidence that, as a result, perhaps 25 percent of families escaped destitution only by sending teenagers into the workforce; more than half of fifteen-year-olds worked for wages.[14]

The rise of new industries, from department stores to locomotive manufacturers, mitigated these problems to some extent because many businesses employed skilled labor and paid a premium for doing so. Living conditions for many workers improved over the course of the nineteenth century and into the twentieth: homeownership became increasingly widespread in Philadelphia, and starting in 1845, Manchester outlawed the worst forms of basement dwellings. Even so, poverty and inequality persisted. In addition, as time went on, the labor market developed new forms of inequality as it became increasingly segmented and structured by noneconomic or extra-economic factors. Age and gender played important roles. In Philadelphia, married white women rarely worked (fewer than 3 percent in the 1800s, and only breaking above 15 percent in the 1920s), but teenagers of both sexes did; the situation was reversed in the black community. In Manchester, meanwhile, patriarchy and paternalism, both at home and in the workplace, reasserted themselves from the 1850s forward, and spinning in particular became defined as male skilled labor.[15] The most notable form of labor market segmentation, however, was ethno-racial, which became more pronounced as the decades advanced and the cities became more fully industrialized. Because this type of inequality is so deeply bound up with migration patterns, I postpone a detailed discussion of it until the next chapter.

Although manufacturing in both cities revived during World War II (Trafford Park, for example, the massive industrial estate just west of Manchester, reached an all-time high of 75,000 jobs during the war years), many local manufacturing establishments were essentially living on borrowed time. Still, Table 3.2, which shows employment by industry for the cities and their surrounding regions between 1950 and 1951 and 2000 and 2001, demonstrates that their employment patterns did not change significantly until well after the war. Both cities still had more than 40 percent of their total workforces in manufacturing industries between 1950 and 1951, and regionally the percentage was even higher—46 percent for the Greater Manchester Council (GMC), and 50 percent for Philadelphia's primary metropolitan statistical area (PMSA).

Postwar economic changes manifested in three main ways: through a decline in industrialization, a rise in service industries, and an increase in suburbanization. Manufacturing employment dropped by more than 80 percent in both cities and by more than half in both regions. Philadelphia's once powerful textile industry lost more than 90 percent of its jobs. Beyer Peacock stopped making locomotives in Manchester in 1966; Baldwin moved out of Philadelphia to the suburbs in 1928 and shut down in the 1950s. Ford closed down at Trafford Park in 1946 and others increasingly followed suit; jobs there declined to 52,000 in 1965 and 24,500 in 1985. The worst of the manufacturing decline was concentrated between 1965 and 1985. In 1970 Lancashire's unemployment rate exceeded the national average; by 1982, it had reached nearly 22 percent (compared to the national rate of 12 percent). Between 1971 and 1975, even jobs in Manchester's office and service sectors fell. Manufacturing employment is now below 10 percent of the total jobs in both cities. The remaining manufacturing employment in both regions concentrates in "new economy" industries like pharmaceuticals, scientific and medical instruments, and synthetic-fiber textiles.[16]

Meanwhile, as manufacturing sectors in the cities were being hollowed out, other industries began to expand. "Professional services," such as engineering and consulting, showed swift rates of growth; architecture and law increased by 150 percent in Greater Manchester between 1951 and 1976. The financial sector (FIRE), by contrast, grew only modestly in the city of Philadelphia (although more substantially across the region as a whole); it showed more significant growth in Manchester. Health care and education, however—the "meds and eds"—were the real drivers of post–World War II employment growth. As overall employment in Philadelphia dropped by nearly a quarter, jobs in both health care and education grew more than twentyfold, and even more in the region as a whole. The University of Pennsylvania is now the region's largest nongovernmental employer, with more than 20,000 jobs, and Manchester University grew into Europe's largest medical school. The medical and education industries, which between them account for almost 30 percent of jobs in Philadelphia and more than 20 percent in Manchester, could be considered the new manufacturing. They are giant sectors that export a significant portion of their production by serving clients and customers from elsewhere, even if those customers have to travel to the region to access the services.[17] Indeed, service-sector growth was so substantial in Philadelphia that it picked up *nearly all* of the slack from manufacturing's decline in the city, about 300,000 jobs, and far outweighed that decline (245,000 jobs lost versus more than one million gained) in the region as a whole.

Consideration of the changing regional employment pictures points to the importance not only of new industries, but also of suburbanization. Those industries that moved to the suburbs first—trade and construction

TABLE 3.2 EMPLOYMENT IN SELECT INDUSTRIES IN PHILADELPHIA AND MANCHESTER, 1950–1951 AND 2000–2001 (IN THOUSANDS)

Industry	Philadelphia City			Philadelphia PMSA			City/PMSA 2000 (%)
	1951	2000	% Change	1951	2000	% Change	
Total employment	773.6	606.5	−21.6	1146.5	2194.1	91.4	27.6
Construction	39.1	13.0	−66.6	64.1	101.9	59.0	12.8
All manufacturing	355.6	42.4	−88.1	576.1	231.4	−59.8	18.3
Food	31.7	7.6	−75.9	43.6	23.1	−47.1	33.0
Textiles	43.3	1.5	−96.5	66.1	4.2	−93.6	35.5
Apparel	48.3	3.6	−92.4	65.0	8.1	−87.5	45.0
Printing/publishing	32.0	4.2	−86.9	35.3	22.3	−36.9	18.9
Chemicals	17.6	2.9	−83.4	29.8	19.9	−33.0	14.6
Steel/metals	7.0	.3	−95.3	29.3	8.9	−69.8	3.7
Tools/metal products	35.5	3.6	−90.0	52.0	27.3	−47.5	13.0
Machinery	31.0	1.6	−94.8	46.6	15.4	−66.9	10.4
Electrical machinery	27.6	3.4	−90.6	47.7	30.0	−48.8	11.3
Transportation	45.0	28.6	−36.5	55.6	63.5	14.2	44.9
All trade	191.6	75.1	−60.8	260.7	391.3	50.1	19.2
Wholesale	66.5	24.1	−63.8	76.3	123.2	61.4	19.6
Retail	125.1	51.0	−59.2	184.4	268.0	45.4	19.0
Finance, insurance, and real estate (FIRE)	49.8	58.1	16.6	61.0	189.4	210.5	30.7
All services	64.9	364.7	461.9	89.0	1106.4	1142.8	33.0
Information		18.4			66.2		27.8
Business services	12.4	93.9	657.9	13.8	349.0	2426.8	26.9
Legal	2.3	18.0	677.4	3.1	31.9	924.7	56.4
Engineering/consulting	3.0	30.2	917.4	3.6	101.5	2720.3	29.8
Education	2.0	56.9	2819.7	3.1	97.9	3090.5	58.2
Health	4.3	117.3	2636.7	6.7	321.4	4707.0	36.5
Nonprofit	6.2	18.0	191.1	8.7	53.6	513.6	33.6

Industry	Manchester City			Greater Manchester (GMC)			City/GMC 2001 (%)
	1951	2001	% Change	1951	2001	% Change	
Total employment	359.9	286.3	-20.5	829.4	1122.6	35.4	25.5
Construction	20.4	7.0	-65.8	43.9	47.6	8.4	14.7
All manufacturing	146.7	21.0	-85.7	380.9	168.3	-55.8	12.5
Food	4.5	3.1	-31.4	10.6	28.7	171.0	10.8
Textiles	12.3	2.7	-77.9	83.3	18.4	-77.9	14.8
Apparel	33.2	1.4	-95.7	55.7	7.1	-87.2	19.9
Printing/publishing	5.7	2.8	-51.9	9.9	13.7	37.8	20.1
Chemicals	2.6	2.0	-24.0	5.2	15.0	186.3	13.4
Steel/metals	7.3	suppressed		17.8	suppressed		
Tools/metal products	7.1	1.2	-83.6	16.5	17.6	6.8	6.6
Machinery	18.7	2.3	-87.7	44.0	16.3	-63.0	14.1
Electrical machinery	7.7	1.7	-78.1	16.4	11.2	-31.3	15.1
Transportation	21.7	31.1	43.0	46.3	52.6	13.6	59.0
All trade	43.6	43.0	-1.5	92.7	208.0	124.3	20.7
Wholesale	18.6	13.6	-27.1	36.8	61.8	68.0	21.9
Retail	25.0	26.6	6.0	56.0	124.4	122.4	21.3
Finance, insurance, and real estate (FIRE)	1.9	26.4	1304.8	4.4	61.0	1289.9	43.3
All services	96.1	121.8	26.7	194.7	403.0	107.0	30.2
Clerical	42.4			81.8			
Hospitality		14.0			60.2		23.3
Business services	18.1	48.4	167.0	39.7	137.1	245.1	35.3
Legal	.1			.4			
Engineering/consulting	3.7	4.0	8.0	9.1	13.6	50.2	29.6
Education	4.1	32.8	702.2	9.4	105.0	1013.1	31.2
Health	4.0	27.3	589.5	15.5	112.8	628.7	24.2

Sources: Great Britain, Office of Population Censuses and Surveys, *Census of England and Wales* (London: HMSO, 1953 and 2001); U.S. Department of Commerce, *County Business Patterns* (Washington, DC: Government Printing Office, 1953 and 2003). U.K. data for 2001 ordered from the Annual Business Inquiry via NOMIS (http://www.nomisweb.co.uk) on 14 May 2007; U.K. data for 1951 downloaded from the Vision of Britain Web site, part of the Great Britain Historical GIS Project (http://www.visionofbritain.org.uk), accessed 8 May 2007 (copyright © Office for National Statistics).

Notes: The initialism "PMSA" stands for "primary metropolitan statistical area." Industries not strictly comparable across cities because of differences in definition. Some cells are blank because the category does not exist for that particular census. Manchester and GMC 1951 data refer to residents rather than to workplaces. GMC 1951 data underestimate because "Tameside" did not exist as a reporting unit, and because Stretford was substituted for Trafford; also, "clerical" should be distributed across other industries.

in particular—were the ones in which proximity to consumers and markets was important. They were soon followed by manufacturing; today, there are more manufacturing jobs in suburban Montgomery County alone than there are in the city of Philadelphia. But the star performers were the various service industries, in which suburban job growth outstripped even the fantastic growth rates in the central cities. This suburban boom was much more prevalent in Philadelphia than in Manchester, largely because Philadelphia was historically more dominant over its region, and so it had farther to fall; while Manchester never held a majority of its region's jobs, Philadelphia did hold such a majority until the 1970s. Philadelphia's share of total regional employment dropped from 67 percent in 1950 to about 28 percent in 2000, while Manchester's decline was more modest, from 43 percent to 26 percent. Even so, Manchester still holds a greater concentration of employment than of population (it has only 16 percent of regional population), while Philadelphia's current share of regional employment is in rough parity with its 30 percent share of regional population. The meds and eds, together with transportation and some business services, like law, are the industries in which the city still holds a disproportionate advantage.

These economic shifts have been wrenching. The largest direct cause of economic dislocation was the deindustrialization and job loss of the 1970s, which reached epic proportions as factory after factory closed or moved away. The structural shift toward service industries and new sources of growth took off in both cities in the 1980s and consolidated in the 1990s, but this shift and new growth occurred in ways that reinforced the decline of the hardest hit portions of the workforce and added new layers of labor market segmentation. Unemployment in Manchester, for example, declined from its 1982 high of 22 percent to 9 percent in 2000, but it did so by increasing the number of part-time and female jobs; the crisis in male full-time employment that began in the 1970s remains. Despite the fact that the number of jobs paying more than twice the median income doubled in the 1980s in Philadelphia, this growth left many people behind; the city's poverty rate was more than 22 percent in 2000. A great ring of poor neighborhoods—with unemployment rates in the high teens or worse, heavy housing abandonment, abundant crime, and elevated school dropout rates—persists, surrounding both downtowns. Once again, however, race and ethnicity structured the experience of poverty and unemployment. While only 12.7 percent of Philadelphia's non-Hispanic white people were poor and less than 6 percent of white people across the region as a whole, 29 percent of black people in the city, 30 percent of Asians, and fully 42 percent of city Hispanics fell below the poverty line.[18] In other words, the reinvigoration of global economic integration in Manchester and Philadelphia has not resolved the economic pain of deindustrialization; rather, it has contributed to and even exacerbated the stratification of the population by class, gender, neighborhood, and particularly, race and ethnicity.

The Global Geography of Corporations

In addition to employment patterns, Manchester and Philadelphia also display distinctive patterns of headquarters and TNC activity. Of course, TNCs are a relatively recent development, and it can be difficult to trace the changing organizational forms of international economic life back through earlier time periods. Historically, firms and investors have pursued globalization in a variety of ways. Trade was presumably the oldest form of globalization: the firm stayed put, but its products traveled around the world. Portfolio investment (the purchase of foreign stocks and bonds) took off in the nineteenth century. And family partnerships, in which heads of firms ("houses") established additional business locations in other cities— under the control of sons, brothers, or long-trusted associates—were for centuries an early, pre-corporate form of FDI. All three activities were ways to pursue economic globalization in the past; the first two, of course, still exist, although the third has faded in importance.

Because the issue of trade is so intimately linked with the provision of transportation infrastructure—seaports, airports, and railroads—a larger discussion of trends in import/export activity occurs in Chapter 6. Both cities produced far more than they could use themselves, however, and so they exported a large percentage of their production. Baldwin, for example, routinely exported a third or more of its locomotives. Nearly all of Manchester's yarn and woven output was destined for export; "in 1913 the home trade took only an eighth of Lancashire's production." British cotton exports—Manchester accounted for the vast majority of them—were approximately 42 percent of British export earnings in 1850, 36 percent in 1860, and 37 percent in 1870. They grew from 1.2 million square yards, or £25 million, in 1850, to 5.2 million square yards, or £69 million in 1896. Over time, the most important destinations for exports shifted from Europe to India, China, and Japan, with South America remaining an important market as well. As a result, Manchester drew hundreds of foreign merchants, of whom Germans were the most numerous, while other nationalities included Dutch, French, Italian, and Turkish.[19] Thus, Manchester in particular played a crucial role in the overall integration of the world economy via trade.

A second option for firms and investors was to engage in international portfolio investing, buying the stocks or bonds of various concerns simply to make profits or dividends, rather than to exercise managerial control. Europeans invested widely in the securities of U.S. states, canals, and railroad companies from the 1830s forward. Although I have been unable to gather any systematic information of this kind, the case of the Pennsylvania Railroad (Pennsy) can serve as an illustration. Foreign investors, mostly British, owned 40 percent to 50 percent of Pennsy stock in the 1880s and 1890s. In the 1850s the Pennsy sold bonds denominated in pounds sterling to Barings Bank and others, and in 1906 the company sold approximately $50 million worth of bonds in Paris denominated in francs. (International portfolio investment remains important today, as does international investment in land and property. Dutch pension funds, Japanese insurance companies, and the government of Singapore were among the owners of shopping malls and downtown office buildings in the Philadelphia region in the 1980s and 1990s.)[20]

FDI, the third major option, has historically taken more than one form. Before incorporation became widespread, FDI was generally pursued via family-centered partnerships or "houses." Each house would be located in a different city, and each would have a separate written agreement among the partners covering ownership, division of profits, and responsibilities. The houses would be linked both by the expectation that they would support one another's activities and by common partners, particularly family members—fathers and sons, brothers or cousins. Indeed, the partnership form was primarily intended to expand the range of what was explicitly considered a family business, with the Rothschild banking house in the nineteenth century being perhaps the most famous example. Such multicity partnership arrangements were well-known in Philadelphia and Manchester before the twentieth century. David Sassoon from Baghdad, for example, managed a trading empire that spanned England, the Levant, China, and India, with British offices established in Manchester, London, and Liverpool in the 1860s. Another example was Friedrich Engels, who came to Manchester in the 1840s to look after his father's interests in the Godfrey Ermen and Engels partnership in Salford; Engels lived in the city for more than twenty years. A. J. Drexel and Company, the Philadelphia bankers who eventually merged with J. P. Morgan, had offices in London and Paris before 1870. And department store magnate John Wanamaker established buyers in foreign cities in 1880; the Paris office, entrusted to one of his sons, was the first foreign office of any U.S. retailer. Wanamaker went on to establish additional offices in Yokohama, Japan, and in London.[21]

The partnership form disappeared in the twentieth century, replaced by the corporation. In some cases it is even possible to trace the transformation and growth of an individual firm from partnership to corporation to full-fledged TNC, thereby turning its home city into a headquarters location. The Philadelphia chemicals firm Rohm and Haas, for example, progressed neatly through a series of stages of internationalization. The company began as an international partnership between Dr. Otto Röhm, who remained in Germany, and Otto Haas, who migrated to the United States in 1909.[22] The firm originally concentrated on technology transfer from Germany and on chemicals to facilitate the processing of leather, but it expanded into other products over time; the company established sales offices in South America as early as 1913, although they were closed in the 1920s. Haas incorporated in 1917, in part to get around the political difficulties of having a German partner during World War I, but close relations with Röhm in Germany continued until World War II. The most successful product produced by Rohm and Haas was Plexiglas, invented on the German side in 1933. Buoyed by Plexiglas, Rohm and Haas opened sales offices in London and Canada, and its first foreign factory opened in Buenos Aires in 1939. After World War II, the company established plants in Milan, Newcastle, Paris, São Paulo, and Toronto, as well as a joint venture in Japan. In the 1960s the company transformed itself into a multinational corporation by naming London its European regional headquarters and opening additional plants in a dozen countries. In the 1980s the company centralized global production of some products in Europe; the decision to source the U.S. market from abroad was significant evidence that Rohm and Haas had developed a truly transnational strategy and firm organization. In 1997 the corporation had thirty-nine foreign subsidiaries on five continents, concentrated around the Pacific Rim and in Europe.

This process of corporate development tended to occur more frequently in manufacturing firms than in finance or services—the textile giants Tootal and Coats Viyella in Manchester, for example. Still, truly transnational corporations—those that have large numbers of foreign subsidiaries in many nations and decide what to produce in which countries on the basis of a global strategic plan—are rare. (In 1973, 45 percent of companies with foreign subsidiaries had operations in only *one* foreign country and 35 percent had operations in two to five foreign countries.) Philadelphia's Smith-Kline is a paradigmatic example of a true TNC. Like Rohm and Haas, SmithKline's roots stretch back into the nineteenth century, when its ancestor firms were partnerships producing chemicals and early, relatively unsophisticated drugs. Also like Rohm and Haas, SmithKline made its reputation in the middle decades of the past century with name brands like Thorazine, Tagamet, Contac, and Sine-Off. It developed itself into a multinational corporation in the 1960s; by 1972, it had thirty-three foreign subsidiaries, primarily in Canada and Europe, but also in Latin America, Southern Africa, South Asia, and the Pacific Rim. Unlike its Philadelphia cousin, however, SmithKline followed a different path to globalization and TNC status; it chose a merger of equals with Beecham plc of England in 1989 for $8.25 billion, at the time the largest corporate transaction ever. "The company that resulted—now called SmithKline Beecham—comes close to meeting the definition of a true transnational corporation. . . . [R]oughly 40 percent of the sales and profits are from North America, 40 percent are from Europe, and the remainder are from Japan and other countries around the world." The new company purposely internationalized its board of directors and split its headquarter functions: corporate headquarters were located in Brentford, a suburb of London, but operational headquarters remained in Philadelphia. This arrangement continues now that SmithKline has merged with Glaxo Wellcome to form GlaxoSmithKline.[23]

These anecdotes are useful in understanding how cities' homegrown companies develop into TNCs, turning the cities into important locations for headquarters. But they fall short of a systematic analysis of a city's role as a headquarters location and its position in the NIDL. Table 3.3 depicts change during the course of nearly thirty years in the number and direction (inward or outward) of FDI connections for Philadelphia and Manchester.[24] It tracks their positions in corporate hierarchies at four points—1972, 1980, 1990, and 1998—enabling what may be the first systematic longitudinal analysis of the urban NIDL. Table 3.3 measures not firms but the number of international subsidiaries that have each city as a node: it is the number of international connections or linkages that matters. Thus, if a Philadelphia-headquartered company had five foreign subsidiaries around the world in 1990, it is counted five times; if a Milan-based firm owned one Manchester subsidiary in 1990, it is counted only once. Manchester's total number of linkages nearly tripled, to more than 1,200, and Philadelphia's total increased slightly during the twenty-six-year span, from 586 to 601. The greater number of total links in Manchester is partly a product of geography, resulting from the different sizes of the United Kingdom and the United States—England is a small country, and Manchester TNCs or subsidiaries located in France are counted as foreign. However, a Texas or California subsidiary of a Philadelphia company does not register in the database.

Total FDI can be broken into two components—"outward" FDI, in which Philadelphia- or Manchester-headquartered companies own subsidiaries in other countries, and "inward" FDI, in which one of the two cities is the subsidiary location for a foreign parent corporation. Both cities have been significant locations for outward FDI, with several hundred overseas

TABLE 3.3 FDI LINKS: SELECT YEARS, 1972–1998

Year	Manchester			Philadelphia		
	Outward FDI	Inward FDI	Total	Outward FDI	Inward FDI	Total
1972	370	68	438	584	2	586
1980	510	129	639	387	28	415
1990	772	337	1109	513	135	648
1998	541	684	1225	470	131	601
Change (%)	46.2%	905.9%	179.7%	–19.5%	6450.0%	2.6%

Sources: Compiled from *Who Owns Whom* (London: O. W. Roskill, 1973 and 1974; London: Dun and Bradstreet, 1981; High Wycombe, UK: Dun and Bradstreet, 1991 and 1998); *International Directory of Corporate Affiliations* (Skokie and Wilmette, IL: National Register Publishing, 1981 and 1991); and the *Directory of Corporate Affiliations* (New Providence, NJ: National Register Publishing, 1999) and supplemented by local industrial directories and other sources (such as banking directories and newspapers).

subsidiaries of local firms throughout the last third of the twentieth century. Manchester's importance as a global headquarters location has increased remarkably, by 46 percent, to the point where it has now overtaken Philadelphia. Philadelphia's importance as a global headquarters location dropped significantly in the 1970s, and then partially recovered, declining by 20 percent during the time period as a whole; in 1998 there were still nearly five hundred Philadelphia-controlled subsidiaries in other countries. Few of these local companies are as large as SmithKline or Rohm and Haas, however. In 1998, Manchester had eleven companies, and Philadelphia thirteen, with more than ten foreign subsidiaries apiece and therefore potentially constituting true TNCs. Most of the locally headquartered firms had only one or two foreign subsidiaries—53 percent in Philadelphia and fully 77 percent in Manchester.

Inward FDI has boomed in both cities, particularly since 1980. The growth of inward FDI in Manchester has been spectacular, increasing by an order of magnitude. In Philadelphia, on the other hand, there has been a kind of replacement process—inward FDI has grown from virtually nil and has slightly more than compensated for the decline of outward FDI. Much of this replacement is accounted for by international mergers in a single industry—pharmaceuticals—of which the SmithKline merger described above was the most significant instance. Even in that case, however, operational headquarters remained in the city after the merger. Overall, while it is true that foreign control of local assets is increasing, this is accompanied by only some, if any, loss of local control of foreign assets. These cities have become more globally integrated during the past several decades but not necessarily less powerful.

The post-1980 rise in inward FDI in both regions is consistent with NIDL theory, which sees growth in inward FDI across all developed nations as part of the transition away from an older international division of labor. In the "old" economic geography, corporations from core countries, like the United Kingdom, the United States, and France, invested primarily in poorer countries, especially their own peripheries. In the NIDL, on the other hand, there is greater cross-investment among richer countries.[25] The changing geographic patterns of FDI for Manchester and Philadelphia aptly illustrate these trends, as Table 3.4 shows. Overall, linkages are shifting in favor of the more developed countries: the European core (for both cities), the United States (for Manchester), and the most important of the Asian economies (for Philadelphia). The most important growth regions were East Asia for Philadelphia and the United States and Western Europe for Manchester. In these growth regions, both components of FDI surged between 1972 and 1998, and inward FDI in particular took off. For Manchester's "Commonwealth I" countries, including Australia and Ireland, outward FDI was stable and inward FDI grew substantially, as corporations from those countries began to invest in the former motherland.

TABLE 3.4   REGIONAL PATTERNS IN INTERNATIONAL CONNECTIONS, 1972 AND 1998

Region and Type of Link	Manchester		
	1972	1998	% Change
Total	438	1,225	180
Outward	370	541	46
Inward	68	684	906
United States	*59*	*299*	*407*
Outward	22	91	314
Inward	37	208	462
Western Europe	*138*	*601*	*336*
Outward	118	282	139
Inward	20	319	1,495
Commonwealth I	*111*	*174*	*57*
Outward	104	100	–4
Inward	7	74	957
Commonwealth II	*51*	*8*	*–84*
Outward	51	7	–86
Inward	0	1	

Region and Type of Link	Philadelphia		
	1972	1998	% Change
Total	586	601	3
Outward	584	470	–20
Inward	2	131	6,450
Western Europe	*263*	*265*	*1*
Outward	261	184	–30
Inward	2	81	3,950
East Asia	*18*	*81*	*350*
Outward	18	57	217
Inward	0	24	
Americas	*176*	*110*	*–38*
Outward	176	101	–43
Inward	0	9	

Sources: Compiled from *Who Owns Whom* (London: O. W. Roskill, 1973 and 1974; London: Dun and Bradstreet, 1981; High Wycombe, UK: Dun and Bradstreet, 1991 and 1998); *International Directory of Corporate Affiliations* (Skokie and Wilmette, IL: National Register Publishing, 1981 and 1991); and the *Directory of Corporate Affiliations* (New Providence, NJ: National Register Publishing, 1999) and supplemented by local industrial directories and other sources (such as banking directories and newspapers).

Notes: For Manchester, Western Europe means Belgium, Denmark, France, Germany, Italy, the Netherlands, Spain, Sweden, and Switzerland; Commonwealth I includes Australia, Canada, Hong Kong, Ireland, and New Zealand; Commonwealth II includes India, South Africa, and Zimbabwe. For Philadelphia, Western Europe includes Belgium, France, Germany, Italy, the Netherlands, Spain, Switzerland, and the United Kingdom; East Asia includes China, Hong Kong, Japan, and Singapore; Americas includes Brazil, Canada, Colombia, and Mexico.

The only regions to register declines in total FDI were the Americas in Philadelphia's case and "Commonwealth II" in Manchester's. These two regions represent former colonial or quasi-colonial peripheries (for example, Mexico and India). In both instances, the decline is entirely accounted for by reductions in outward FDI from Philadelphia and Manchester—in other words, locally headquartered TNCs have left or been bought out of those countries. This decline was not replaced by a rise of inward FDI; virtually no foreign companies from these countries established Manchester or Philadelphia subsidiaries. Outward FDI for Philadelphia also fell in the Western European region, although it was almost precisely matched by a rise in inward FDI from European countries. This switch is in keeping with the long-term trend of post–World War II economic growth in Europe and the rise of European TNCs.

Unfortunately, the business directories and other sources are too fragmentary to allow a comparison of direct city-to-city linkages over time, but it is possible to compile a reasonably complete record of city-to-city FDI patterns for Philadelphia for 1998. In that year, specific city linkages exist for 576 of the 601 total linkages, representing 196 different cities. Nearly two-thirds of the cities (125 of 196) have only one link to Philadelphia. The top tier of global cities far and away leads the pack of partner cities: London has fifty-three links to Philadelphia (9 percent of the total) and Tokyo and Paris have thirty-five apiece (6 percent). The top eleven cities (I include eleven because the last two are tied), in order, are London, Paris, Tokyo, Toronto, Singapore, Sydney, Mexico City, Brussels, Milan, Frankfurt, and Hong Kong. All are well-recognized global cities, with perhaps the exception of Brussels; together they account for 240, or 42 percent, of the total linkages. Interestingly, the FDI linkages with the top three cities are fairly balanced with regard to control (i.e., which city is the parent or headquarters location and which the subsidiary): sixty-eight of the links are outward FDI, and fifty-five are inward. For the rest of the top eleven, Philadelphia is much more likely to be the headquarters location—104 outward links and only thirteen inward links. The groups of cities with which Philadelphia has between three and nine links include global cities, such as Madrid, São Paulo, Seoul, and Zurich, as well as peer or second-tier cities, like Birmingham, Düsseldorf, Lyon, Manchester, Melbourne, Monterrey, Montreal, Munich, Rotterdam, Stuttgart, and Vancouver, along with capital cities of uncertain global rank, like Auckland, Santiago, and Stockholm. Most of these FDI linkages are also outward rather than inward.

The combined patterns for both cities show increasing integration among the most advanced economies and with the most swiftly growing of the developing countries; they are less connected than previously with economies on the periphery. In part, this reflects the growth of indigenous ownership and control of manufacturing assets in peripheral and semi-peripheral countries. But whatever the cause, an older international and interurban division of labor (in which Manchester firms established subsidiaries in British colonies, for example) has withered. Yet neither Manchester nor Philadelphia has disappeared from the "new" international division of labor. They are globally integrated both as headquarter locations and as sites for the subsidiaries of foreign corporations. In direct city-to-city linkages, based on limited information from one recent year in Philadelphia, these cities, in their patterns of FDI, tend to reach upward toward the global cities, and they tend to exercise a substantial measure of control in their economic relations with both global and peer cities.

The Question of "Leading Industries"

Corporate headquarters and FDI alone, however, are insufficient measures of how cities are integrated into the global economy. One must also examine the critical sectors that enable economic actors (primarily TNCs) both to coordinate their own globally dispersed activities and to exercise control over the decisions of other firms and places. Increasingly, Saskia Sassen in particular has argued, the tools and mechanisms of this global coordination have been outsourced from TNCs themselves to "producer service complexes"—spatially concentrated agglomerations of both large and small firms providing specialized inputs to other firms. It is these agglomerations—in accounting, advertising, architecture, communications, engineering, finance, and law—that are the critical drivers of economic globalization and that make economic globalization work. In the most reductionist version of this argument, there is really only one critical sector: finance, especially international financial markets or exchanges. In more nuanced and sophisticated versions, the impact of finance, or FIRE, is distinguished from the rest of the producer services, and more weight is given to producer services.

The pattern of globalization in FIRE looks very different in second cities than in global cities. Financial sectors that are both large and primarily internationally oriented are almost exclusively found in the world's major financial markets—Chicago, Frankfurt, Hong Kong, London, Milan, New York, Paris, São Paulo, Singapore, Tokyo, and the like, together with a few offshore banking centers in the Caribbean and elsewhere. In the early 1990s, for example, New York held more than half of all financial industry assets in the United States, while Philadelphia financial firms controlled less than 5 percent; daily turnover in the London, New York, and Tokyo foreign exchange markets in 1989 was more than $100 billion apiece, while Philadelphia and Manchester simply were not even on the map. Furthermore, most of the growth in international financial activity from the 1970s to the late 1990s has been captured by the leading centers, rather than being spread more broadly.[26]

This is true despite the fact that, as Table 3.2 shows, there is substantial employment in the FIRE sector in both Manchester and Philadelphia.

Not all financial jobs or firms are equally important; the existence of retail banking for residents and businesses does not signify the presence of an international financial sector. There are relatively few foreign banks and insurers with even a modest presence in either city—a dozen in Philadelphia and twenty-five in Manchester.[27] Broader data on employment trends support this conclusion; growth in the FIRE industries has been small in both cities since 1970, although it has expanded greatly in the Philadelphia suburbs, in large part because residential populations there have boomed. Manchester has never been much of a financial center; even at the height of "Cottonopolis," most of the banking and credit activity ran through or out of London. The city's largest locally headquartered bank, the Co-operative Bank, has no overseas branches.

Philadelphia, furthermore, in keeping with its long-term legacy of loss of global city potential, has witnessed a gradual two-hundred-year slide in the prominence of its financial institutions. From being the nation's first financial center, the city has slowly shed firms across the decades. The fall of the Second Bank of the United States was a day of reckoning for the city. From that time forward, New York grew into its current position as the nation's financial center. It took the lead in financing the railroads and was the first city to establish a clearing system for bank-to-bank transactions. By the 1850s, Philadelphia had slipped to third place in banking capital, behind not only New York but also Boston. When Philadelphia's Jay Cooke organized banking syndicates to underwrite U.S. government bond issues for the Civil War, he had to turn to New York and London to raise the funds. By 1866, Cooke conducted all of his international business from New York, not Philadelphia. The last of Philadelphia's great financiers was A. J. Drexel, who tutored J. P. Morgan; in the 1860s he formed partnerships in London and in Paris. The leadership and even the name of Drexel's firm, however, passed to Morgan and New York in the 1890s. A century later, in 1998, Philadelphia even lost the last of its major locally headquartered banks (CoreStates Financial) to an acquisition by First Union.[28]

Finance, of course, is not just banking; it is also insurance, financial markets and exchanges, and money management. Philadelphia and Manchester rarely show up on lists of important centers in these categories. The Philadelphia region does have a sizable locally headquartered insurance industry, led by CIGNA, and it has the United States' second-largest mutual fund firm, Vanguard; these two giant companies in particular lead to the city's presence on some "league tables" of insurance and institutional investment. In addition, regional stock exchanges were located in both Philadelphia (founded in 1790, the oldest in the United States) and Manchester (1836), although there has been a relentless trend toward consolidation. Manchester's exchange merged into the London Stock Exchange in the 1970s and closed in the 1990s. The Philadelphia Stock Exchange (PHLX) has in the past been a pursuer in the game of

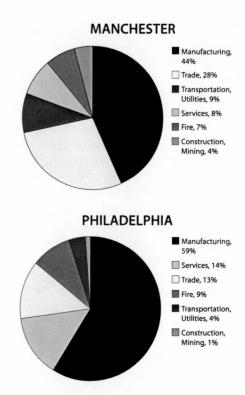

MANCHESTER

- Manufacturing, 44%
- Trade, 28%
- Transportation, Utilities, 9%
- Services, 8%
- Fire, 7%
- Construction, Mining, 4%

PHILADELPHIA

- Manufacturing, 59%
- Services, 14%
- Trade, 13%
- Fire, 9%
- Transportation, Utilities, 4%
- Construction, Mining, 1%

Figure 3.2: International firms by sector, 1998.

financial consolidation—it bought out the Washington and Baltimore exchanges after World War II—but it is increasingly pursued by others. In 1998, the exchange's board even voted to join the Amex/Nasdaq merger and move all trading to New York. Although the deal fell through at the time, it was finally concluded in 2008.[29] Economic globalization in these cities, in contrast to global cities, is not really about finance, and their indigenous financial sectors have been under serious pressure for decades.

More broadly, the overall sectoral distribution of TNCs in Philadelphia and Manchester is markedly different from that in global cities. Figure 3.2 describes the breakdown across industries of internationally connected firms in 1998 (the total number of firms is 833 in Manchester and 245 in Philadelphia). Although the fastest-growing sectors since 1972 have been trade, services, and transportation, both cities' international connections clearly stress manufacturing over other sectors (44 percent in Manchester and 59 percent in Philadelphia). The combined manufacturing and trade sectors account for more than 70 percent of international companies in both cities. The domination of manufacturing among second city TNCs has declined over time, to be sure: manufacturing firms were 68 percent of Manchester's internationally connected firms in 1972 and 77 percent of

Philadelphia's. But the most internationalized subsectors in each city show marked continuity with older economic specializations—that is, machinery, chemicals, textiles, electronics, plastics, and metalworking in Manchester and chemicals, electronics, machinery, and printing and publishing in Philadelphia.

This concentration in manufacturing helps establish the distinctiveness of second cities. Manchester and Philadelphia differ from global cities not in whether they exercise command and control functions at all but in the specific sectors in which they exercise those functions. They developed TNC-sized firms and specializations with global reach in manufacturing and increasingly in services as well, but not in international finance. Financial firms account for less than 10 percent of each region's internationally connected or globalizing companies. This pattern differs as well from the overall pattern of outward FDI for Germany, Japan, and the United States, in each of which service subsidiaries outnumber manufacturing subsidiaries.[30]

Their pattern of development in producer services is harder to tease apart. There is some evidence, from both the employment numbers and from anecdotal reports, that Philadelphia and Manchester have developed into "full-service" producer service complexes. By the early 1990s, one newspaper analysis noted that Manchester's "increasingly self-standing" downtown, nicknamed the "half mile," contained half of all the producer service jobs in the entire Northwest region. In addition, locally based service firms are just now beginning to globalize. Dechert Price and Rhoads, for example, a Philadelphia law firm, merged with a long-term English partner in summer 2000; it now has eleven American and nine foreign offices. Much of this incipient globalization occurs in ways different from Sassen's argument about producer service complexes, however, via the growth of single giant firms. Philadelphia's Aramark, to give just one instance, provides food service outsourcing in fifteen countries and has 150,000 employees worldwide; it is in effect a producer-services version of Rohm and Haas or other manufacturing TNCs.[31]

Globalization is also occurring in another kind of service industry altogether: universities. Since they are either nonprofit or government enterprises, the activities of these organizations do not show up in conventional directories of economic activity or FDI, and thus an increasingly important aspect of economic globalization is not captured at all in existing data. Globalization is proceeding at universities through both the increasing enrollments of foreign students and the expansion of university structures to include foreign campuses. In Philadelphia, for example, Temple University runs campuses and degree programs—the equivalent of corporate subsidiaries—in London, Rome, and Tokyo. International student enrollment at Manchester University grew from 2,303 in 1994–1995 to 3,077 in 1998–1999, and in the latter year there were 867 foreign students at the University of Salford in Greater Manchester. There are thousands of foreign students attending the Philadelphia area's dozens of colleges and universities. Temple University alone has nearly 1,400 full-time and 400 part-time foreign students. Even Philadelphia's hospitals have begun marketing themselves to international patients, turning themselves into one of the city's export industries.[32] Philadelphia's and Manchester's economies have indeed become more service-intensive during the past several decades, as have most urban economies. But their patterns of globalization, including in finance and producer services, play out quite differently from those of global cities like New York and London.

Conclusion: The Durability of the Second City

Like global cities, Philadelphia and Manchester are—and have been for a long time—deeply integrated into the global economy. But their patterns of integration are enduringly distinct from those of global cities. More than any other single factor, what sets them apart is the relative lack of an internationally oriented financial industry. Manchester has never had such an industry, and Philadelphia has undergone a nearly two-centuries-long process of decay. On the other hand, they have been the sites for distinct economic specialization and strength in manufacturing, which were the bases of their economic success for more than a century and the key sources of their original entry into second city position in the early nineteenth century. Textiles, machinery, and chemicals played particularly important roles in their economies. On these foundations they built for themselves roles not just as production sites, but as headquarters and command centers.

In the past forty years the two cities have endured an economic transformation unlike any challenge they have faced since the early nineteenth century. Urban-based manufacturing has declined by 90 percent, and for the most part, Philadelphia and Manchester no longer make *things* (although manufacturing remains more prevalent throughout their wider regions). But the period of restructuring and transition from manufacturing to services is now over, and both cities have in fact made a successful sectoral shift. Moreover, despite the massive changes in their employment bases and in their economic specializations, they have remained globally integrated centers, not only as branch-plant locations for inward FDI but also as international headquarters locations in their own right and as centers for some kinds of producer services, the new leading industries of the world economy.

This transition is a global phenomenon, not a local one, and as the WCH argues, it has ramifications for both within-city inequality and inequality between places. Within cities, the worst economic dislocation clearly occurred during the deindustrialization of the 1970s, which was simultaneously the death knell of an older global division of labor associated with the British Empire and a straightforward core-periphery model of

FDI. Since then, there has been clear evidence of a resuscitation of both local economies, created by economic diversification, the growth of new service industries, and the two cities' gradual internationalization. There has also been substantial immigrant arrival. But the new growth patterns have not healed the old wounds; indeed, they may have institutionalized them by reinvigorating ethnic divisions of labor on top of the 1970s-produced bifurcations between manufacturing and services, cities and suburbs, employable and unemployable. While some have interpreted this new stratification as a "dual" or "divided" city, both current and previous patterns of stratification are more varied and complicated.[33] Philadelphia and Manchester are stratified and segmented not just by class, but also by gender, education, geography, ethnicity, race, and immigrant status. Chapter 4 examines in particular how both cities' migration patterns have shaped their ethnic, racial, and labor market inequality over time.

Between places, the urban hierarchy has shifted. During the past few decades, new opportunities have arisen for cities to become global (Toronto is one city that has taken advantage, in addition to places like Bangkok and São Paulo), and some formerly global cities or cities with global city potential may have declined (such as Melbourne and Montreal). Also, new opportunities have arisen for places to become second cities (Bangalore, Monterrey, Pusan, and Seattle have all attempted to rise into second position, with considerable success). But for a number of Manchester's and Philadelphia's peers—places like Liverpool, Cleveland, Detroit, Saint Louis—the past few decades of restructuring have brought on a seemingly inexorable decline.[34] The fact that some cities are losing ground is one of the reasons why FDI, restructuring, and economic globalization are politically charged topics. Deindustrialization and economic transformation caused a good deal of suffering and a lot of public discontent. In the United States there was widespread anxiety over the rise of inward FDI by Japanese companies in the 1980s, just as there is concern now over outsourcing to India. At the urban level, growth machine theorists and others have argued that the loss of locally headquartered corporations may reduce local political capacity as the attention of the economic elite shifts away from the region.

A similar concern with FDI's political and social implications has been expressed by a group of Manchester-based social scientists, including Steve Quilley, Jamie Peck, and Peter Dicken. They argue that the rise of inward FDI over the twentieth century—initiated by large U.S. corporations, like Westinghouse and Ford at Trafford Park before World War I—cost the region its economic autonomy. As locally headquartered firms were replaced by subsidiaries of foreign corporations, Manchester's history became a woeful tale of decline and disinheritance. "During the first half of the 20th century, Manchester successfully diversified its economic base, and developed a complex, broad-based manufacturing economy. But it did so at the price of ceding economic sovereignty to large firms based outside the region."[35] Manchester, however, was never really sovereign in the sense of being autonomous, self-reliant, or self-contained. It was always deeply intertwined with world markets; vulnerable to fluctuations in commodity prices, bad harvests, and supply disruptions; and mightily dependent on slavery and empire. Also, it is hard to call the nineteenth century's foreign merchants, like Engels, of whom there were hundreds in Manchester, local or indigenous capitalists. Manchester's economy, like Philadelphia's, was made up of a complex mix of dependence on decisions made elsewhere *and* control over other's decisions.

Philadelphia and Manchester appear to have successfully remade themselves and to have reinvigorated their historic second city economic status on the basis of new economic specializations. They still face difficult problems—poverty and social exclusion in both cities are unconscionably high and it is not clear that either city has the will or the capacity to overcome them. But the durability of their global economic positions during nearly two centuries is still something to marvel at. A crucial question for understanding this persistence is what strategies or mechanisms the cities may have employed to help make it possible. What can the local state do, if anything, to facilitate economic transformation and to preserve or enhance prosperity when restructuring crises occur? One important set of lessons lies in history, for these kinds of challenges are not new. Philadelphia, after all, was quite clearly embroiled in interurban competition in the 1820s and 1830s. Although it lost the struggle for global city status, it discovered a replacement role as an industrial metropolis and an economic path that turned it into a second city. Such questions of policy and urban agency are addressed in detail in Chapter 6. First, however, our description of the second city's position in global flows remains incomplete. In the next chapter, we turn to the issue of migration and the second city as a site for flows of people.

4

Migration Patterns in Second Cities

They joined together by the dozens and then the hundreds, on a busy June workday afternoon in 2000, from Chinatown and from other neighborhoods around the city. They had spent the first part of the day collecting petition signatures and holding a silent vigil; now it was time for the march. More than fifteen hundred strong, they gathered at Tenth and Vine streets, in front of the Holy Redeemer Church, and stepped in a winding line through the neighborhood from Chinatown to city hall. They chanted and shouted, "a boisterous procession of bells, cymbals and drums." Some threatened to sue and others threatened to lay down in front of the bulldozers.[1]

Philadelphia's Chinese community had come together to protest Mayor John Street's decision to locate the new Philadelphia Phillies baseball stadium at Twelfth and Vine, on the northern end of the neighborhood. The Chinese community had been progressively hemmed in, decade after decade, by urban renewal and redevelopment, and enough was enough. Between the Gallery and the transit station along Market Street, the prison to the east, the Vine Street Expressway on the northern side and the new convention center along Arch Street, Chinatown was encircled on nearly all sides by public projects. Chinatown was growing (see Figure 4.1); the route north across the Vine Street Expressway was the only pathway left, and the stadium would cut off even that.[2]

By November, before Thanksgiving, it was all over. The mayor announced, after the protestors had filed a lawsuit, that the city was

Figure 4.1: Philadelphia's Chinatown.

moving the site to South Philadelphia, near the old stadium. Victory meant that the Asian community in Philadelphia—not just Chinatown—acquired new visibility, power, and unity. Chinese of different generations and from across the region, even those who lived in the suburbs, banded together because, in the words of one participant, "Even though I don't live in that small piece of land, I care." The protests even brought together Asian Americans from multiple national backgrounds. "'A lot of Asians are defending Chinatown because it's a metaphor for how Asians in America are treated,' said Helen Gym, the Korean American president of the board of Asian Americans United. 'This is our only Asian neighborhood, and it's come under attack.'"[3] Chinatown and the broader Asian community in Philadelphia came of age politically in a classic redevelopment struggle over the right to control urban space. The struggle thus demonstrates the crucial role that urban politics plays in the eventual incorporation of migrant groups into their host societies and communities. A spatially dispersed, ethnically fragmented, and politically lightweight community defeated a Democratic African American mayor—the city's second black mayor, in fact—in a city that was 43 percent black and overwhelmingly Democratic.

It is still unclear, however, whether the pan-Asian unity will persist and the political awakening in the stadium fight will empower the community in an enduring way, for events like this are rare. It takes a lot of effort for migrant communities to overcome their disempowerment and exclusion—

and in this case, their spatial fragmentation as well—to act forcefully in the public arena. In addition, the relatively small size of the Chinese community (Chinatown had about four thousand residents in 2000, although of course there were many more Chinese and Chinese Americans spread across the region) made its victory all the more striking. Compared with native-born African American and white populations of about 650,000 apiece, the community's size provides an obvious, although not sufficient, motive for Chinese to band together with other nationalities, such as Korean Americans or Vietnamese Americans, in groups such as Asian Americans United.

The numerical dominance of the native white and black communities in Philadelphia also suggests a key fact about second city migration patterns. The relative prominence of internal over international migrants is what sets Philadelphia and Manchester apart from global cities. Internal migration has been more important for them than for global cities, and they received a more selective or narrower range of international migrants than global cities. Their large populations of ethnically or racially distinct internal migrants (most particularly, the Irish in Manchester and African Americans and Puerto Ricans in Philadelphia) dominated much of the low-skill, low-wage end of the labor market, essentially freezing out many poor or low-skilled foreign workers. As a result, they received large numbers of foreign immigrants from only a handful of nationalities, and those nationalities were often middle class or class-diverse rather than predominantly working class or poor. This pattern of migrant receipt has its roots both in the cities' distinctive economic structure and in their historic lack of "gateway" status.

This migration pattern simplifies the dynamics of ethnicity and race in second cities compared with global cities, and leads to different senses of identity, diversity, and intergroup politics. Politics in Manchester and Philadelphia have often revolved around a conflict between an established, privileged native group that holds an inordinate amount of power, and a large, ethnically or racially distinct group of internal migrants who have been systematically excluded for a long period of time. In such a two-player political system, true immigrant groups are likely to be relatively small or few in number. This simplified demographic composition results in a politics that can deflect attention from immigrants, forcing them onto a longer, slower—yet less conflictual—pathway to incorporation than happens in global cities. And all migrant groups, whether internal or international, are likely to face a rather slow process of recognition and inclusion in comparison with the political incorporation process in global cities.[4] In Philadelphia and Manchester, ethnic-minority internal migrants have typically suffered a harsher reception from the existing society than have immigrants.

A focus on the nature of migrant communities and the specifically political relations of inclusion and exclusion that second city migrants encounter naturally entails greater attention to issues of race and ethnicity—identity, discrimination, and the like—than to issues of class. Indeed, questions of racial and ethnic inequality are fundamental to understanding not simply migration and urban politics, but the entire phenomenon of globalization as well. Globalization is a deeply racialized process.[5] Racial, ethnic, and religious inequalities are deeply implicated not just in city politics, but also in the labor market. Ethnic and racial sorting and segmentation play a primary role in shaping the within-city economic polarization that the WCH points to. These ethno-racial inequalities have manifested in distinctive ways in Manchester and Philadelphia compared to the corresponding patterns in global cities.

By 2000, Philadelphia had become a majority-minority city. According to the U.S. census, the city was 43 percent African American, 9 percent Hispanic, and nearly 5 percent Asian. The Chinatown stadium conflict thus took place in a new political context that was, astonishingly, virtually unremarked at the time. The causes of Philadelphia's majority-minority status, however, are strikingly different from those in a global city like New York. In New York this achievement was driven mostly by the arrival of nonwhite immigrants: in 2000 the city was 27 percent African American, 27 percent Hispanic, and 10 percent Asian, but fully 36 percent of the city's population was foreign born, and 80 percent of those were non-European. In Philadelphia the foreign-born population was 9 percent, and majority-minority status was driven primarily by African Americans and Puerto Ricans. These indigenous minorities are historically migrants themselves, even if several generations past, who left declining rural conditions elsewhere to make their way in the city. Although Manchester is not a majority-minority city, the migration story runs parallel; the city's Irish migrants and their descendants played a similar role and experienced similar economic and social situations.

Manchester and Philadelphia have thus been profoundly shaped by internal migration in the same way that global cities are shaped by international migration. Both types of cities get both kinds of migration, but the relative significance of each kind varies. In what follows, I first compare the overall migration patterns in Manchester, Philadelphia, New York, and London. Second, I discuss Manchester's and Philadelphia's migration histories in detail. Third, I analyze the issues of political incorporation, ethno-racial inequality, and intergroup relations. The chapter concludes with a discussion of the relations between migration, local political culture, and urban revitalization.

A Distinctive Pattern

Nearly all writings on global cities stress their roles as magnets for immigration. They receive hundreds of thousands of immigrants from every corner of the globe. Contemporary New York City, for example, vies with Los Angeles for the title of the most diverse population center in the world. In 2000 more than 2.8 million foreigners—or 36 percent of the city's population—called New York home. New York's immigrants represent nearly 10 percent of the national total, and approximately half of all immigrants to the United States live in just five metropolitan regions (Chicago, Los Angeles, Miami, New York, and San Francisco). Similarly, 31 percent (more than 850,000 people) of London's population were immigrants, according to the 2001 U.K. census. Inner London's 866,662 immigrants constitute 22 percent of the national total for all of England and Wales. The most evocative term for these places is "gateway cities"—the places that serve as the main entrance and first settlement points for new arrivals to a country.[6]

Even so, half of all immigrants to the United States and more than three-quarters of those to England settle in other cities. Philadelphia and Manchester are also centers for migration, but in a different way than global cities. Sources for international migration concentrate in just a few countries, and internal migration plays a more significant role. Furthermore, this internal migration is often rural-to-urban migration by people from an ethnically distinct background subject to substantial discrimination. In other words, in addition to receiving a select population of foreign migrants, these two cities in some ways substitute internal for international migrants. The point is not that they lack immigrant populations altogether—rather, their participation in global society is selective and specialized.[7]

Table 4.1 shows the differences in migrant settlement among the cities of Manchester, Philadelphia, London, and New York in 2000–2001. It illustrates three comparisons: the overall number or percentage of immigrants, the number of source countries, and the size of internal migrant populations. While Philadelphia's foreign born constitute 9 percent of the city's population, and Manchester's foreign born nearly 12 percent, the foreign born in New York and London are both more than 30 percent of the cities' total populations. The immigrant population alone in London is larger than all of Manchester; similarly, New York's immigrant population is larger than Philadelphia's total population.

The table also lists the source countries that account for more than 0.5 percent of the cities' immigrant populations from 2000 to 2001.[8] Philadelphia and Manchester have relatively large immigrant populations from just a few source countries—China, India, the Ukraine, and Vietnam for Philadelphia, and Bangladesh, India, Jamaica, Pakistan (all former colonies), and China for Manchester. Despite the higher numerical threshold (because of significantly larger populations in each city), however, London has eighteen and New York seventeen nationalities that exceed the cutoff. Furthermore, the global cities each have several groups with more than 1 percent of total city population. The clearest conclusion from Table 4.1 is that while London and New York are polyglot, receiving hundreds of thousands of immigrants from a wide range of source countries, Philadelphia

TABLE 4.1 MIGRATION IN SECOND VERSUS GLOBAL CITIES, 2000–2001

	Manchester	% of city	Philadelphia	% of city	London (Inner)	% of city	New York	% of city
Population	392,819		1,517,550		2,766,114		8,008,278	
Ratio internal/foreign born	0.550		1.786		0.189		0.278	
Internal	**25,708**	**6.5**	**243,917**	**16.1**	**163,697**	**5.9**	**798,565**	**10.0**
	Irish	2.7	Puerto Rican	2.7	Irish	2.4	Puerto Rican	3.8
	Northern Irish	1.0	African American	8.5	Northern Irish	0.6	African American	3.8
Foreign born	**46,765**	**11.9**	**137,205**	**9.0**	**866,662**	**31.3**	**2,871,032**	**35.9**
	Pakistan	2.4	Vietnam	0.8	Bangladesh	2.5	Dominican Republic	4.6
	Jamaica	0.9	China/HK	0.6	Jamaica	1.7	China/HK	3.0
	India	0.7	India	0.5	Nigeria	1.6	Jamaica	2.2
	China/HK	0.7	Ukraine	0.5	India	1.4	Guyana	1.6
	Bangladesh	0.5			West Indies	1.2	Mexico	1.5
					USA	1.1	Ecuador	1.4
					Australia	0.9	Haiti	1.2
					Turkey	0.9	Trinidad	1.1
					France	0.9	Colombia	1.1
					Pakistan	0.8	Russia	1.0
					Italy	0.8	Italy	0.9
					South Africa	0.8	India	0.9
					Cyprus	0.7	Ukraine	0.9
					Germany	0.7	Korea	0.9
					Somalia	0.6	Poland	0.8
					China/HK	0.6	Philippines	0.6
					New Zealand	0.6	Bangladesh	0.5
					Portugal	0.5		

Sources: Great Britain, Office for National Statistics, *Census of England and Wales* (London: TSO, 2001); U.S. Department of Commerce, Bureau of the Census, *Census of Population and Housing* (Washington, DC: Government Printing Office, 2001).

Notes: The Office for National Statistics acknowledged in 2003 that it missed more than twenty-five thousand people in Manchester ("Census 'Lost' 25,000 People" 2003). Total numbers of London internal and international migrants are estimates calculated from census percentages. "Internal" means outside the states of Pennsylvania and New York, respectively, for Philadelphia and New York City, and outside England for Manchester and London (the U.K. internal migrant numbers are therefore underestimates).

and Manchester exhibit a more selective or niche pattern of immigrant settlement; they may get immigrants from many countries, but only a few nationalities arrive in substantial numbers.

Internal migration, in contrast, plays a more significant part in the demography of the second cities than it does in the global cities. In Manchester in 2000, although the internal migrant population is smaller than the foreign migrant population, the ratio of internal to international migrants (0.5) is nearly three times the ratio in London (0.189). And Philadelphia's ratio of 1.786 is more than six times higher than New York's. Also, the crucial role played by ethnic-minority internal migrants is evident. In Manchester, they are nearly one-third as large as the total foreign-born population and larger than any single immigrant group, while in Philadelphia, Puerto Rican and African American migrants together outweigh the whole immigrant population. In London and New York, these ethnic-minority internal migrant groups are much smaller relative to the foreign-born populations, and the overall percentages of internal migrants are much smaller than those of the foreign born—one-fifth as large in London and about two-sevenths as large in New York.[9]

Additional U.S. Department of Commerce figures on internal migration, from both countries' censuses, substantiate the contrast. The difference is clearest for Philadelphia. Overall, 6.1 percent of Philadelphia's population in 2000, but only 4.4 percent of New York's, lived elsewhere in the United States in 1995; only 2.8 percent of Philadelphians lived in a foreign country in 1995, compared with 6.6 percent of New Yorkers.[10] In sum, Manchester and Philadelphia have sizable immigrant populations, on the order of 10 percent each. But their ethnic-minority internal migrants play a larger role in creating and defining the demographic and cultural diversity that the foreign born create in global cities.

This second city migration pattern is not a new development. According to the U.S. census, in 1980, 22 percent of U.S.-born Philadelphia residents came from outside the state of Pennsylvania; this percentage was virtually unchanged in 1990, and native migrants outweighed international migrants by a factor of more than three. For both 1981 and 1991, the U.K. census reported that 29,000 people had moved into the Manchester "conurbation," or region, from other parts of Britain in the previous year, three to five times the number from foreign countries. In Manchester in 1981 internal migrants born within the United Kingdom but outside England (e.g., in Ireland, Scotland, and Wales) slightly outweighed international migrants, 7.7 percent to 7.1 percent. In London (both inner London and Greater London) by contrast, international migrants as a percentage of total population outweighed internal migrants by a factor of roughly 2.5 to 1.[11]

Indeed, the migration differences between cities extend back into the nineteenth century. Table 4.2 shows population statistics for these four cities at intervals between 1850 and 1991. New York and London consistently

TABLE 4.2   PERCENTAGE FOREIGN-BORN RESIDENTS: SELECT YEARS,
1850–1991, SECOND CITIES VERSUS GLOBAL CITIES

City	1850–1851	1890–1891	1910–1911	1970–1971	1990–1991
Manchester	0.8	2.2	2.3	4.3	7.9
Philadelphia	29.8	25.6	24.7	6.5	6.6
London	1.7	4.3	4.7	20.3	24.1
New York	45.7	38.7	40.4	18.2	28.5

Sources: Great Britain, *Census of Great Britain in 1851* (London: Longman, Brown, Green, and Longmans, 1854); Great Britain, *Census of England and Wales* (London: HMSO, 1891, 1913, 1973, 1991); U.S. Bureau of the Census, *Compendium of the Seventh Census* (Washington: AOP Nicholson, 1854); U.S. Department of Commerce, Bureau of the Census, *Census of Population and Housing* (Washington, DC: Government Printing Office, 1892, 1914, 1972, 1992).

Notes: Manchester and London figures do not include those born in Ireland. Denominator for U.S. cities in 1850 is white people plus free black people only; the percentage listed for New York in 1850 represents Manhattan only. U.S. figures for 1890 and 1910 represent foreign-born white people only. The figure for Manchester in 1851 is an estimate based on foreign-born people in the county of Lancashire; the figure for London in 1891 is actually from 1901.

have foreign-born percentages greater than those for Philadelphia and Manchester; the divergence exists across time, although it has become starker since 1970. New York has a foreign-born population that is consistently at least 10 percentage points higher than Philadelphia's, and even at its lowest London essentially doubles Manchester's percentage. Internal migration, by contrast, displays the opposite pattern. Other population data culled from U.K. and U.S. censuses figures also support this conclusion. In 1870, for example, 9.2 percent of all Philadelphia residents were born in another U.S. state; this figure had reached 10.4 percent by 1880. In New York City, by contrast, only 4.1 percent of the population was born in some other state in 1870, and 6.3 percent in 1880. The Irish born, who were for all intents and purposes internal migrants, constituted 13 percent of Manchester's population in 1851. Although this percentage declined during the rest of the century, Manchester's proportion of Irish consistently exceeded London's, which was 4.6 percent in 1851 and only 1.1 percent by 1991.[12]

The factors that shaped these divergent migration patterns include geography, transport and communications infrastructures, migrant social networks, and the global reputations of the cities. The most important influence, however, is probably the nature of the receiving-city labor market.[13] There is an interaction between labor market structure and group migration patterns. In Manchester and Philadelphia, internal migrants play a bigger role at the bottom of the labor market, making the city less attractive to the working-class international migrants who make up the bulk of foreign workers. There is certainly a low end of the labor market in these cities—just as low as in global cities, if somewhat smaller. But a much larger percentage of those jobs are filled by domestic minorities with a historic background of migration and discrimination. Some immigrant streams never get started, or never take off, because the right kinds of opportunities do not exist. Philadelphia and Manchester, of course, do not lose their attractiveness to immigrants entirely—they are still large and diverse economies, with broad opportunities plus transportation and communication links to enable ongoing contact with home. But because the number of available "ethnic niches" is smaller or fewer, they tend to fill up faster, which means fewer opportunities for new immigrant groups. In other words, a combination of local native residents and internal migrants effectively crowd out some opportunities for immigrants. The more detailed migration dynamics in Manchester and Philadelphia, to which I now turn, do indeed suggest that a kind of substitution of internal for international migrants is and has been occurring.

International Migration to Philadelphia and Manchester

Manchester and Philadelphia underwent massive spurts of migrant population growth in the first half of the nineteenth century. Table 4.3 lists the raw population numbers for the major migrant groups in both cities for select years since 1850. Both cities have experienced successive waves of immigration, usually highly concentrated in just two or three groups at any given time. In Manchester this meant Germans and Russian Jews before World War I, and Chinese, Jamaicans, and South Asians since World War II. In Philadelphia it primarily meant British, Germans, and Irish in the middle of the nineteenth century; Italians, Poles, and Russian Jews between 1890 and World War I; and Chinese, Indians, Ukranians, and Vietnamese in recent decades. Each group continues to have a slowly dwindling presence for decades after migration has peaked. Long-standing political relationships, whether imperial (most of Manchester's immigrants come from former British colonies) or military (Korea and Vietnam for Philadelphia), appear at least as important as standard economic factors in explaining which countries of origin provide immigrants to these cities. The largest immigrant flows (the Irish in Philadelphia and east European Jews in both cities) arose suddenly due to an economic or social crisis in the originating country.

Table 4.3 makes the wavelike pattern of immigration clear. In Philadelphia, peak immigrant population was associated with the massive wave of Irish immigrants that the city received in the mid-nineteenth century; it began in the 1830s but took off as a direct result of the potato famine of the 1840s. To this day, this wave of Irish arrivals remains the single largest immigrant stream Philadelphia has ever received. As the Irish-born population declined, new groups did not match the statistical importance of earlier immigrants; by the turn of the century, Philadelphia was the most native of America's major industrial and commercial cities. The mid-nineteenth

TABLE 4.3 MIGRANT GROUP POPULATIONS IN MANCHESTER AND PHILADELPHIA: SELECT YEARS, 1850–2001

City		1850–1851	1890–1891	1910–1911	1970–1971	1990–1991	2000–2001	2000–2001 Region	City as % of Region
Manchester									
Internal	Population	303,382	505,368	714,333	543,870	404,861	392,819	2,482,321	16
	Irish	28,534	23,005	18,410	28,365	18,465	10,708	31,399	34
	Scottish	4,112	7,599	9,065	9,160	6,864	6,938	32,088	22
International	Total	2,355	11,260	17,434	23,495	27,974	46,765	134,214	35
	Pakistan				3,440	6,637	9,471	29,350	32
	Jamaica				5,230	3,693	3,368	5,635	60
	East Asia (mostly China/HK)			58	915	3,683	2,871	6,743	43
	India			855	2,995	2,554	2,700	18,159	15
	Bangladesh					1,220	1,958	10,618	18
	Germany			1,318	1,190	1,105	1,382	6,869	20
	Russia			7,487	1,290	652	1,332	5,414	25
Philadelphia									
Internal	Population	408,672	1,046,964	1,549,008	1,949,996	1,585,577	1,517,550	5,100,931	30
	African American (total)	19,671	39,371	84,459	653,791	631,936	655,824	1,027,021	64
	Puerto Rican (born in PR)				14,939	30,623	41,267	68,873	60

City		1850–1851	1890–1891	1910–1911	1970–1971	1990–1991	2000–2001	2000–2001 Region	City as % of Region
International	Total	121,699	268,249	382,578	126,896	104,814	137,205	357,421	38
	Vietnam					5,670	11,533	20,111	57
	China/HK	17	785	997	1,317	4,928	10,354	23,775	44
	Ukraine						8,326	14,265	58
	India			87	801	4,218	7,610	29,030	26
	Jamaica				1,033	3,812	6,994	11,821	59
	Italy	516	6,799	45,308	25,629	9,279	6,097	18,066	34
	Russia	94	7,879	90,696	23,349	11,024	5,275	9,940	53
	Korea				303	5,286	5,209	21,198	25
	Poland	146	2,189	19,859	11,116	4,830	3,765	8,293	45
	Germany	22,750	74,971	61,480	10,849	4,770	3,078	14,381	21
	Great Britain	17,500	48,658	46,736	9,514	3,673	2,332	14,072	17
	Ireland	72,312	110,935	83,187	6,060	2,004	1,359	5,172	26

Sources: Great Britain, *Census of Great Britain in 1851* (London: Longman, Brown, Green, and Longmans, 1854); Great Britain, *Census of England and Wales* (London: HMSO, 1891, 1913, 1973, 1991); Great Britain, Office for National Statistics, *Census of England and Wales* (London: HMSO, 2001); U.S. Bureau of the Census, *Compendium of the Seventh Census* (Washington: AOP Nicholson, 1854); U.S. Department of Commerce, Bureau of the Census, *Census of Population and Housing* (Washington, DC: Government Printing Office, 1892, 1914, 1972, 1992, 2001).

Notes: In 1850 Philadelphia numbers are for Philadelphia County. The U.K. census in 1851 and 1891 did not provide detailed information about the foreign born. "Austrians" are used to estimate the number of Philadelphia Poles for 1910. "Russia" primarily means Jewish migrants, in both pre–World War I and contemporary streams. For 2001, "Russia" in Manchester is approximated by "other eastern Europe."

century also marks the crest of the long wave of German and English migration to Philadelphia, and the high point of Manchester's German merchant community (although as quantitative data on immigration to Manchester during the nineteenth century are sparse, the numbers for this group and others are not reflected in the table). By the 1970s, as the table shows, these immigrants were a dwindling presence, their descendants long since absorbed into the larger population.

The second wave in both Manchester and Philadelphia was most noteworthy for the heavy representation of Jewish immigrants fleeing poverty and religious violence in Eastern Europe. Jews became by far Manchester's largest immigrant group. Although a handful had been present for nearly a century, larger numbers of Jews started settling when the U.S. Civil War shut down migration to America. By 1881, immigrant Jews made up more than half of a Jewish population of perhaps 15,000. By 1901 (data not shown in table), Manchester's largest immigrant groups were from Austria, Germany, Italy, Poland, Russia, and the United States; Jews dominated the eastern European groups. Similarly, although some Jews had been in Philadelphia since the mid-eighteenth century, the first pogrom-fleeing contingent of 225 Russian Jews landed in Philadelphia in 1882. The community grew rapidly and reached 55,000 by 1905. By the 1890s, there were about 2,000 Russian Jews arriving every year. The other large group of immigrants in the second wave was the tens of thousands of Italians who came to Philadelphia to settle. There were other groups, of course—Christian Poles, Hungarians, and Slovaks in Philadelphia, and smatterings of Italians and Levantine traders in Manchester—but they were, for the most part, small.[14]

The third wave began during World War II, when black West Indians started arriving to work in the Trafford Park industrial estate. Black demobilized servicemen settled in Manchester after the war, as did a few students from both the West Indies and British Africa, like future Kenyan president Jomo Kenyatta. By 1955, people of color numbered about five thousand. Overall, Manchester's new migration streams were primarily postcolonial, from the countries of the New Commonwealth, and occurred in three mini-waves: Caribbean migration (more than half from Jamaica) peaked in the early 1960s, Indian and Pakistani in the late 1960s to early 1970s, and Bangladeshi in the 1980s.[15]

Philadelphia's third wave got off to a slower, later start and was still subdued as late as 1980. It has been dominated overwhelmingly by Asians: Koreans and Chinese first, then Vietnamese—who have now become the city's largest immigrant group—and finally Indians. Their presence has been supplemented by the rise of black migration from Jamaica and by the post-Soviet rekindling of Russian and Ukrainian (now tallied separately for the first time) migration. Given overall contemporary U.S. migration

Figure 4.2: Philadelphia's emerging ethnic economy.

patterns, what stands out is the lack of Spanish-speaking Latin American immigrants—this makes Philadelphia much different from other cities in the United States. Only very recently, since 2000, have Mexican immigrants begun arriving in the city in substantial numbers (see Figure 4.2), although their presence is more noticeable in the suburban and agricultural areas of the region. All the while, the oldest immigrant groups have maintained a gradually dwindling presence.[16]

Many of Manchester's Jamaicans arrived in the city indirectly; they moved to the city after first landing, and often working, elsewhere. This pattern of immigrant communities forming more through secondary than initial settlement is common to both cities. Manchester has never been a main port of entry or gateway, and although Philadelphia was a major immigrant port in the eighteenth century, it lost that distinction in the nineteenth. Most Italians traveled to Philadelphia from somewhere else in the United States. Fewer than 3,000 Italians landed at the port of Philadelphia between 1880 and 1890, and yet the Italian community had nearly 7,000 residents by 1890; the population grew swiftly to slightly more than 45,000 by 1910. In addition some groups that did arrive in Philadelphia did not stay: English, Norwegians, Poles, and Swedes all had at least twice as many arrivals as residents in this time period.[17]

The question therefore becomes which groups settle, and why? A large part of the answer is related to immigrants' skills and occupations.[18]

Recognizing the imperfect nature of any classification, it makes sense analytically to group immigrants into three broad economic categories: unskilled laborers, skilled workers and tradesmen, and professionals. Nineteenth-century international migrants clustered overwhelmingly in manufacturing and related industries. Despite this fact, unskilled laborers formed a smaller proportion of the immigrant stream to these two cities than most accounts would lead one to expect, and the skilled group was comparatively larger. The single largest group of unskilled immigrants was the Philadelphia Irish. The Irish entered Philadelphia at perhaps the time of its greatest economic growth, after the depression of 1837–1843 was over. Second only to African Americans, however, they remained stuck at the lower end of the occupational scale in the second generation and beyond. Researchers for the Philadelphia Social History Project found that fully 30 percent of Irish immigrant men worked as laborers, as did 15 percent of the second generation.[19]

Other than the Irish, unskilled immigrant groups were relatively small, a few thousand people each—most notably Poles in Philadelphia and Jamaicans and West Indians in Manchester. They were small in part because of the cities' industrial structures, which provided a relatively small number of unskilled jobs in occupations like domestic service, stevedoring, basic steel, and general labor. Instead, much of their manufacturing was in skilled trades, such as metalworking, tooling, printing, engineering, and machining. These groups were also small because of the presence of large numbers of unskilled, internal-migrant minorities at the bottom of the labor market.

Although most of Philadelphia's Italian immigrant community first worked as laborers, they quickly transitioned to skilled occupations. Most Italians traveled to Philadelphia from somewhere else in the United States for temporary work; the railroad and public construction were the most important employers. Many settled and decided to stay in Philadelphia, however, because they had craft or merchant skills and could move out of unskilled labor, given the particular character of the city's industrial patterns. Italians in Philadelphia moved into skilled trades like masonry, and also out of construction entirely into retail and personal services (e.g., barbers); Italian women worked in the needle trades.[20]

Indeed, substantial numbers of these two cities' immigrants came with trade or entrepreneurial skills, finding their way into skilled positions and small business ownership. Philadelphia's textile industry was filled with immigrants from the British Isles, both as workers and owners. The city's German immigrants, meanwhile, concentrated in the crafts and skilled trades, including the food processing industries, like brewing and baking, as well as skilled metalworking and printing. Over time they moved into white collar and clerical occupations as well. In recent decades in both cities Asians are thriving economically as small business owners have concentrated in food, restaurants, clothing manufacture, wholesaling and distribution, and personal services, like nail salons. Koreans in Philadelphia, like in the United States generally, are highly concentrated in self-employment and small business ownership, particularly in textiles and retailing, as are Pakistanis in Manchester.[21]

Finally, there have always been small but important groups of professional immigrants—those who arrived with substantial amounts of economic or human capital and took up high-status occupations. The prototype of these groups was the German merchant community in Manchester. Lancashire had the second-largest concentration of Germans in England. The group was never large but it was wealthy and prominent; from the mid-nineteenth century forward they were joined by traders from the eastern Mediterranean, including Greeks, Arabs, Turks, and Armenians.[22] Many of Manchester's German merchants were Jewish, and these merchants provided the original base from which grew the city's late-nineteenth-century Jewish community. Indian immigrants today, especially in Philadelphia, fit this pattern of a high-status professional group.

Thus, Philadelphia's and Manchester's appeal to immigrants was selective. The textile and weaving sectors displayed this selectivity well, although they employed immigrant labor differently in the two cities. In Manchester textile workers were primarily native or internal migrants, with Irish hand-loom weavers at the bottom and English master spinners at the top. Foreign migrants, such as the Jews of the late nineteenth century, were almost as likely to be merchants or firm owners at the upper end of the occupational spectrum as they were to be workers. After the Lancashire weaving industries declined precipitously in the 1950s, a new wave of South Asian immigrants, particularly Pakistanis, began to infiltrate the remnants of the broken industry as both workers and small firm owners, revitalizing some industrial quarters and regional satellite towns. In Philadelphia's Kensington and Manayunk neighborhoods in the nineteenth century, by contrast, the textile industry was very largely an immigrant sector. Immigrants from the British Isles constituted the bulk of both owners and workers, later joined by Jewish immigrants.[23] Ethnic succession in the textile industry was more frequent and rapid in Philadelphia than in Manchester, switching from Irish and British to Jewish, Italian, and eventually, as the industry went into prolonged decline after World War II, Puerto Rican, then most recently to Korean and Chinese.

Manchester's and Philadelphia's local industrial structures thus affected the composition and size of migrant labor streams via the "match" they provided with the skills and talents of various migrant groups. This is the phenomenon explained by the sociologist Roger Waldinger's concept of the ethnic niche: a specific occupation in which a particular migrant group is overrepresented. A few particularly large niches dominated these two cities' industrial patterns. Once these were taken over by a particular group, opportunities for other groups of migrants were significantly reduced because the incumbents often held on to their niches for decades. Lower numbers of unskilled jobs overall combined with preexisting Italian and Irish populations made Philadelphia relatively unattractive to Polish workers, for example. And large numbers of internal Irish migrants in Manchester made that city unattractive to many less-skilled foreign workers. This "crowding out" was less true for global cities, which had greater occupational diversity; even their large niches were not as dominant in the local economy, leaving more room for multiple ethnic groups. At other times, niches were "handed down" to successive groups: one group vacated a niche and in so doing opened opportunities for others to enter it. The Vietnamese in Philadelphia appear to be replicating the Italian pattern in shop keeping, and Chinese, Koreans, and Pakistanis are filling niches once dominated by Jews—as shopkeepers, wholesalers, and small textile producers, with a growing number of professionals, such as lawyers and doctors.[24]

While "occupation" is a factual description of what immigrants do in the labor force, it is not simply about skills or qualifications, since many immigrants may work in lower-status jobs than the fields they trained for. East Asians in both cities began as a small stream of Chinese immigrants who became entrepreneurs because other fields were closed to them. This is also clearly true for many Korean small business owners. Those who arrive with skills or other resources do not long remain at the bottom of the occupational ladder, however. Jews, for example, rapidly moved up via education and entrepreneurship. Germans and British in Philadelphia became economically assimilated relatively quickly, and their class profile became similar to that of natives. Upward mobility has also been noticeable among many Chinese, Koreans, and Pakistanis, to such a degree that in 1978, 24 percent of Manchester's Asians were in professional occupations, compared with 10 percent of the general population; only 12 percent of Asians worked as unskilled or manual laborers.[25]

The configuration of ethnic niches resulting from the interaction between local economic structures and migration patterns deeply shaped local inequality in both cities. On the one hand, a sizable proportion of immigrants followed one of two patterns: they entered the middle rather than the bottom segment of the labor market or they did not stay at the bottom for long. The exceptions to this pattern were placed in a low position through markers of religious or racial differences: the Irish in Philadelphia and black West Indians in Manchester. A study for Manchester city government in 1978, for example, found that those of African descent, mostly Caribbean people, were overwhelmingly concentrated in unskilled occupations—25 percent of the black workforce in 1978. Less than 1 percent of Manchester West Indians were in professional occupations.[26] On the other hand, the worst economic outcomes, at the bottom of the labor market, were experienced by native, internal—yet ethnically distinct—migrants. Thus, ethnicity and migration status combined as perhaps the most important factors in the creation of local inequality; these internal migrants were confined to the lowest economic positions for social more than for strictly economic reasons.

Internal Migration

Internal migration has played, and continues to play, a crucial role in these cities. There is a continuous flow of internal migrants in and out of both cities, swollen by occasional waves (see Table 4.3). It is helpful to split these internal migrants into two subgroups. One subgroup is composed of majority-group natives (essentially, white Protestants, although in the contemporary period one should arguably drop the religious restriction); this migration was especially important in the nineteenth century, in the cities' high-growth decades. The Manchester region was the site of massive migration from Scotland and the English counties surrounding Lancashire as industrial and factory employment started to replace work at home, and textile manufacturing became concentrated in Lancashire and West Yorkshire. In the late nineteenth century, the largest groups of internal migrants to Philadelphia were from the neighboring states of New Jersey, Delaware, Maryland, and New York—and as already noted, they made up about 10 percent of the city's population. Historian Russell Kazal suggests that, in addition, there was a steady stream of native whites of German descent into the city from the surrounding rural counties.[27] Native whites, both indigenous and migrant, held a disproportionate share of the better-paid occupations.

The second major form of internal migration was the arrival in the city of natives from ethnic-minority groups: the Irish in Manchester and African Americans and Puerto Ricans in Philadelphia. The numerical impact of these ethnic minorities was truly immense and helped define the cities in ways that immigrants do in global cities. In Manchester, for example, approximately 20 percent of the city's population was Irish born in 1831. Mini-waves of Irish migration occurred in the 1790s, around 1820 and after 1840, and Lancashire was the center of English Catholicism, with 43 percent of England's practicing Catholics. Although the Irish as a percentage of total population declined steadily during the succeeding decades, they still constituted 2.7 percent of the city's population—more than 11,000 people—in 2001.[28]

Philadelphia long had the largest black urban population in the North, and it was the antebellum center of black institutional life. The city had the first black church in America, some of the first schools for black people, and a thriving artisanal and entrepreneurial class. This preexisting group of natives made the city a magnet for black people leaving the South, with notable groups of arrivals in the 1820s and after Reconstruction. W.E.B. DuBois, in his famous book *The Philadelphia Negro*, found that in 1897 more than one-half of Philadelphia's black population had been born in the South, most in Virginia and Maryland. In the twentieth century, as Table 4.3 shows, the city's black population grew nearly 800 percent from more than 84,000 in 1910 to about 650,000 in 2000. Included in these figures, but not reflected in the table, are 128,000 African Americans born in other states; in other words, black internal migrants nearly equaled the city's entire immigrant population. Philadelphia's other group of minority internal migrants was the Puerto Ricans. The first arrivals were recruited during World War II to work for the Campbell Soup Company in Camden. Others were recruited for farm labor after the war but soon moved to the city. By 1970, there were nearly 15,000 Puerto Rican–born residents of the city; together with Puerto Ricans born on the mainland, the total community had grown to 26,702. Philadelphia was the third-largest destination for *puertorriqueños* coming to the mainland after New York and Chicago. By 2000, there were more than 40,000 Puerto Rican–born residents of the city and nearly 70,000 in the region (see Table 4.3). People in the city who could claim Puerto Rican descent numbered more than 90,000.[29]

Ethnic differences combined with labor market discrimination and low skills to push these groups out of expanding industries and confine them to declining ones. African Americans notoriously faced the worst circumstances of all. Philadelphia's early black population, indigenous and migrant, often had craft skills and developed niches in skilled service fields, such as barbering and catering. But from the 1830s forward, African Americans suffered a serious decline in their well-being from unemployment, disempowerment, poverty, and mass intergroup violence; between 1840 and 1850, the city's black population actually fell. Downward mobility was widespread as black people were pushed out of the craft and skilled service industries by competition from similarly skilled European immigrants. During the following century, they moved increasingly into the lower rungs of domestic and personal services (especially black women), and they were almost entirely shut out of expanding sectors, such as machining, most factory employments, and retail and producer services. DuBois found in the 1890s that 45 percent of employed black men were laborers and 34 percent were servants; among women, 44 percent were domestic servants and 43 percent were day laborers.[30]

While African Americans undoubtedly suffered the most severe economic and social exclusion, the other two groups faced surprisingly similar stigmas. Manchester Irish employment was largely in unskilled occupations—construction, trade, factory labor, and handloom weaving; they were occasionally employed as strikebreakers. The Irish continued to concentrate in handloom weaving even as the occupation itself declined, suffering reduced wages and replacement by power looms. A segregated labor force emerged and persisted well into the twentieth century, in which the Irish took over entire occupations that English workers increasingly refused to perform. Puerto Ricans too were concentrated at the lower reaches of the occupational hierarchy, particularly in industrial work, and were hit hard by the deindustrialization of Philadelphia and Camden; they entered manufacturing at precisely the time when both the number and the wages of these jobs began to shrink. "Puerto Rican women became overwhelmingly concentrated in the city's manufacturing jobs. Puerto Rican men, on the other hand, were overrepresented in the service sector, especially in hotels and restaurants, and also found manufacturing jobs." Indeed, while the Irish and African Americans are no longer so economically excluded as they once were, these groups are still—150 to 200 years after their arrival—poorer than the population at large. More than 20 percent of those who self-identified as ethnic Irish in Manchester in the 2001 U.K. census, for example, still worked in what the British call "elementary" occupations—unskilled manual and office labor. In Philadelphia 28.5 percent of African Americans and 46 percent of Puerto Ricans were below the poverty line in 2000.[31]

African Americans in mid-nineteenth-century Philadelphia were crowded out of skilled service trades by the arrival of immigrants, and this displacement forms an important part of the history of black disadvantage. More often, however, it appears that immigrants and minority internal migrants *substituted* for one another—where one group was particularly large, others tended to stay away, either by choice or because job networks were monopolized by the incumbent group and closed to outsiders. The less desirable occupational niches became the preserve of the ethnic-minority internal migrants and their descendants, and as a result, upward mobility has been harder and more constrained for them. Thus, compared to global cities, Manchester and Philadelphia tended to be relatively unfavorable locations for working-class and poor immigrants. Rather than competing directly in the labor market, to a large degree the two populations instead flowed to different regions, different cities. The presence of these ethnically distinct internal migrants has also had significant, lasting impacts on the politics, culture, and character of each city. When there has been competition or conflict in either city, it has tended to happen between different groups of natives, rather than between natives and immigrants.[32] The prevalence of between-native conflict has had important implications for working-class conservatism and for the difficult struggles over political incorporation minority-group internal migrants have experienced.

Politics, Violence, and Incorporation

In Manchester and Philadelphia, struggles over incorporation and political inclusion centered primarily on conflicts between different native groups—

ethnic majorities versus ethnic-minority internal migrants—rather than between natives and immigrants. Conflict between natives and immigrants has not been absent, but it has been less common. Ethnic-minority internal migrants and their descendants have faced a significantly harsher social reception than immigrants, and these internal migrants have remained at the bottom of the economic and political systems for very long periods. Their relatively narrow class profile, combined with religion, culture, and race differences, serves to distinguish them from other internal migrants and from immigrants. They generally have suffered for decades from a quadruple segregation—ethnic or racial, occupational, political, and residential—from the public life of much of the city.

Even today, ethnic-minority migrants remain spatially segregated. The last column of Table 4.3 lists the percentage of each migrant group's regional population residing inside the central city in 2000–2001. Using the overall concentration of immigrants in the central city (35 percent for Manchester and 38 percent for Philadelphia) as a gauge, one can distinguish groups with central-city concentrations significantly above this level from groups that are more spatially assimilated. As one would expect, the older immigrant groups have spatial distributions that look very much like the population as a whole, and many of the newest groups—Ukrainians, Vietnamese, and Chinese—are moderately or highly concentrated in the cities. The most striking figures, however, show the continuing spatial distinctiveness of the ethnic-minority internal migrants. The Irish in Manchester are still as concentrated as if they were immigrants, and 60 percent or more of African Americans and Puerto Ricans live in the city of Philadelphia. This is true despite the fact that the Irish and African Americans have been present for more than 150 years. The ongoing spatial concentration of internal migrants speaks to the long-term difficulties these groups have faced, including widespread poverty and prejudice. For African Americans, this reflects continuing patterns of residential segregation and housing discrimination that have forced them to play by different "ecological rules."[33] Manchester's Irish population too remains more poor and working class than one might expect after nearly two centuries of migration.

These groups experienced sustained efforts to subordinate them through collective violence, poverty, and political exclusion. In addition, they were typically more actively despised by the native majority than were immigrants. African Americans and the Irish faced mass, collective violence directed against their settlement and presence in the cities. There were at least a half-dozen serious racial, ethnic, and sectarian riots in Philadelphia in the 1830s and 1840s, with black people almost always suffering the worst outcomes in terms of property damage (usually by arson), injury, and death. Thomas Scharf and Thompson Westcott, chroniclers of old Philadelphia, wrote of one race riot that lasted three days in August 1833, near South and Seventh streets: "The negroes, whenever they were caught, were assaulted and beaten mercilessly, and the most savage feeling prevailed. . . . In these proceedings the whites who resided in the neighborhood escaped injury by reason of displaying lights in their windows." In the North of England, anti-Catholic and anti-Irish violence exploded in response to massive Irish immigration. This anti-Catholic violence was linked to declining prospects for native Protestant craftsmen in the face of industrialization and to the later emergence of working-class Toryism. The Stockport riot of June 1852 (just south of Manchester), for example, lasted for three days, destroying two dozen homes and injuring scores.[34]

This violence occurred for several reasons. African Americans and the Irish were concentrated at the lower end of the labor market, and they began entering the cities in large numbers at a time when deskilling and the factory were rapidly replacing earlier craft occupations. They were unable to rely upon the foreign-language, group-recruitment methods that have been written about by so many historians of immigration; as native English speakers, they were more directly in competition with native whites in the labor market. They were ethnically and religiously distinct and stigmatized, and thus made ready targets for a variety of social dissatisfactions. In essence, African Americans and the Irish were just socially distant enough to be credible targets and just close enough to be perceived by native artisans as serious competitors or threats. Furthermore, social and political institutions in this era were under incredible strain and proved themselves increasingly unable to cope with the increase of population and the mass outbursts of protest and violence.

Antipathy between Protestants and Catholics in Manchester lasted into the twentieth century. "Protestants held a series of beliefs about the 'Micks' which for the most part precluded any genuine friendship between them. People assured one another in the shop, I remember, that nearly all Roman Catholics were dirty and ignorant and even the cleaner ones could never be trusted." Racial violence persisted throughout the twentieth century as well. It continues to simmer in Philadelphia even today, in neighborhoods where internal ethnic minorities mix with whites. In July 1953, a riot broke out between several hundred whites and Puerto Ricans in the Spring Garden neighborhood, and there were five nights' worth of riots in October 1966, after a black family moved to Kensington. The Grays Ferry neighborhood too has been on the ethnic and racial front lines for more than a century, and there have been several incidents of racial violence in recent years. In Manchester, three nights of rioting against police brutality, primarily by black people of Caribbean heritage, rocked Moss Side in July 1981.[35] Social peace was a fragile achievement, ever likely to be disrupted; moreover, it was largely built on the success of the majority-group natives in achieving their goals of fear and discrimination.

The strength of the majority-group natives led to a strongly exclusionist political system. Because of popular resistance by majority-group natives against internal migrants, mobility for them was frequently transformed from an economic into a political process. Philadelphia, for example, developed a Protestant and native Republican political machine—not a Democratic or immigrant one—that thrived on delaying or frustrating minority aspirations. African Americans had lost the Pennsylvania franchise in 1838, and they did not win it back until Reconstruction. In the 1870s, they quite naturally entered the voting lists for the Republican Party, but they saw little political advance and continued oppression. After nearly a century and a half of struggle, African Americans fought their way into the political system in the 1960s and 1970s through the local Civil Rights movement, protests against police brutality, and militant tenant activism. Community activists like Cecil Moore and the brothers John and T. Milton Street led black incorporation, but they led it into the (now Democratic) political machine or regulars, not into the reformist camp. They won few benefits in terms of jobs, power, and patronage until the late 1970s and early 1980s, as black population growth and politicization increased and African Americans began to win elective city offices. Philadelphia is now one of the only major U.S. cities that has had three black mayors, two of whom served for two terms. African Americans have *become* the city's political establishment, if not its economic establishment. The other internal groups have suffered similar patterns of long-term exclusion, with meaningful returns to participation delayed for decades.[36]

In Manchester in recent years, white discontent and high unemployment among both whites and British Asian youth in the old textile towns surrounding Manchester—particularly Oldham and Burnley—led to several riots, spurred by interethnic fights, strong police tactics, and mutual resentment. Tellingly, most of the Asian British participants were second- or third-generation youth, born and schooled in England. In newspaper interviews, they noted that it was feeling *both* British and excluded that fueled their frustration. One neighborhood mosque official said, "The older generation has always put up with it, but young people who have been born and bred here just won't take this kind of rubbish." Their experience counterintuitively confirms the point that conflicts over incorporation in second cities run deepest between majority-group natives and ethnically different native minorities.[37]

In addition, the severity of the conflict between majority natives and minority internal migrants helped delay political inclusion for all migrant groups. While the violence between native whites and native minorities flared, immigrants were often left on the sidelines. Their incorporation was frustrated, or it was accomplished but delivered little in the way of real power. In Philadelphia, for example, the Irish had established the pattern of using their incorporation as a tool for group mobility through the entry of the Irish into the Democratic Party before the Civil War— but the Democrats were a losing political party. After the Civil War, the

Republicans built one of the most corrupt city governments in America by using control of public construction contracts for roads, street railways, and public buildings as tools to generate support while retaining ultimate power and control. Prominent second-generation Irishmen were contractors and Irish laborers worked on the projects, but they won little in the way of political power. The Republican machine ran the city almost without interruption until the end of the 1940s, and in contrast to other machine cities, Philadelphia did not have an Irish-American mayor until the 1960s, when James Tate rose to the office after Richardson Dilworth resigned.[38]

The belated incorporation of migrants into the urban political process had seemingly contradictory effects. For the minorities themselves, a lack of return on political investment has been characteristic of the means by which they have been incorporated. Yet the widespread discrimination and violence practiced against the ethnically distinct internal migrant groups by the majority ironically promoted the formation of autonomous, institutionally complete communities as a protective mechanism. Each time ethnic or racial relations worsened, African Americans and Irish migrants responded by building independent, autonomous community institutions. They developed their own rich networks of self-help and mutual aid organizations; the Irish, through the sponsorship of the Catholic hierarchy, erected an almost entirely separate set of social institutions, including schools and newspapers.[39] This cultural separateness lasted even after their incorporation and provided a strong basis for an enduring neighborhood and community identity.

On the other hand, the paradox is that their inclusion, which the majority fought against for so long, brought the city significant benefits. The cultural autonomy of migrant communities had several effects that reflected back on their host cities' global status. First, this rich ethnic cultural life was a significant wellspring of the pop-culture innovations I describe in Chapter 5. By promoting institutional closure among the ethnic-minority internal migrant groups in particular, exclusion and subordination fostered the development of networks of cultural and musical innovators. Second, their cultural distinctiveness added to the city's diversity and helped produce an atmosphere of tolerance, openness, and cosmopolitanism. Ethnic-minority internal migrants gave the cities a remarkable social diversity that the cities would not otherwise have possessed, given their selective appeal to international migrants. This multicultural, cosmopolitan sensibility has become one of the key mobilizing principles of the attempts to build new political regimes and to reinforce a second city identity in the 1990s. Political actors have also discovered that this cosmopolitanism can be a global marketing tool for the city (see Figure 4.3).

Finally, migrants of color during the last several decades have begun to force changes in the cities' racial and ethnic dynamics, as the story of the Chinatown protests at the start of the chapter shows. Their incorporation

Figure 4.3: Woman parading in Manchester's Caribbean carnival celebration.

has been critical to claims of inclusiveness on the part of ruling political coalitions. This is most apparent in Philadelphia, where whites may no longer be even a plurality of the city's population. With Hispanics and Asians totaling 13 percent, politics and neighborhood relations are swiftly becoming more subtle and variegated.[40] These changes are driven as much by internal Puerto Rican migration as by international migration; in the fall of 2001 the Hispanic community forced a debate over the creation of a Hispanic-plurality city council district.

Conclusion: Migration and Population Decline

Manchester and Philadelphia are indeed connected to world society by patterns of migration and settlement, but their patterns differ substantially from those of global cities. They receive very large numbers of internal migrants, especially from internal ethnic minorities, and immigrants from a limited or select group of sending countries. In addition, the class composition of the migrant stream differs from global cities—many of the working-class and poor migrants are internal, and these internal migrants substitute in many cases for poor foreign immigrants. This class composition in effect cuts off some of the "bottom" from the immigrant stream. The inequalities that globalization produces are not only economic, however, but also racialized. Because migration is ethnically organized by social networks and migration chains, the type and extent of inequality in globally integrated cities, whether global or second, is likely to be noticeably ethnic or racial in character. Migration in general is a core feature of globalization, and it is through migration that globalization produces some of its deepest impacts on inequality. In short, globalization as a process is shot through and through with race and ethnicity.

Today, these historic migration patterns are intertwining with more recent demographic realities: Philadelphia and Manchester are cities whose populations are declining. Their surrounding regions are growing, but the cities themselves have lost a third or more of their residents to the suburbs since 1950. Yet both cities have seen increases in their downtown populations during the past decade, largely accounted for by well-educated upper-middle-class residents choosing to live downtown for its proximity to work and cultural amenities. More important, they have been witness to rising migrant populations in the working-class neighborhoods that ring their downtowns.

The structural context into which migrants are moving is markedly different from the one into which pre–World War I migrants moved, however. The fact of migration means very different things in a situation of population and tax-base decline than in one of growth. These are neighborhoods that during the past half century have been emptied of their working- and middle-class populations. The cities themselves have faced funding and revitalization crises, including near-bankruptcy in Philadelphia. With fewer voters and representatives, they have less clout in national assemblies. As they become more diverse, therefore, the cities are weaker politically than they have been at any time since the 1830s or 1840s. This political weakness may combine with the growth of organizations and institutions within migrant communities to give migrants more power to negotiate favorable terms for their incorporation. Philadelphia's recent controversy over Mayor John Street's attempt to build the new baseball stadium in Chinatown is a case in point.

There has been much talk in recent years about whether a city like Philadelphia should try to encourage greater immigration. The prior experience of these two cities does not promise much success. Their patterns of immigrant receipt have historically been selective and it seems unlikely that any short-term state action would change that selectivity. Certainly, local governments can subsidize labor recruitment or even engage in recruitment directly, but they cannot really—except in a very long-term sense—impact local industrial structure in ways that might be conducive to migrant settlement. Local governments can also offer services to ease immigrant adjustment, or to assist upward mobility. Historically, however, they have done a poor job of providing such services, and there is little reason to think they will do much better now. Immigrants of the past were either left by the local state to make their own way until they became politically powerful enough to demand attention or were actually harmed by local government antagonism. The historical reality of the ethnic division of labor in second cities is that Philadelphia and Manchester both relied heavily on internal migrants for many of the jobs that immigrants perform in a city like New York.

Do populations of new migrants, both internal and international, have the potential to revitalize these cities? The anthropologist Pnina Werbner clearly believes the answer is yes, pointing to Pakistani immigrant entrepreneurs who "utilised empty warehouses and workshop space, creating new businesses in the abandoned landmarks of Manchester's former industrial glory." James Kenney, a member of the Philadelphia City Council, held hearings in the fall of 2000 on how to promote the city as a destination for international migrants. He argued that immigrants were the primary way in which struggling cities could maintain their populations and tax bases, by investing in rundown neighborhoods and starting small businesses.[41] The migrant experience implies, however, that it is not simply a question of numbers. It is also a question of how those numbers and people are arranged and mobilized. The secret of revitalizing the second city for the next several decades lies in political and institutional transformation. That has been the means for urban revitalization in the past and that will be the means in the future as well, if it is to be achieved at all. The historical lessons and future potential for these transformations are the subjects of Chapters 6 and 7.

5

Making Global Culture

Ideas and Innovation in Second Cities

•

uring the 1992 presidential campaign, third-party candidate
Henry Ross Perot commented that the proposed North American
Free Trade Agreement would result in the "giant sucking sound"
of U.S. jobs leaving for Mexico. The phrase swiftly became one of
the most memorable sound bites of the 1990s, encapsulating the protectionist side of the voluble debate over free trade. Perot and other
partisans of both neoliberalism and nationalism in the economic
sphere—presidents and prime ministers, columnists and pundits, protestors and the corporate elite—became increasingly strident over the
ensuing decade. Many people characterized these positions as simple
reflections of material or economic interests, and sometimes they were.
But often they were more—they were different worldviews or interpretations of what globalization was and of what it meant for the whole
world to be interconnected. They served as examples of a growing
world culture: people's attempts to construct meaning out of the changing global circumstances of their lives.

Along with the more material manifestations of globalization
discussed in Chapters 3 and 4, the development of a world or global
culture is one of the most prominent features of globalization. This
chapter examines how Manchester and Philadelphia have contributed
important, even essential, elements to that global culture. This culture
is incredibly diverse and not by any stretch internally coherent or consistent. Islam and Christianity are part of it, but so are many of the

professions, such as architecture and planning, which increasingly think of themselves as global or universal rather than national. It includes both ideas that have a fully worldwide distribution—such as doctrines of human rights—and ideas and practices that are not fully global in extent but have spread across multiple spatial contexts, such as hip-hop.[1]

This chapter demonstrates that much of what we ordinarily understand to be a relatively freely circulating, disembedded global culture actually has its origins in very specific places. Just as goods for global trade need to be manufactured and just as global migrants have particular home countries from which they originate, the ideas, practices, and beliefs that make up global culture need to be produced and need mechanisms for diffusion and circulation. Manchester and Philadelphia have played a crucial, frequently unrecognized role in this production and circulation of culture. They specialized in the innovation, incubation, and production of pragmatic and utilitarian cultural endeavors, such as political ideologies, professions, and disciplines, rather than in spiritual or religious contributions, or in the aesthetic products of "high" culture. For example, both free trade and protectionism, as we currently understand them, are in large part bequests to the world from Philadelphia and Manchester. In this chapter, I present the story of those ideological gifts. The lessons drawn from this story then serve as a spur to the more general question of the global cultural role of these cities. This question is put to the test with examples from other spheres: the professions (medicine and management) and academic disciplines (chemistry and physics). I conclude with some thoughts on the implications of Philadelphia's and Manchester's historic roles in cultural production for the emerging field of cultural policy.

The Manchester School and the Vespers Circle

As is the case in the contemporary world, for much of the nineteenth century, free trade and protectionism were the chief contending ideologies of how the world economy should be organized. Laissez-faire liberalism—the gospel of global free trade—may not have been invented in Manchester, but the city became virtually synonymous with this ideology in the nineteenth century. The theory of free trade was even named the "Manchester School" by British Prime Minister Benjamin Disraeli in 1848, just as it was called "Manchestertum" by the Germans. Throughout Queen Victoria's reign, the rising bourgeoisie of manufacturers and merchants, known locally as the "Manchester men," were the chief ideologues of an intellectual-political movement for free trade. They made it the official development policy of England and exported it to the world.[2]

In the wake of the successful battle for incorporation as a city, and in the face of the depression that followed the Panic of 1837, Manchester's merchants and factory owners turned their attention to trade and tariffs.

In December 1838 they formed an Anti–Corn Law Association, which soon thereafter became the Anti–Corn Law League (ACLL), dedicated to reducing British tariffs on imported grain and to pursuing free trade around the world. The league's politicians and activists pioneered modern mass political techniques. Free traders took over not only the city's chamber of commerce but also the Manchester City Council. After 1842 the league became an immense national electoral organization, primarily Liberal but fundamentally a single-issue interest group outside of the existing political parties. It was an unparalleled propaganda machine with pamphlets and its own newsletter, campaigns to pad the electoral rolls, mass challenges to the voter registrations of opponents, by-election challenges to political adversaries, and extensive fundraising campaigns. The Manchester office kept "a complete set of electoral registers for the whole country" and updated them according to reports from its own agents across the nation. The league paid several newspapers an annual fee in exchange for favorable editorial treatment and sometimes made mass purchases of editions with pro-ACLL articles. In 1843 it even helped found the *Economist* magazine— still a prominent global voice in favor of economic liberalism—through the financial incentive of several thousand subscriptions. The league created the tools of modern mass mobilization in Britain and schooled a generation of political leaders in their uses.[3]

The heart of the league was its council, which met in Manchester daily. The league's core organizers came from the most politically active and radical of the city's bourgeois factory owners.[4] The most famous and influential members were two mill owners turned politicians and MPs. John Bright, a Quaker from the Lancashire industrial town of Rochdale, had been the country's foremost radical factory owner for four decades and spoke eloquently in defense of progressive causes. He supported not only free trade but also extending suffrage to the working class. Richard Cobden—the chief organizer and proselytizer for free trade—was the moving spirit behind the city's incorporation movement in the 1830s and the ACLL in the 1840s, and he was the negotiator of the Cobden-Chevalier Treaty in 1859–1860.

Ideologically, the Manchester School stood for a profoundly internationalist and meliorist capitalism: "neither provincial nor sectarian, but catholic and cosmopolitan—the proclamation of the continental as against the self-contained theory of life." Beyond mere economic benefits, its adherents promised that, if enacted faithfully, free trade would usher in worldwide harmony and was indeed "the surest guarantee for peace." In a public address in 1838, supporters argued, "In order that mankind may be united as one family, it requires only that they may be allowed to interchange freely the benefits which nature has so variously and superabundantly bestowed upon the different countries of the earth." Cobden himself, in a letter to friend and fellow manufacturer and free trader Henry Ashworth, argued, "Free Trade, by perfecting the intercourse, and securing the dependence of countries upon one another, must inevitably snatch the power from the *governments* to plunge their people into wars."[5]

Free trade was celebrated for its worldwide effects in promoting sympathy and understanding. It would bring about global peace and reciprocity and contribute to the flowering of human civilization and culture. Manchester merchants would be both teachers and students to others the world over. "We may be the instruments, as we have been and now are, of conveying the knowledge of the arts and sciences, the blessings of civilization, and the truths of religion."[6] This vision of world peace and cultural enlightenment brought about through trade has lain at the core of arguments in favor of a global economy ever since. The rhetorical origins of neoliberal and cosmopolitan arguments for free trade in the 1990s can be traced directly to the nineteenth-century city. The political scientist Samuel Huntington's "Davos Man"—the archetypal member of a post-national corporate elite—is the son of Manchester.

Similarly, many of the intellectual and rhetorical roots of contemporary economic nationalism, free trade's main ideological antagonist, lie in Philadelphia. Philadelphia's manufacturers and publishers cemented a local, ideological commitment to protectionism as a philosophy of political economy that ruled the city's politics, formed the fertile soil for the emergence of the Republican Party in Pennsylvania, and governed U.S. economic policy for decades.[7] They argued strenuously against the laissez-faire ideology and its idealistic humanism in favor of an exclusive focus on the autonomous, independent nation-state and its internal prosperity as the proper concerns of development policy. As with the Manchester School, Philadelphia's protectionists not only restructured their nation's politics but also bequeathed their enduring ideology to the world.

The local partisans of national protection formed a closely interconnected and broadly influential circle, including the father-and-son publishing team of Mathew and Henry Carey. Mathew Carey founded the Philadelphia Society for the Promotion of National Industry in 1819. The society published Friedrich List's famous protectionist tract, *Outlines of American Political Economy*, in 1827. The core group of protectionist advocates, however, arose from the city's next generation of intellectual and business leaders. Mathew Carey's son, Henry, like his father, was one of the city's most active civic leaders. He was a founder of the Union League, the city's oldest Republican club, and played an important role in defining the Republican Party's platform, partly through his role as an economic adviser to newspaper publisher Horace Greeley. The party's first presidential nominating convention was even held in the city in 1856, and in Philadelphia, at least, it was the party of protectionism and high tariffs even before it was the party of Lincoln or of emancipation. Henry Carey gathered about him an important coterie of supporters. The circle convened regularly through his salon Vespers to discuss issues of political economy and to hear lectures by invited speakers. Attendees included Philadelphia's major heavy-industrial manufacturers, such as Joseph Wharton, and future Congressman E. Peshine Smith.[8]

Wharton, the Quaker industrialist, became a national leader on the issue after the Civil War. He wrote and lectured widely and in 1881 he gave $100,000 to the University of Pennsylvania to establish the School of Finance and Economy, the world's first business school. The main condition he placed on his gift was that the school must be firmly protectionist; ironically, the Wharton School—today perhaps the world's foremost business school—began its life dedicated to the defeat of free trade. Robert Ellis Thompson, the first dean of the school and first professor of "social science" in the United States, carried out this command in his courses and in his textbook, *Social Science and National Economy*, as did economics professor Simon Patten in *The Economic Basis of Protection*.[9] Through the school's efforts, protectionism entered not just the halls of parliamentary debate, but also the academic curriculum, and it spread to new generations of students, politicians, civil servants, journalists, and reformers.

Culturally, the doctrine of national protection became one of the primary theories of how economic development ought to be pursued and policy enacted. Protectionists vilified England; they maintained that Britain's free trade policies deliberately and horribly impoverished other nations, which became trapped in dependent or colonial roles. Wharton even directly decried the "Manchester philanthropist, with his moral pocket-handkerchiefs and his relentless extermination of the simple habits and industries of weaker people." In contrast, protectionists recommended a development policy that restricted international trade and focused primarily on national economic autonomy and independence. Directly opposing themselves to the Manchester School's vision, they maintained that nationalist development policies would help countries to fit "themselves for a prosperous existence, were they even wholly debarred from intercourse with the outer world."[10]

For protectionists, the nation—not the individual or the firm—was the proper, fundamental economic unit. According to Wharton, "The doctrine of protection to home industry, no matter by what means, grows directly and inevitably from the idea of nationality. The nation exists of itself and for itself, not by the grace or for the benefit of any beyond its boundaries." Each of these nation-states was independent but structurally or institutionally homologous; each had a complete division of labor and a similarly diversified economy, with its own political institutions, school system, and national literature. This vision of an independent national economy inspired much of national development planning in the twentieth century. Its descendants include the "import substitution industrialization" theory of development as pursued in Latin America and elsewhere. More broadly, it influenced the entire discourse of development in post–World War II policy making.[11]

Both schools—free trade and national protection—agreed on the fundamental social goals they wanted to pursue: prosperity, economic development, the flowering of civilization, and the promotion of citizens' talents. But they envisioned starkly different roads to achieving those goals, forming two opposite poles along the spectrum of modern international economic theory. Each in its own way contributed to the formation of an idea of the world as a whole. Now, especially in the wake of communism's collapse, the starkly opposed choices they recommend resonate in our own time—in Lee Kuan Yew's developmental state in Singapore, in the arguments of labor unions lobbying for import controls, and in the words of *Wall Street Journal* editorialists, presidents, and trade ministers.

The Cultural Roles of Second Cities

These stories of the growth of global political economic ideologies suggest three lessons about the origins of global culture in general. First, these ideas resulted not from the efforts of single individuals but from networks of like-minded industrialists and activists. Cultural innovation is most often a collective process and occurs in the context of a tightly knit social network of cultural producers that possesses a common class or ethnic identity. Such networks of innovators and producers are most often spatially concentrated; it is their location in a particular place that allows them the opportunity to meet with one another frequently and to be influenced by each other. As new groups and occupations arise, they criticize older orthodoxies in favor of new sources of expertise and knowledge that are designed in part to benefit themselves and the communities or cities from which they come. The Manchester School was only the most obvious example of this kind of cultural network. There was thus a clear relationship between bourgeois social dominance and the rise of practical and professional cultures; in Philadelphia and Manchester rising middle classes created professional and instrumental cultures.[12]

Second, the cultural systems or schools these networks built were, in a broad sense, pragmatic or utilitarian. During the past two centuries, a stream of such "technical" cultural enterprises has reshaped the world and human social life—through medicine, political ideologies, new professions, and new scientific disciplines and advances. There has been an explosion of educational credentials and certificates, systematization of claims to expertise, and codification of knowledge in a wide variety of fields. Philadelphia, for example, was where the medical profession enacted the most important battles in defining itself. The city had the most prominent physicians in the Americas, the first hospital in the British colonies (Pennsylvania Hospital, founded in 1751), and was a central point for professional discourse, learning, and exchange. Over time, the city incubated an unsurpassed combination of hospitals and medical schools. The profusion of institutions and the lack of formalized criteria for training or professional accreditation, however, led to conflict. Formally trained physicians were a minority of all practitioners, and they competed for prestige among themselves as well as with pharmacists, quacks, and herbal healers.[13] Increased anxiety over professional status and access to patients led to calls for the creation of a national medical society. The founding conference of the American Medical Association was held in Philadelphia in 1847. The key organizers were Philadelphian and among them were Isaac Hays and John Bell.

The new organization's code of ethics, adopted at the meeting, was signally important in defining the medical profession and defending its status against competitors. It also was a crucial cultural innovation with global significance. Bell's committee, in charge of drafting the new code, tried to freeze out alternative practitioners, such as homeopaths, by limiting the ability of licensed physicians to consult with them. More important, Bell and Hays strove to update the previous codes of medical ethics that had stressed the physician's personal character as a gentleman and thus affiliated the profession with older, feudal notions of gentility, virtue, and nobility. Bell and Hays moved away from this aristocratic reliance on personal honor and enumerated the duties doctors owed to patients, establishing "an egalitarian professional medical ethics based on ideals [of] reciprocity."[14] For the very first time, this code defined what patients had a right to expect in terms of their medical care, and it also defined what the public as a whole had a right to expect from the profession. The science historian Robert Baker argued that the code constituted a new, egalitarian basis for the medical profession's cultural authority that was better suited to the age of Jacksonian Democracy than older, more aristocratic conceptions.

Philadelphia was thus the key arena in the nineteenth-century battle over professional standards of training, accreditation, and practice in medicine, through which the profession elaborated its definition of itself and its claims to expertise and social utility. Moreover, as a trailblazer in this process of professional redefinition for a modern, democratic, and bourgeois society, the 1847 code of ethics also served as model for other professions. "The 1847 AMA Code of Ethics is the world's first national code of *professional* ethics, the world's first national code of *medical* ethics, and the ancestor of all professional codes of ethics, medical or nonmedical."[15] So although the nascent profession was spatially grounded in Philadelphia, it did not remain that way; the innovations generated in the city subsequently spread around the globe, providing a hitherto unrecognized legacy of second city cultural production.

Philadelphia's professional innovations in medicine highlight the third important lesson: these sorts of cultural innovations and production are profoundly urban centered. Scientific and technological innovations, medicine, public health, and planning all originated in cities during the course of the nineteenth century, and they are still overwhelmingly located there.[16] Philadelphia and Manchester in particular have been critical, overlooked sites for these instrumental and pragmatic cultural innovations. They were drawn to their cultural specializations through the deep, complicated relationship between their local social structures and citizens' appreciation of their global position relative to other cities. Their second-tier global position promoted among residents a self-conscious striving to maintain their position relative to other cities. In turn this consciousness pushed them toward a greater focus on practical cultural efforts that emphasized distinctive claims to knowledge and status based on their utility and that assisted them in their competition with other cities. That competition was not simply economic. It occurred on the basis of prestige or recognition as well. In other words, it was the combination of a pragmatic intellectual and cultural focus with a second city consciousness that made these two cities distinctive in the long run, rather than the presence of either element in isolation. Over time, these cultural innovations would move from their origins in informal networks to become institutionalized in universities and then diffuse more broadly across the globe. This confluence of factors is best illustrated by the rise of new professions in Philadelphia and by the growth of academic disciplines in Manchester.

Professionalization, Academic Disciplines, and Universities

Philadelphia between the Civil War and World War I was the epicenter of a set of technical, managerial, and professional developments that were swiftly recognized as having global implications. The business school, the business manager's claim to special expertise, and the profession of management consulting—endeavors that have transformed the world in multiple and profound ways—were all pioneered in Philadelphia by a closely interconnected network of people. The luminaries of this set of innovations were Joseph Wharton, the protectionist who ran Bethlehem Steel and founded the Wharton School, and Frederick W. Taylor, the consultant who transformed Wharton's company and developed scientific management. The soil that nurtured their achievements, however, was a much larger circle of Philadelphia manufacturers, professors, and reformers. It included the following:

- William Sellers: president of Midvale Steel, trustee of the University of Pennsylvania, president of the Franklin Institute in the 1860s
- Carl Barth: teacher at the Franklin Institute, disciple of Taylor's
- James Mapes Dodge: vice president of the Franklin Institute, proprietor of the Link-Belt plant
- Henry Towne: engineer at Midvale Steel and Cramp's Shipyard, partner in Yale and Towne lock company

- Wilfred Lewis: engineer at Midvale Steel, manager of Tabor Manufacturing
- Morris Cooke: disciple of Taylor's, director of public works under Mayor Rudolph Blankenburg

Frederick Taylor, born in 1856 into a prominent Quaker family, pioneered the scientific reorganization of industrial production. Taylor described his program as the substitution of "scientific for rule-of-thumb methods"; he more than anyone else sought to reorganize factory work on a planned, "scientific" basis.[17] In his famous time and motion studies, he broke down factory tasks into discrete parts and reassembled them, prescribing the precise order and speed at which workers should perform them for maximum efficiency. He attempted rigorous observation of the coordination of activities on the factory floor, replanned the factory's physical layout to achieve improved efficiency, and instituted planning departments, cost accounting, and productivity-based wage incentives.

Precisely at the time of the growth of large corporations, Taylor created a new sphere of expertise that would be the manager's alone. The scientific manager's job involved "gathering together all of the traditional knowledge which in the past has been possessed by the workmen and then of classifying, tabulating, and reducing this knowledge to rules, laws, and formulae." Taylor argued that the role of the manager should be expanded relative not only to that of the worker but also the owner or entrepreneur. "Both sides must recognize as essential the substitution of exact scientific investigation and knowledge for the old individual judgment or opinion, either of the workman or the boss, in all matters relating to the work done in the establishment." Through this enlarged role for the engineer-manager, he essentially invented the profession of management consultant. In this new role, he expected the full cooperation not only of workers but also of entrepreneurs, directors, and presidents; everyone in the organization was to be guided by his scientifically based assessment of best, most efficient practices. Through claims to possession of an objective, systematized, expert knowledge produced in accordance with scientific principles, he elevated the status and power of managers.[18]

Taylor first envisioned the need for a consultant's position in the 1880s while employed at William Sellers's Midvale Steel in Philadelphia and then at the Manufacturing Investment Company. The owners of these companies gave him free reign to work on experiments, and while there he made some of his most important discoveries. He then went on to enact the consultant's role at Joseph Wharton's Bethlehem Steel from 1898 to 1901, and then at Tabor Manufacturing Company and Link-Belt Engineering. Afterward, he retired from active consulting and went on to the lecture circuit. He wrote articles, gave tours of Tabor and Link-Belt, and perhaps most important he trained a group of disciples who were deeply devoted to him and who popularized and extended his work. These disciples introduced scientific management to more than 150 plants between 1900 and the advent of World War I. In 1911 they formed the Taylor Society to spread scientific management further.[19]

Morris Cooke, the most important of Taylor's disciples, synthesized Taylorist ideas with the emerging Progressive movement and remade public administration according to scientific management principles. When Rudolph Blankenburg was elected mayor of Philadelphia in 1911 on a reformist platform, he hired Cooke to be director of public works. Cooke revamped the department by creating an increased role for professional administrators and implementing the ideas and research of reformers from the Wharton School. It was Cooke who spurred Taylor to write his most important work, *The Principles of Scientific Management*, and who worked hardest to turn Taylor's ideas into a general philosophy for management and administration. With Cooke's assistance and encouragement, Taylor traveled to Canada and Europe to lecture; the French in particular were converted to Taylorism, including the firms of Renault and Michelin. By the 1920s, the *Principles* had been translated into Chinese, Dutch, French, German, Italian, Japanese, Russian, Spanish, and Swedish, and in the newly formed Union of Soviet Socialist Republics Lenin called for the practice of Taylorism to improve productivity.[20]

Simultaneously, the University of Pennsylvania institutionalized one of the most far-reaching of all contributions to world culture—the belief in a "science" of business that could be codified, written down, and transmitted from instructor to pupil, thereby creating the prominent Wharton School. Joseph Wharton envisioned the school providing the sort of training in industrial leadership that used to come from apprenticeship to other merchants and entrepreneurs, and the school in fact nurtured the conviction that management was a science—that it could be codified and put into a curriculum. Both Taylor's and Wharton's disciples pursued the ideal of a science of management applicable not just to the economy but also to public affairs and government. In the process they provided the impetus for the professionalization of several new fields. Professors Robert Ellis Thompson, Edmund Janes James, and Simon Patten, along with Wharton himself, all became active in the Philadelphia Social Science Association. James in particular was energetic, organizing (together with other Wharton affiliates) the American Academy of Political and Social Science in 1889 and the National Municipal League in 1893. He later established another business school at the University of Chicago. The Wharton School also hired W.E.B. DuBois to research conditions in Philadelphia's African American neighborhoods, an effort that became one of the pioneering empirical research efforts in sociology, *The Philadelphia Negro*. And Wharton alumni were the organizers in the late 1890s of the first social work training programs in the United States.[21]

Cultural innovations like Taylor's originated in dense, spatially concentrated, informal networks of practitioners and amateur theorists. Over time, however, these innovations became centralized in formal institutions, particularly in universities. Medical training, of course, moved from apprenticeship to formal schooling during the nineteenth century. For management and engineering, though Taylor himself preferred practical, on-the-job training to a university education for engineers and managers, the credential-oriented path defined by Wharton eventually became dominant as well. It was in Manchester, however—where the development of scientific disciplines occurred simultaneously with the founding and growth of a new university—that the connection between professionalization, formal education, and middle-class culture took shape most strongly.

Cultural innovation in Manchester focused on scientific disciplines, especially chemistry and physics, which simultaneously served the utilitarian technological needs of the local economy and elaborated a new, middle-class professional identity as "scientist." The key transformation was to turn science—the production of knowledge—into an activity that one could and should pursue for a living. This transformation redefined the scientist as middle rather than upper class, and occurred side by side with a provincial, city-based chauvinism that celebrated middle-class Manchester's innovatory culture against the stifling, aristocratic conceptions of scientific activity pursued in the capital's royal societies and at "Oxbridge." These innovations had their beginnings in a dense local network of amateur intellectuals in the early nineteenth century. Its original core, described in Chapter 2, was a circle of physicians, entrepreneurs, and amateur scientists who belonged to the Manchester Literary and Philosophical Society (Lit&Phil). Much as Philadelphia's development of management and social science relied on a symbiotic connection between entrepreneurs and the more intellectually inclined academics and experimenters, so Manchester's disciplinary innovations depended on an intimate connection between men of business and increasingly professionalized and academic scientists.[22]

Under the leadership of John Dalton, president of the Lit&Phil from 1817–1844, a new generation of "devotees"—men deeply committed to the pursuit of scientific knowledge but who did not make a living from research—came to dominate the society. The most important figures included the following:

- George Wood: vice president of the Lit&Phil, 1822–1843, backer of Owens College
- William Fairbairn: boiler manufacturer, engineer, cofounder of the Manchester Mechanics' Institute, backer of Owens College

- Benjamin Heywood: banker, cofounder of the Manchester Mechanics' Institute and the Manchester Statistical Society, trustee of Owens College
- James Joule: Lit&Phil officer, experimenter in electromagnetics and chemistry, prime contributor to the theory of the mechanical equivalent of heat
- Lyon Playfair: chemist, consultant, public expert, organizer of a research circle of industrial chemists
- Robert Angus Smith: chemist; fellow student of Playfair's in Germany; researcher on sanitation, air quality, and sewage disposal
- Eaton Hodgkinson: Lit&Phil officer, experimenter at Fairbairn's firm
- John Mercer: textile chemist, member of Playfair's circle, inventor of "mercerizing" process for fabrics
- Henry Roscoe: chemistry professor at Owens College, board member of Manchester Mechanics' Institute

These men took it upon themselves to improve the facilities for pursuing science in the city, and to make them attractive to men interested in doing science for a living. As the size of Manchester's scientific community expanded, the degree of professionalization and disciplinary specialization grew. This growth proved a powerful attraction to several cohorts of budding scientists. Some of these men—Henry Roscoe, James Joule, and Arthur Schuster—had grown up locally, but others were students together at Scottish or German universities and moved to town to pursue their careers. There were even a number of direct teacher-to-student relationships among them: John Dalton provided lessons to James Joule, Lyon Playfair trained John Mercer, and Balfour Stewart taught physics to Arthur Schuster.[23]

Increasingly, the devotees differentiated themselves by subject into chemists and physicists. Manchester, with its economy devoted not just to the textile industry but also to engineering, offered a supportive environment for both disciplines. The physics circle mixed engineers like William Fairbairn with devotee scientists like James Joule. A brewer's son who studied under Dalton, Joule used his research on electricity and resistance to theorize the mechanical equivalent of heat, helping establish the law of conservation of energy. The chemists, lured to the city by opportunities in the textile industry, began arriving in the 1830s to work in dyeing and bleaching. They were the first people to make a living at scientific research. Lyon Playfair was chief among them, and although he left Manchester for London in 1845, he played a crucial role in solidifying the city's reputation as a center of scientific ferment and innovation. He hired researchers and also invited several of his schoolmates to join him, including Edward Schunk and Robert Angus Smith. Playfair inculcated a public service ethos among his colleagues and followers, arguing that science should serve the public good, whether that meant aid to industry and manufacture or the promotion of public health. Smith, for example, studied the deterioration of Manchester's air quality due to factory fumes and smoke, helping to improve sewage treatment and sanitation. Playfair also established an informal circle of chemists and entrepreneurs who met regularly to discuss and critique one another's work. These men and others innovated new coal-tar and synthetic dyes, resulting in the formation of legendary local firms like Clayton Aniline.[24]

But what held this network of men with such a variety of disparate interests together was not simply their mutual interest in scientific knowledge and its application to material progress. They also elaborated and shared a civic identity that was middle-class, practical, and specifically Mancunian. Through "the adoption of science as the mode of cultural self-expression by a new social class," Dalton, Joule, and their colleagues reinterpreted a historically upper class, leisurely activity in new pragmatic and utilitarian terms. Their provincial pride set them self-consciously apart from London, the royal societies, and the ancient universities, with their aristocratic approach to science. This ethos tapped deep roots of religious nonconformity as well. Oxford and Cambridge were barred from granting degrees to religious Dissenters, and many Manchester factory owners were dissenting.[25] In good Bourdieuian fashion, the Lancashire industrialists turned the necessities of their own restricted social position into virtues. The scientists, in turn, used business owners' commitment to science both to expand their professional opportunities and to claim enhanced social status for their pursuits.

The protagonists of Manchester science felt keenly their geographic and social marginality to England's cultural and economic elite. In response, they proclaimed their civic chauvinism, a dedication to a uniquely Mancunian spirit of enterprise and invention that was superior to the stuffy, hidebound attitudes found in London and the south. It is difficult today, perhaps, to imagine how deeply the connection to science was felt in the city: "When Dalton died in July 1844, he was accorded a civic funeral with full honors. His body first lay in state in Manchester Town Hall for four days while more than 40,000 people filed past his coffin . . . [in] a display of civic pride by what in his lifetime had become the pre-eminent provincial city."[26] It was in large part this civic and municipal identity—a belief in the value of a distinctive, pragmatic Manchester ethos hospitable to both science and industry—that held the scientists and the businessmen together. Five decades later Roscoe claimed that "the more robust and stimulating air of sturdy northern independence and intelligent northern activity" was more fertile soil than Oxford or Cambridge for scientific innovations.[27]

The network of scientists and businessmen sought to institutionalize its commitment to science, particularly through the founding of new educational institutions. Playfair, for example, "urged the establishment of technical colleges and the alteration of existing colleges and universities into

Figure 5.1: The University of Manchester's gothic front entrance.

technical schools." The city's chief businessmen took up Playfair's challenge with enthusiasm. At first, these institutions—the Manchester Mechanics' Institute, the Royal Manchester Institution, the Royal Victoria Gallery, and others—were designed primarily for the practical, skills-related education of workers, artisans, and lower-level clerical employees.[28] In addition to technical institutes for educating their operatives, however, both scientists and manufacturers came to believe that they needed special institutions dedicated to advancing science, training future owners and managers, and providing an education for their own sons.

The culmination of this need for superior training was the founding of Owens College. The cotton merchant John Owens left in his will a £100,000 bequest to fund a new college, which opened its doors to students in 1851. Trustees of the college included the most prominent manufacturers and politicians of the day, such as Richard Cobden, Benjamin Heywood, and William Neild. Owens College allowed Manchester to institutionalize its commitment to pragmatic science in a very public, prestigious way, led above all by chemistry professor Henry Roscoe. Appointed in 1857, Roscoe during the following four decades transformed Owens into the University of Manchester, pictured in Figure 5.1. He recruited prestigious faculty, nurtured departments, and together with his colleagues wrote histories of Dalton's and Joule's research that emphasized the city's contributions to the growth of scientific knowledge. While Thomas Ashton and other trustees led a successful campaign in the 1870s to raise £250,000 for the college, Roscoe campaigned tirelessly for Owens to win fully independent, degree-granting status (until the 1880s students had to register for degrees at the University of London).[29]

Under Roscoe's leadership, "later Victorian Manchester became the center of Britain's first fully professional school of chemistry." He also strove to hold manufacturers' allegiance to the school, in particular through the engineering program. Following the initiative of a group of local engineers and entrepreneurs—such as Fairbairn, Charles Beyer, William Mather, and Joseph Whitworth, who in the 1860s and 1870s donated more than £100,000 for endowed chairs in engineering—Roscoe recruited Osborne Reynolds, who became the college's first engineering professor, in 1868. He also established "what was perhaps in its time the most important school of physics in the world," hiring Balfour Stewart as professor of physics in 1870. Arthur Schuster, the son of German Jewish immigrants to Manchester, first attended the college and then worked there, replacing his teacher Stewart in 1888. In 1906 Schuster recruited Ernest Rutherford. Rutherford's research team included Hans Geiger (inventor of the Geiger counter) and Niels Bohr.[30] It was at Manchester that Rutherford carried out the experiments that led to the discovery of the atom, permanently cementing the university's reputation.

Rutherford, Dalton, Playfair, Joule, Roscoe, and others "enabled Manchester to present a face . . . to the world, as a 'scientific' city." They fought to escape the influence of London, Oxford, and Cambridge, to be modern where the others were "ancient." This local network formed an enduring nucleus that reinvigorated itself over time and that proved a powerful stimulus to innovation. In turn, the network and its innovations connected with a broader, nascent global community of similarly professionalizing and discipline-founding scientists. Many of the city's chemists, for example, including Roscoe, Playfair, Robert Angus Smith, and Edward Schunk, were schooled in Germany under Justus von Liebig or Robert Bunsen. The movement toward the professionalization of intellectual activity was increasingly both global in orientation and municipal or urban in practice, pursued at urban universities around the world.[31]

Manchester's and Philadelphia's major contribution to world culture has been their specialization in new professions and disciplines, such as management, medicine, social science, chemistry, and physics. The pursuit of applied science and expertise has been more important in these cities than the pursuit of knowledge for knowledge's sake. As historian Walter Licht argues, "Classical learning never occupied in Philadelphia a dominant place in educational theory or practice." Philadelphia and Manchester became centers of technical development and excellence dedicated to educating the middle classes. This middle-class status depended on the pursuit and development of new spheres of knowledge and on credentials proving the acquisition of that knowledge. As Owens College grew, for example, it became increasingly possible to envision and redefine the practice of science as a professional identity. The scientists saw the development of formal experimental-scientific education in chemistry and physics as the basis for the achievement of a secure middle-class status through credentialed scientific training.[32]

Although this attitude toward culture was native to the upwardly mobile bourgeoisie, or middle classes, the business elite and academic professionals in both cities—including such men as George Wood, Benjamin Heywood, Samuel Vaughan Merrick, Frederick Fraley, Matthias Baldwin, Richard Cobden, and Isaiah Lukens—worked hard to instill it in the working classes as well. They funded and established mechanical and scientific institutes for adult education in skills that were just as pragmatically oriented as the universities they were funding for their own sons, but with no expectations that the graduates would become leaders or social equals.[33] Over time, the most successful of these institutes grew into universities and became in their own right significant contributors to each city's cultural production. Their growth entailed the formalization and professionalization of education for workers, artisans, and clerks.

Perhaps the best example of such an institution was the Manchester Mechanics' Institute (MMI), founded in 1825. The MMI's original purpose was to sponsor lectures and to educate workers in the technical and mechanical arts; it offered popular courses in construction, mechanical drawing, and other practical subjects. In 1837 it began offering art and design exhibitions as well. The school grew in the 1880s under the leadership of J. H. Reynolds, and in 1892 it was taken over by the city and renamed the Municipal Technical School. Over time, through a series of mergers with other institutes (a normal school, a school of design, and the "College of Commerce"), it was transformed into Manchester Polytechnic, the largest polytechnic in the country. By the 1990s, when it became a full-fledged university and changed its name again, to the Manchester Metropolitan University, it had more than twenty thousand students. A similar story could be told about Philadelphia's Franklin Institute (founded in 1824) and its spin-offs, the Philadelphia College of Textiles and the Philadelphia School of Design for Women (later the Moore College of Art).[34]

These two-centuries-old foci have endured and persisted; indeed, they have shaped Manchester's and Philadelphia's patterns of cultural specialization and production to the present day—most notably through a vast expansion of professionally oriented higher education. From the 1970s, Manchester developed a "higher education precinct," concentrating nearly

70,000 students in a few square miles, perhaps the largest such grouping in Europe.[35] Students make up more than 10 percent of the contemporary city's population, and in recent decades Manchester University has become Europe's largest medical school as well. The Philadelphia region has one of the densest higher education concentrations in the United States, if not the world—a quarter of a million students in more than fifty institutions, and it still retains its stellar collection of medical schools. The University of Pennsylvania is the city's largest nongovernmental employer, providing more than twenty thousand jobs, and the university's Wharton School has remained perennially one of the top-ranked business and management education programs. Temple University, also located in the city, claims to confer more professional degrees than any other institution in the United States.

High and Pop

Manchester's and Philadelphia's concentration on professional and pragmatic cultural achievements has in turn implied a lack of emphasis on or specialization in other kinds of cultural production: there has been less focus on and achievement in the spheres of high and popular culture, for two reasons. First, consciousness of being in second position meant that the approach to high culture in the two cities was almost invariably instrumental. The focus on pragmatic and professional cultural endeavors like chemistry, engineering, political ideologies and management spilled over and became an instrumental attitude toward culture in general. High culture, for example, tended to be shown or displayed in second cities more than it was actually created in them. This is not to say there was no high culture in Philadelphia or Manchester—both cities, for example, had well known orchestras, but there was little or no indigenous tradition of composing in either city. Manchester's Hallé Orchestra was formed in 1857 in part as a showcase, explicitly conceived as a tool for competition with other European and British cities. The point was to demonstrate Manchester's "arrival" as a city of international importance—to display simultaneously the city's parity with London and its superiority to other English cities.

Second, the global cities exerted a strong pull on high-culture producers, which militated against the formation of the dense local networks that were at the core of cultural innovations. Global cities are enormous media centers and universally acknowledged as cultural capitals; they house emergent movements in painting and other arts and exert a constant gravitational pull on high-culture practitioners, which tended to sap lesser cities of their native talent in these areas. High-culture innovators, therefore, when they existed in Manchester and Philadelphia, were likely either to be single figures or to be seduced away to New York or London.[36]

There was, on the other hand, sufficient native soil in Philadelphia and Manchester for the emergence of pop-culture innovations. The foundation for such innovation was a densely connected local network of practitioners, innovators and creators; thus, in origin and process pop-culture innovation was similar to the professional and scientific innovations described previously. The most famous, prominent example was the diffusion and popularization of football, or soccer. As with many sports, football originated as an upper-class, exclusively amateur pastime in the south of England. The practice of paying players, however, and thus the origins both of football's professionalization and its mass popularity, began in the textile cities surrounding Manchester in the late 1870s and early 1880s, at Blackburn, Bolton, and Darwen. Paying players allowed teams to win more consistently; more important, it opened up the opportunity to play to working-class and poor youth. Lancashire became the institutional home of organized football; its teams won a third of all Football Association cup titles through the 1930s. From this heritage arose legendary teams like Manchester United, and football spread around the world. United has remained the most popular and successful team in all of football, if not the entirety of professional sports, with a network of literally thousands of supporters' clubs around the world.[37]

What most differentiated pop-culture innovation from the scientific and professional endeavors detailed earlier was the class or stratification location of the network. Pop-culture innovators derived primarily from the ranks of working-class and minority groups rather than from the historic elite or professional occupations. In particular, the ethnic-minority internal migrant groups identified in Chapter 4 played a large role. Twentieth-century popular-culture innovation patterns were thus part of the historic legacy of migration, economy, community, and class formation outlined in previous chapters. Just as with high culture, however, pop innovation in Manchester and Philadelphia has been continually at risk of attrition to the global media centers of New York, Los Angeles, and London. As DJ and scene chronicler Dave Haslam wrote about the dilemmas facing post-punk musicians, "Although being in Manchester gives you more credibility, the location of all the major record labels, music publishers, magazines and media in London creates something of a glass ceiling."[38] These processes of second city pop-culture production can be seen clearly in the popular music of both cities during the past several decades.

During the punk explosion of the late 1970s, for example, Manchester developed a distinctive musical style, rooted in dense local networks of creators and entrepreneurs. Musicians and small business owners (nightclub and record shop proprietors) came from the same neighborhoods and knew one another. Many of these "working-class bohemians" grew up in the city's oldest blue-collar and immigrant neighborhoods, located on the western and southern edges of downtown—Hulme, Moss Side, and Salford. Salford was home to members of New Order, the Fall, and Happy Mondays, as well as Tony Wilson, who as the owner of Factory Records and co-owner of the Hacienda nightclub was the most important entrepreneur associated with the city's musical reputation. Hulme and Moss Side housed members of the Smiths, the Stone Roses, and James, among others; nearby Burnage was home to the Gallagher brothers of Oasis.[39]

Manchester punk and post-punk were deeply rooted in the ugliness of the 1970s deindustrialized landscape. This environmental influence shows in both the apocalyptic propulsiveness of Joy Division and the morbid gloom of the Smiths, and it also inspired the development of a distinctive minimalist design ethos, displayed most characteristically on the album covers released by Factory Records. As the bands' popularity grew, and students at the nearby universities became involved in the scene, both the network and the aesthetic of the music underwent significant changes.[40] A transformation of musical style occurred. In the mid-1980s New Order took advantage of these changes to lead a rapprochement between punk and disco that ushered in the DJ era. Manchester bands became dominant figures in the intertwining of rock, disco, and DJ styles. Groups like the Chemical Brothers were lauded by both fans and critics, and Oasis became the world's best-selling band in the mid-1990s.

In addition, the music scene galvanized the higher education and culture industries as the city became an important gathering place for youth. "In the summer of 1988 the city became a latter-day Haight-Ashbury, as young people from all over England and Europe flocked to a club scene, dubbed 'Madchester.'" Manchester musicians and innovators helped give the city a reputation for creativity and trendiness; Manchester University and Manchester Polytechnic applications rose nearly 30 percent in 1990. In turn these changes jump-started downtown regeneration. Local programs in commercial art and design graduated young people who reconfigured the city's bars, restaurants, and clothing stores, and who opened new businesses in graphic design, fashion, and interior design in the old downtown. "Clubs took over old buildings in rundown areas (often attracted by the low rents and rates, occasional refurbishment grants, and a lack of local residents and businesses likely to lodge planning objections) and thus achieved a trailblazing position at the forefront of city centre regeneration."[41]

As Manchester has made its mark with punk and dance music, so Philadelphia has had recurring waves of innovation in African American music since World War II. Philadelphia jazz, soul, and hip-hop have relied on social networks that were grounded in specific black social institutions and spatially concentrated in historically black neighborhoods. Many performers attended school together or lived on adjacent blocks. Each wave emerged by focusing renewed energy on black people's identity as a distinct group and by reasserting a claim to a distinctive black musical aesthetic. These claims fueled innovations that won much wider audiences for the music.

The first such stylistic innovation was the "hard bop" jazz of the 1950s, which incorporated significant elements from blues and black church music.

The Philadelphia region was perhaps the music's most important center, home to performers like Clifford Brown, Benny Golson, John Coltrane, Hank Mobley, Philly Joe Jones, Jimmy Heath, and McCoy Tyner. In the late 1960s a second period of stylistic innovation occurred as a community of musicians and producers converged on Philadelphia International Records, including the O'Jays, Harold Melvin and the Bluenotes (with alumnus Teddy Pendergrass), and MFSB (Mother Father Sister Brother). At Philadelphia International (see Figure 5.2), Kenny Gamble and Leon Huff created a signature sound, mixing irresistible dance rhythms with arrangements for large horn and string sections, and they combined it with a commitment to black ownership that made them a crucial symbol for and representative of the Philadelphia black community. They pioneered the anthems of soul, like the twelve-minute theme from *Soul Train*, that would in the late 1970s become disco music. In the 1990s a subsequent generation of musicians and producers configured a new hybrid that combines soul with hip-hop. Musicians and producers like the Roots, Bahamadia, King Britt, and James Poyser have made Philadelphia a center for a distinctive African American club music, which uses live instruments rather than synthesizers and drum machines, and which integrates the social themes of Gamble and Huff's songs with rap.[42]

Continuous threads of black musicianship, cultural innovation, entrepreneurship, and independence run through all three genres. This music

Figure 5.2: Philadelphia International Records, on South Broad Street's Avenue of the Arts.

has also been Philadelphia's public face to the world in the past several decades, representing the city to others far and wide. Gamble and Huff's Philadelphia Sound in particular convincingly embodied a community sensibility, with its earnestness growing out of struggles for civil rights, even as it conveyed a suave, cosmopolitan feel that explicitly addressed both local and global audiences. Through its influence on late-1970s disco, the Philadelphia Sound became one of the building blocks of global pop music. In their own ways, these pop-culture innovations and networks have contributed not just to the social and cultural life of these cities, but to their global reputations and to a burgeoning global consumer culture. Cultural production is one of the most important ways in which Philadelphia and Manchester developed international reputations.

Conclusion: Cultural Innovation and Cultural Policy

Different cities participate in cultural innovation and development in different ways. Manchester's and Philadelphia's primary concentrations in cultural production lie in a group of innovations and activities with a pronounced middle-class, pragmatic character, dedicated simultaneously to trumpeting the social position and achievements of a rising social stratum and to proclaiming the virtues of their provincial status. Over the course of the nineteenth century, both cities became key sites for the transformation of knowledge production and the development of new occupations and disciplines. This process had cultural and historical roots in the eighteenth-century character of each place and resulted in a legacy that continues to shape cultural production into the present day. These cities were not solely centers for professional formation and education, however. While high-culture projects and incentives from the top down have often been only modestly successful, certain pop-culture innovations have repeatedly made a significant impression. These innovatory scenes, in both cities, occurred independently of mainstream, middle-class, or elite cultural trends. Moreover, they were unrecognized and largely unassisted until after they were already successful.

Similarly, the contributions to professional, ideological, and technical cultures described in this chapter are also underappreciated. Their status as part of the substance of a world culture, or of cultural globalization, is largely unacknowledged. These innovations emerged not out of individual efforts but from collaborations among people strongly tied to one another by networks of employment, neighborhood, education, class, and ethnicity. But these networks and the cultural products that spring from them are fragile resources. They are subject to the lures and attractions of global city media concentrations and are dependent on a long history of experimentation and collaboration in which a successful outcome is in no way assured. Even the cities themselves did not fully appreciate their own cultural histories, cultural specializations, and cultural resources. From a policy point of view, what is so often striking about cultural policy initiatives—building a museum or a new performance venue—is the disjunction between a city government's cultural priorities and the cultural history and reality of that city. This is just as true of cultural policy in Philadelphia and Manchester as it is in other places.

Chapters 3 and 4, as well as this chapter, analyze three different ways or fields in which Philadelphia and Manchester are imbricated in global exchanges and relationships. Those fields—the components of the global urban system—define a *position* for each city in the flows and networks of goods, money, people, and ideas. What makes Manchester and Philadelphia second cities, so far, is not so much intentional, collective action by "the city," but more the sum of actions by individual, microscale actors—corporations, migrants, workers, innovators, small-group networks. The city itself, particularly the local state, has not exercised much agency or been the locus of decision making. Each chapter also, at its end, brushes up against questions of policy and politics: Should city government encourage migration as a way to reverse population decline? What kinds of cultural policy and subsidy should the city pursue? And how best can the city increase the number of high-paying jobs in globally integrated industries?

Chapters 6, 7, and 8 tackle these questions explicitly. They address the city—especially city government—as an actor in its own right. City governments shape and plan the city's space, activities, and identity with global considerations in mind. They design and build transportation linkages to the world as a whole in order to secure or reinforce their positions in global flows. They also use large-scale cultural planning to articulate a global urban identity. As the city governments of Manchester and Philadelphia devise and carry out these plans, the two cities cease to be mere effects of a globalization process whose genesis lies elsewhere, and the cities themselves become contributors to and sustainers of globalization.

6

Municipal Foreign Policy

Planning for Global Integration

In the early autumn of 1859 Michel Chevalier, France's leading free trade advocate, visited his old friend Richard Cobden in England to begin secret negotiations for a free trade treaty between the two countries. Cobden then traveled to Paris in October with an under-the-table brief from the British government to conclude an agreement. He met with sympathetic French ministers and Emperor Charles-Louis-Napoléon Bonaparte (Napoleon III) to discuss the parameters of the agreement and strategies for getting approval from the political classes in each country. Over the ensuing weeks, he drafted and revised what would become the Cobden-Chevalier Treaty, which was signed on 23 January 1860. The treaty lowered tariffs and established free trade relations between Britain and France. Cobden returned to France from April to November in order to negotiate the specific tariff clauses and rates on a host of goods, from yarn to iron. By 1877, the treaty had resulted in a near tripling of trade between Britain and France. Moreover, it inaugurated an era of lowered trade barriers and bilateral trade negotiations across a range of European countries.[1]

Cobden, leader of the movement for municipal incorporation, long-time MP for Stockport and later Rochdale, tribune of the Anti–Corn Law League, and the most politically astute of Manchester's cotton merchants, was the ideal candidate to serve as Britain's negotiator. He had unimpeachable credentials both at home and abroad, not only in support of free trade but also as a proponent of liberal idealism more generally. In 1846 and 1847, in the wake of the victory against the Corn Laws, he had undertaken a months-long European tour to lobby in favor of free trade, traveling to Berlin, Bologna, Hamburg, Madrid, Milan, Moscow, Paris, Rome, Seville, Turin, Vienna, and elsewhere. He met with ministers, merchants, and intellectuals. And he began his twenty-year acquaintance with Chevalier, which was further cemented in 1849 at the international Peace Congress in Paris. He became widely known as a spokesman in favor of peaceful international relations and against war and colonial adventures. Cobden even refused a Cabinet position in prime minister Lord Palmerston's Liberal government of 1859, in large part because he opposed what he saw as its overly militaristic and imperialist foreign policies.[2]

Cobden was certainly the most well-known, idealistic, and vocal of the "Manchester men" to inject themselves into foreign affairs, but he was far from the only one. Prominent lobbying campaigns by businessmen in support of clear economic interests were common, carried out through the Manchester Chamber of Commerce (MCC) and the region's parliamentary delegation. In March 1860, for example, the MCC sent a delegation to London to meet with the secretary of state; they protested a recent rise in India's tariff rates on imports and asked for a return to the older low rates.[3] The merchants did more than simply lobby against other countries' and territories' tariffs, however. They also made international contacts around the world with thinkers and merchants of similar inclinations, they organized schemes (although with little success) to expand cotton cultivation to new countries, particularly West Africa, and they pushed to keep cotton-supplying regions from developing their own spinning or weaving industries.

India, which constituted by far the largest market for Manchester's goods, was a particularly important case. The most consistent interest of Lancashire, expressed by the MCC, the Cotton Supply Association, petitions, letters to political figures, and local MPs, was that India should serve as both a raw cotton supplier and a market for Manchester goods. The MCC worried that Indian tariffs might promote the increase of yarn and textile manufacture in India, particularly Bombay. As part of their campaign to focus India's economy on cotton growing rather than weaving or manufacturing, cotton merchants and spinners lobbied strenuously for the British government to fund infrastructure improvements, especially railroads, that would enable more efficient transport of India's raw cotton exports.[4]

While the backers of these efforts certainly had their own material interests in mind, it would be too simplistic to interpret such lobbying only as an effort to secure straightforward class interests. The attempts of the urban economic elite to project its influence beyond the national sphere into an international or global arena flowed into deeper currents of urban and regional politics, culture, and identity. These mobilizations were self-consciously urban, Mancunian, and regional—they celebrated the North's distinctiveness from London, its specifically regional manufacturing prowess, and the glory of Manchester in particular. The attempt to influence foreign relations became a kind of partisanship on behalf of the city in general rather than just on behalf of class interests. Furthermore, when push came to shove, the city government and urban elite placed municipal interests ahead of national or imperial interests. Evaluating the debate over whether to repeal India's tariffs, for example, the economic historian Peter Harnetty concluded, "In public, the justification for repeal of the duties was the theory of free trade. . . . Privately, however, both [Indian Finance Minister Evelyn] Baring and the Viceroy, Lord Ripon, agreed that it was political pressure rather than fiscal arguments which had led to general repeal of the duties, and that India had been sacrificed on the altar of Manchester."[5]

City government increasingly took on the burden of representing and embodying those interests. The definition of a specifically urban interest relied on the growth of an underlying sense of identity that was political more than economic and cross-class in its appeal, connected in complex ways to the activities of the local state and the interests of a wide swath of the local or regional community. Indeed, it was in part the mobilizing of larger coalitions in support of the projects—including local politicians, workers, and the public at large—that drove the rationales for the projects beyond narrow class interests toward broader political and cultural concerns. Few if any of these activities, of course, were supported unanimously by locals. But concern for the city's welfare and global standing increasingly became a public issue, relevant to most of the community's members and not reducible to a single group's interest; it was an issue that could and should be taken up by the local state.

Municipal Foreign Policy

The previous chapters detailed Manchester's and Philadelphia's positions in global flows of capital, goods, ideas, and people during the course of nearly two hundred years. The cities did not attain these positions automatically, however; they had to be worked at and pursued. In this chapter and the next I analyze the cities' explicit attempts to preserve or enhance their positions—that is, to actively pursue deeper global integration. These efforts by city governments to achieve a collective city interest at the global level, and to project the city onto the global stage, constitute what I defined in Chapter 1 as "municipal foreign policy" (MFP). Local governments are usually conscious of their positions on the global stage, not just economically, but also in terms of prestige and political autonomy. They regularly seek to reinforce that autonomy and prestige through a variety of strategies. They are certainly not always successful, and their visions are not always clear or accurate, but they do have visions of their places in the world and they work to try to achieve them.

Local states engage in MFP in multiple ways. The simplest version is probably the municipal trade mission to a foreign country or city. Another form of MFP involves resolutions on foreign affairs designed either to express the will of local people or to influence the national government's conduct (for example, divestment or contract bans with regard to South African companies in the 1980s). Cities are also increasingly developing direct city-to-city political ties that bypass national governments, such as sister city programs and the Eurocities association.[6] Most of these kinds of MFP are easy, cheap, and of limited impact. There are, however, much more substantial actions and projects that require extensive planning and directive control on the part of the local state. This last category includes transportation projects like airports, that are designed to better connect the city to the world, and planning for global cultural events, like the Olympic Games, that burnish the city's international reputation and prestige. In all these ways and more, cities actively engage in globalization processes and with other actors in order to bolster or maintain their own positions.

Municipal foreign policy provides the context in which cities and lower levels of government come closest to having their own independent set of interests vis-à-vis globalization. The local state is directly and deeply involved as planner, sometimes manager, and often as chief investor as well. These multiple directive roles give substance to the claim that the projects really are *municipal* foreign policies, and MFP is thus where city governments come closest to challenging the policy-making authority and sovereignty of the nation-state. It is a set of regionally chauvinist policy tools, and may show little concern for national priorities, national planning, or the national interest. (When I portray "the city" or "the cities" as actors, I mean city government or the local state.) These efforts in turn propel the city more solidly onto the global stage and often have significant effects at the global level—by manipulating the flow of trade, for example. Therefore, through their MFP and planning activities, local states actually further globalization by making choices that lead to increased world-system integration. The causal arrow here runs from cities to globalization: cities by their choices make globalization happen.

This chapter details the efforts of local states to deepen the locality's integration with the world economy and the world polity. In particular cities have tried to capture an increasing portion of global flows—the movements through space of goods, people, capital, and information. These flows require a material infrastructure of transportation facilities, shippers, processors, offices, and warehouses to support and enable them. The most important MFP projects a local government conducts are global transportation infrastructure projects, such as airports, designed to better integrate the city into these global networks and to enhance the city's role as a node. That is, planning is not merely or primarily about making more of the city's own goods, but rather about increasing the city's gravity and allowing it to capture some larger portion of trade and other flows.

In this chapter, I analyze five such transport infrastructure projects in the two cities: the Pennsylvania Railroad and the Manchester Ship Canal in the nineteenth century, the port of Philadelphia across the entire time period, and the international airports of each city in the later twentieth century. Local governments undertook them to serve three simultaneous purposes: to achieve deeper global economic integration, to facilitate their success in intercity competition, and to catalyze local economic diversification. Together they constituted the major initiatives through which each locality sought to maintain its competitive position relative to other city-regions in global networks of trade, opinion, and circulation. Moreover, the effects of these projects on the global roles and profiles of the cities endured for decades, even a century. They were the most important drivers of Philadelphia's and Manchester's positions in the world urban system.

These critical initiatives were undertaken by a coalition of the local state with the regional economic elite. In some cases private interests were the initiators and in others public agencies, but the local state played a leading role in each instance, not simply as planner, but also as manager, owner, or investor. The projects themselves were so big that often the state was the only local actor with sufficient resources to make them happen. In addition, they carried such momentous consequences for local well-being—economic, environmental, social—that government became the only local institution with enough legitimacy and power to handle the disputes and negotiations surrounding their construction. These projects thus represented a kind of urban mercantilism, in which the city government deliberately tried to extend its tentacles and influence beyond its immediate hinterland to the world at large.

These projects can be understood in part as examples of urban "growth machines": local political coalitions dominated by capital and property development interests that pursue changes in land use to bolster their own profits.[7] These projects are different, however, in that they constitute a particular subset of the usual range of projects and controversies studied by growth machine theorists. Because they focused on long distance transport, backers portrayed them as having few local "losers"; these portrayals were often successful. In other words, supporters argued that the projects were not zero-sum for local residents, and many residents were persuaded. Proponents focused on the risks of interurban competition and the opposition of outsiders from other cities. Indeed, there was substantial resistance to these projects from other places whose residents believed that a particular project would harm their own interests, and often this conflict of interest *between* places was more significant than the conflict of interests *within* Philadelphia or Manchester over a particular project.

The Pennsylvania Railroad

Philadelphia's transport infrastructure was shaped by the city's shift from an incipient global city to a second city. By 1840, the Bank of the United States was in decline and would soon close its doors forever. Financial, commercial, and mercantile supremacy had passed to New York. The city was beginning to capitalize on two of its other advantages—its proximity to Pennsylvania's anthracite coalfields and its strong heritage of high-skill craftsmanship—to make the transition to the industrial era. It was already the country's largest textile producer and one of the key centers for chemicals. To these it added a reputation for the most extensive and advanced metalworking and tools industries in the nation, including saws, boilers, textile machinery, instruments, ships, and, crucially, locomotives.

One impact of these shifts was to make the economy more locally focused. Philadelphia integrated a large hinterland along the Delaware River and deep into Pennsylvania, but it became less of an international trading hub. The Philadelphia port, of course, was the city's original connector to the outside world and to its flows of people, goods, and information. Despite the port's importance to the city's economy and to its ability to compete with other seaboard cities, Philadelphia had difficulty keeping its position among Eastern maritime centers. From first rank in the import and export trade in the 1790s, the city fell to fourth in 1840, behind New York, Boston, and New Orleans; in that year it also dropped behind its neighbor Baltimore in export tonnage, although it maintained the lead in the import trade. Philadelphia was at risk of being shut out of international trading and economic circuits, and the city could not hope to maintain its standing without increasing or at least restoring its importance as a trading hub.[8]

The city's trading route over the Appalachian Mountains was also a problem. In order to compete with New York's Erie Canal, the state of Pennsylvania had built the Main Line of the state works to Pittsburgh, but the Main Line was cumbersome, unprofitable, and too inefficient to provide real competition with other modes of transport controlled by other cities. By the time the Main Line opened in 1834, Baltimore had already begun laying track toward Pittsburgh and Ohio via the Baltimore and Ohio Railroad (B&O). Also, New York was trying to augment its Erie Canal with a cross-state rail line that would eventually become the New York Central. Most historians agree, however, that New York's lead in foreign trade and commerce was, by the 1830s, virtually unassailable. In reality, whether they realized it or not, other cities—particularly Baltimore and Boston, along with Philadelphia—were competing for positions in the second tier.[9]

Philadelphia, despite its historic importance and the wealth of its elite, barely built a railroad in time to maintain its competitive lead over Baltimore; once it did so, however, the city's fortunes stabilized and grew. It

became the senior partner among the group of cities that jockeyed for position behind New York. More than any other institution, the Pennsylvania
Railroad (the Pennsy) was the engine that pulled Philadelphia along the
second city track and made it the country's premier industrial metropolis
from the 1840s through the end of the century. The Pennsy was chartered
by the state in 1846, and the line to Pittsburgh was completed by 1854. The
railroad expanded rapidly, to more than 6,500 miles and 95,000 employees
by 1882, becoming the largest corporation in the world. It had more than
200,000 employees in every year between 1910 and 1927, save 1915, and
more than 10,000 miles of track. Figure 6.1 shows the eventual extent of
the Pennsylvania system.[10]

The Pennsy, designed primarily to beat Baltimore over the Allegheny
Mountains to Pittsburgh and Ohio, was promoted by a cross-section of
the city's elite. Of the railroad's first board of directors, six were primarily merchants, with Liverpool packet entrepreneur Thomas Cope the most
prominent among them. Two were bankers (including William Patterson,
who became the Pennsy's second president) and seven were primarily manufacturers, including Samuel Vaughan Merrick. Many of the railroad's officers
and board members were descended from long-established Philadelphia
families. The manufacturers among them, however, were more likely to be
first-generation wealthy and represented the industrial turn the city's economy had taken. Merrick, for example, had moved to the city from Maine
and, with his partner John Towne, owned the Southwark Iron Foundry,
which designed and built engines and boilers; Merrick was also a founder of
the Franklin Institute. Stephen Colwell, another iron manufacturer, was a
close associate of protectionist writer Henry Carey. The Pennsy thus helped
effect a merger of older commercial and newer industrial capital in the city.

These men and others lobbied the public and the state legislature in
early 1846 for approval of the railroad and formed a committee to raise
stock subscriptions. The Philadelphians, however, had trouble garnering
statewide support. Pittsburgh was impatient; the city badly wanted a better
connector to the coast than the state's Main Line provided and contem-
plated making arrangements with New York for a railroad. People in the
rest of the state were suspicious of Philadelphia's wealth and power, and
many in central and southern Pennsylvania were geographically closer to
Baltimore (the B&O had in fact tried as early as 1829 to get a Pennsylvania
franchise to Pittsburgh). In addition, a new railroad would disrupt established commercial interests, such as innkeepers, along the state's Main Line
and existing canals and turnpikes; these interests opposed the railroad. Both
the B&O and the backers of the Pennsy went to the Pennsylvania state legislature. As a way of balancing the conflicting interests, the state gave the
Pennsy the chance to build first but specified certain conditions that had
to be met. Only if these conditions were satisfied would the Pennsy's route
to the West be secure. Also, worried about the effects of a rail line on state

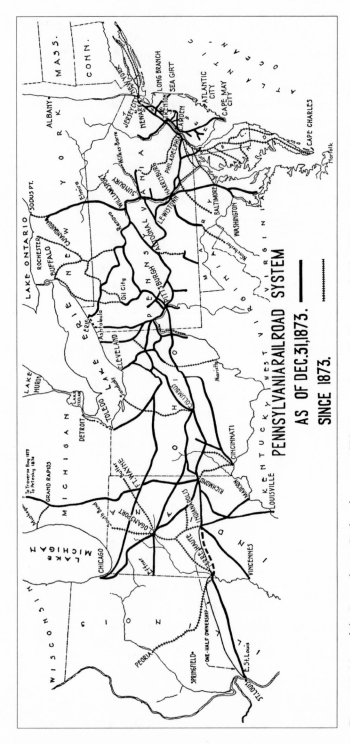

Figure 6.1: Map of the Pennsylvania Railroad system, 1873. (Source: George H. Burgess and Miles C. Kennedy, Centennial History of the Pennsylvania Railroad Company [Philadelphia: Pennsylvania Railroad, 1949], 318–319.)

revenues from canals and the Main Line, state officials enacted a tonnage tax on the Pennsy's rail freight.[11]

Local governments invested heavily in the railroad, especially as private subscriptions lagged in the early days. The cities at the railroad's two termini, Pittsburgh and Philadelphia, led this effort. Allegheny County (Pittsburgh) subscribed $1 million, and the townships of Spring Garden and Northern Liberties several hundred thousand dollars apiece.[12] When the city of Philadelphia did not move quickly enough, almost six thousand Philadelphians signed a petition urging the city to buy shares, and the citizens elected several pro-railroad candidates to city council in the fall of 1846. This tipped the balance of political power in the Pennsy's favor. The Pennsy was thereby transformed from a mostly private effort into a quasi-public project, lending city government resources and legitimacy to the railroad and making the city responsible for its success or failure. The city agreed to match private subscriptions up to $1.5 million, and subsequent purchases eventually brought the total city stock ownership to $5 million. By the end of 1851, more than two-thirds of all stock purchases were from local governments. The city held the stock until 1879, when the Pennsy bought out its stake.

The Pennsy thus began its life explicitly as a mixed public-private enterprise. Private investors could not succeed on their own. Since many Philadelphians thought the railroad would promote the general good of the city, they demanded a partnership between the railroad's backers and the local state. Not only was the city of Philadelphia the largest investor, but the tracks at the railroad's Philadelphia end were initially owned by the city, not the company. Also, the public entities demanded board representation in return for their investments, although they remained in a minority position; Philadelphia controlled three of fourteen positions, and Allegheny County two. Both the public and Pennsy executives long held on to a perception of the railroad's civic importance. At the 1892 shareholders' meeting, Pennsy President George Roberts asked the shareholders "to be [the city's and state's] bulwark and protect their interests in the competition that exists between the seaboard cities for the commerce of this great Country."[13] Such a perception was more than likely not universal, but the argument for the Pennsy's role in capturing commerce for the city that would otherwise have gone to rival cities tended to carry the day against skeptics.

Overall, the railroad provided exactly the economic revitalization its backers had sought: "More than any other single factor, [the railroad] rescued Philadelphia from the disasters of 1840, and set the city once more on the road to prosperity."[14] The Pennsy and affiliated industries generated vast amounts of wealth and a great number of jobs for the city, helping it to prosper for decades. In part because of its transport connections, Philadelphia became the quartermaster's supply headquarters for the Army during the Civil War. Untold legions of city workers churned out uniforms, cast munitions, and riveted ships. The city received troops by the thousands, both as soldiers on their way to battle and as returning wounded, requiring treatment and convalescence.

After the Civil War, the Pennsy defended its business—and Philadelphia's—against challenges from Baltimore's B&O and New York's Erie and New York Central lines. For much of the period between its founding and World War I, the Pennsy was guided by a pair of visionary executives intent on expansion. From 1850 to 1874, under the presidency of J. Edgar Thomson, the Pennsy devoted most of its attention to expanding its geographic coverage. Thomson squeezed the B&O by building a series of competing rail lines. These ran from Baltimore to Buffalo, and also from Baltimore to Washington and then south into Virginia. In addition, he won federal approval to build a passenger terminal on the Mall in Washington, D.C. When in 1869 the New York financier Jay Gould used his control of the Erie in western New York State to try to buy out the Pennsy's operating agreements west of Pittsburgh, Thomson responded by securing direct control of lines into cities like Fort Wayne and Chicago, building a great, self-contained system. And in 1881, Pennsy Vice President A. J. Cassatt (brother of the painter Mary Cassatt) outbid the B&O for the Philadelphia, Wilmington, and Baltimore Railroad, a crucial link between New York and Washington, in what was the largest business deal ever undertaken in the United States at the time. The Pennsy became the dominant railroad in the country for decades, well into the twentieth century, and it pulled Philadelphia's economy along with it (see Figure 6.2).

The great railroad was a main force behind the city's economic diversification. It helped focus the city's industry on high-skill manufacturing, such as in locomotives and ships; this focus in turn significantly benefited the entire workforce and the city as a whole. The most spectacular instance is probably that of Baldwin Locomotive; founder Matthias Baldwin and the Pennsy's J. Edgar Thomson were close friends, and Baldwin's firm supplied engines for the Pennsy, the Reading Railroad, and many other rail companies. Baldwin's production grew from only eight locomotives in 1841 to 2,250 in 1905; it was the country's largest capital equipment firm, employing 15,000 hands in the early twentieth century at wages that were among the highest in the city. "The Philadelphia giant accounted for 30 to 45 percent of all locomotive production in America in every decade from the 1870s to the 1930s." The Pennsy's demand for engines, and Baldwin's needs, fostered the rise of dozens if not hundreds of smaller suppliers, especially in metalworks, machine tools, instruments, and boilers. Midvale Steel, for example—the firm at which Frederick Taylor would conduct some of his most important management studies and experiments—began in the 1860s with the recruitment of William Butcher of Sheffield to Philadelphia, to design and forge steel tires for the railroads.[15] The growth of the Pennsylvania Railroad played a critical role in the maturation of Philadelphia's industrial economy

AMERICA'S SMARTEST TRAIN

THE ALL-ROOM

Broadway Limited

LEADER OF

THE FLEET OF MODERNISM

What an amazing advance in rail travel this distinguished new flyer represents! Privacy? Yes . . . for everyone . . . from the compact and cheerful Roomette with every personal convenience, to the Master Room with its own bathroom with shower.

Relaxation? Time passes pleasantly in the colorful, clublike surroundings of the highly decorative bar-lounge, the observation car with its glass-enclosed solarium, or the glamorous setting of the brilliant new dining cars.

Service? There are valet, barber, manicurist, maid and train secretary to serve you, as well as a selected staff of other attendants to smooth your way.

Speed? Sixteen hours . . . timed for the most convenient departures and arrivals at Chicago and New York . . . so spaced for the most convenient evening departure and morning arrival at either end. Over the shortest route between east and west to assure maximum speed with minimum effort.

16 hours

NEW YORK – CHICAGO

Lv. New York . . . . 6:00 P.M.
Lv. North Philadelphia . . . . 7:19 P.M.
Ar. Chicago (Union Station) . . . . . 9:00 A.M.

Lv. Chicago (Union Station) . . . . . 4:30 P.M.
Ar. North Philadelphia . . . . 8:08 A.M.
Ar. New York . . . . 9:30 A.M.

Figure 6.2: Advertisement for Pennsylvania Railroad passenger service. (Source: Douglas Wornom, History, Passenger Train and Through Car Service: Pennsylvania Railroad, 1849–1947 [Chicago: Owen Davies, 1974].)

and helped give the city the distinctive profile in skilled manufacturing that was its hallmark from the 1840s through at least the 1920s.

The Pennsy also contributed to Philadelphia's integration with the world economy. The railroad itself was perhaps the most important provider of port improvements. In 1861 the Pennsy completed a link to the port terminals on the Delaware River at Washington Avenue, and during the ensuing decades, the railroad built more than a dozen piers. In 1871 the Pennsy invested in the American Steamship Company, which started running steamers (built at Cramp's Shipyard in the Northeast section of the city) between Philadelphia and Liverpool; the Red Star Line and the International Navigation Company, traveling between Philadelphia and Antwerp, opened soon after. These developments preserved Philadelphia's status as an international trade center. By 1891, the Philadelphia seaport received $59.4 million in imports (ranking third in the country, behind New York and Boston), and it disbursed $33.4 million in exports, ranking eighth nationally; by 1911, imports had grown in value by more than 40 percent and exports more than doubled. Other Philadelphia firms also undertook their own international connections. Baldwin, for example, exported 20 percent to 40 percent of its production every year, to buyers in places like Russia, the Middle East, England, Australia, and South America; the firm even opened a sales office in London.[16]

Beyond these impacts on the city's economy, the railroad stimulated a less visible form of economic globalization: the international flow of investment capital. As I noted in Chapter 3, during the course of the nineteenth century, foreign portfolio investment came into its own as an outlet for capital, stimulated in large part by the sale of stocks and bonds for transportation companies. Foreign investors owned about a quarter of all railroad bonds in the 1850s, and foreign ownership of railroad stocks also boomed. Foreign investors held 29 percent of Pennsy stock in 1881 and 47 percent in 1895, and they owned a majority of the other great Philadelphia railroad, the Reading. Because this international investment was channeled primarily through New York, however, the very growth of the Pennsy and other railroads cemented New York's position ahead of all other cities as the nation's financial market. It was in the 1840s and 1850s, during the period of railroad growth and after the fall of the Second Bank of the United States, that New York consolidated its paradigmatic global city function of international capital market.[17]

The reverse side of New York's rise to global city status was Philadelphia's acknowledged exclusion from that position. New York was the undisputed leader in trade as well as finance; it became the leading American port in the 1810s, and from the 1850s to 1911, it accounted, on average, for more than 60 percent of U.S. imports and a third of exports. New York's utter dominance left other cities—Baltimore, Boston, New Orleans, Philadelphia, and increasingly San Francisco—scrambling to hold on to positions in the second tier. The historians' consensus is that railroads like the Pennsy allowed the coastal cities to secure and maintain, but not improve, their relative positions in the urban hierarchy. Indeed, even the Pennsy realized that relying on Philadelphia alone would not secure the company's or the city's future. In the 1890s President Cassatt began construction on a Hudson River crossing near Newark that would run its lines directly into New York City. The railroad's tunnels under the Hudson, completed in 1901, represented one of the great engineering feats of the day and were followed by the opening of Penn Station in New York in 1910. But establishing the Pennsy's presence in New York was a mixed blessing.

"Of all Philadelphia's Grand Gestures, the Pennsylvania Station was one of the grandest; but of course made in New York, to impress 'foreigners.' As such, it represents something of a defeat."[18] The price for securing Philadelphia's economic success was the reinforcement of its position as a second, rather than global, city.

The Manchester Ship Canal

Just as Philadelphia had built the Pennsy, Manchester's economic and political elite, in the 1870s and 1880s, pursued the Manchester Ship Canal. It would provide them independent access to world markets "so that goods might be brought from all parts of the world and conveyed direct to all the towns in this locality."[19] The canal, constructed between 1887 and 1893, was thirty-five miles long with a series of locks and an entrance to the sea at Eastham in Cheshire. It was an engineering marvel, crossing the eighteenth-century Bridgewater Canal by means of an ingenious lock-switching system. (Figures 6.3 and 6.4 map the canal.)

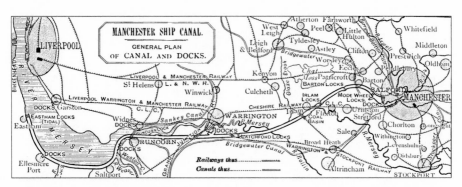

Figure 6.3: Map of the Manchester Ship Canal route. (Source: William A. Shaw, Manchester Old and New [London: Cassell, 1912], 95.)

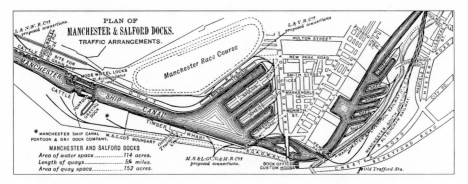

Figure 6.4: Plan of the Manchester Ship Canal docks. (Source: William A. Shaw, Manchester Old and New [London: Cassell, 1912], 89.)

Proponents justified the expense of the canal primarily by the specter of intercity competition. They stressed the rise of foreign challengers in cotton textiles; indeed, Richard Cobden and others had warned as early as the 1830s that Manchester was threatened by competitor cities. They also, however, mirrored Philadelphians' struggle with Baltimore, complaining that their trade routes might be monopolized by their sister city of Liverpool. For most of its history, Manchester had relied on the port at Liverpool, forty miles down the Mersey River, to bring in cotton—its prime raw material—and the two cities had grown in tandem. But many business owners became dismayed at Liverpool's attempts in the 1870s to consolidate, centralize, and extend control over shipping via cartels. Business owners were similarly frustrated with the Liverpool Dock Board's control over shipping charges. Their unease coincided with the beginning of Britain's "Great Depression" in 1873, and they grew more strident at the prospect of manufacturing competition from the United States, Germany, France, and (increasingly) Japan.[20]

In June 1882, boilermaker and canal proponent Daniel Adamson held a dinner at his house in suburban Didsbury that brought together several dozen prominent citizens—including a half dozen local mayors, several aldermen, and cotton spinner John Rylands (the city's wealthiest businessman) to discuss the canal. Out of this meeting arose the Provisional Committee, the entity that drove the proposal forward. The Manchester Ship Canal's early backers derived from three main groups—local manufacturers, smaller merchants and professionals, and Liberal politicians. Manufacturing supporters came primarily from the city's two biggest industries, engineering and cotton. The backers included Adamson, Richard Peacock (the locomotive builder), and the brothers Henry and John Platt of Oldham (the textile machinery manufacturers). There were five merchants on the committee, but none were from the city's largest firms. Local politicians included aldermen and councillors from Manchester and Salford; although some prominent Tories supported the idea of the canal, most proponents were from the Liberal party, including the Manchester MPs John Slagg and Jacob Bright. Bosdin Leech, one of the canal's strongest backers, wore two hats, as both a merchant and a Liberal city councillor. He would go on to serve both as a director of the Manchester Ship Canal Company and as mayor (between 1891 and 1892). Furthermore, in 1907 Leech wrote the two-volume quasi-official history of the canal. By September 1882, the plans for the canal were public and the city council was on board.[21]

Local government was thus, as in the case of the Pennsy, integrally involved from a very early stage. In addition to local government support, however, the Provisional Committee embarked on a public campaign to build a bigger coalition in support of the plan and to raise funds to fight for parliamentary approval. The roster of donors read like a roll call of prominent Lancashire manufacturers and families, including Joseph Whitworth, Edmund Potter, S. L. Behrens, Silas Schwabe and Company, Oliver Heywood, and more. Liverpool's strenuous opposition to the waterway was the main reason the campaign to win parliamentary approval was so protracted and expensive. Several town councils—Salford, Stockport, Oldham, and Warrington—took up resolutions in favor of the canal, and the city government of Manchester itself donated £18,000. Mass meetings of workers passed resolutions in favor of the waterway in late 1882, and local union leaders from the carpenters, engineers, spinners, typographers, and others spoke publicly in its favor.

To win broader support, canal promoters made three key claims: that the canal would be profitable; that it would offset the high transport costs charged by Liverpool, which were strangling industry; and that it would promote diversification of the regional economy. Although the historian Ian Harford has debunked many of the claims about transport charges, the project would clearly tie the city more closely to global trade circuits, and this appealed to manufacturers who exported a substantial proportion of their output. Jacob Bright, on the stump for the project in Oldham in 1884, argued that "the commercial prizes of the future. . . . won't be won by communities that are guided by timid councils. They won't fall into the hands of men who dare risk nothing."[22] In addition, transforming Manchester into a significant port promised to increase the city's regional economic hegemony, and commercial and service firms that relied on Manchester's centrality would consequently benefit. These groups of businessmen became crucial supporters of the scheme; many of them donated to the approval campaign and served either on the Provisional Committee or on the Manchester Ship Canal Company's board of directors. The prospect of diversification, together with the fact that the waterway would be a huge construction project, helps explain the wave of working-class support that pushed the canal through the approval process. Workers staged mass rallies of support and the local campaign took on some aspects of a social movement:

> Enormous loaves of bread, huge joints of beef, and large packets of tea and sugar were not infrequently used by Liberal campaigners to illustrate the benefits of Free Trade, and a massive loaf made appearances—usually carried in procession—at many of the large Ship Canal demonstrations.[23]

After the canal won parliamentary approval in 1885, however, backers had difficulty translating political support into financing. Only £750,000 worth of shares in the Manchester Ship Canal Company was purchased initially instead of the £8,000,000 the organizers had planned for. The sponsors were forced to pay interest on the shares in order to attract London

finance capital. These funding difficulties combined with construction problems to cast doubt on whether the canal would succeed at all. The work,
which started in 1887, was a huge undertaking, employing between twelve
thousand and seventeen thousand people. Several times sections of the
canal were washed out by floods of the adjacent rivers. After the primary
contractor died in 1889, there followed a period of confusion as his execu-
tors were unable to perform the work. By 1890, more than £9 million had
been spent, and the canal still was not done. Construction, estimated at £7
million, ultimately cost £15 million.

The confusion and cost overruns led to a dominant role for the local
state. From the beginning, there had been a substantial minority that
wanted to make the canal a fully public enterprise; instead, Manchester city
government took on a larger funding role in the midst of construction. This
was done to guarantee project completion and to keep neighboring cities
from playing a directive part. Negotiations between the city and the canal
company led to the rejection of offers of financial assistance from both
Salford and Oldham. Eventually, the Manchester City Council loaned the
company a total of £5 million and the city council demanded eleven of the
twenty-one seats on the newly expanded board in return—although voting
control stayed with the wealthy shareholders. In the process, Manchester
city government both flexed its political muscle and increased its hegemony
over other local governments, shutting them out of participation and keeping them from having a voice in what was the single largest infrastructure
project of the time. As with the Pennsylvania Railroad, a global transportation initiative was lobbied for by the local state, which then went
on to become the single largest investor in the scheme. The difference at
Manchester was that the city government intervened much more forcefully
in the project and retained its board majority until 1987.

The Manchester Ship Canal opened for business on 1 January 1894.
The queen came to lend her official blessing and toured the canal and the
city. The *Manchester Guardian* noted the crowds and the celebration with
pride, and praised Mancunians for following the example of the older canal
at Ravenna, Italy, by putting "the keel where once the plough was." The
"wonderful transformation" of direct access to the sea had effects similar
to the Pennsy's in Philadelphia. The canal quickly made Manchester the
fourth largest port in Britain and deepened the city's trade linkages with
the world economy. On that first day, foreign ships arrived from the cities of Antwerp, Christiania (now Oslo), Huelva, Rotterdam, Rouen, and
Valencia; soon others would come from British Honduras, Jamaica, and
Norway, from the Canadian provinces of New Brunswick and Nova
Scotia, and from the U.S. cities of Galveston, Mobile, and New Orleans.
By 1902, Manchester had ships traveling at least monthly to more than
one hundred foreign ports. The value of trade grew from £6.8 million in
1894 to £47.2 million in 1910. By 1950, the port of Manchester handled

6.7 percent of British imports and 4.2 percent of exports, and the value of trade reached £264.3 million. This was a substantial achievement for a city with no natural outlet to the ocean.[24]

The ship canal not only made Manchester the fourth largest port in England; it stimulated diversification of the regional economy. The city built facilities for fruit, cold storage, cattle, and oil. The canal company itself became the largest firm in Manchester; it served as port authority, navigation regulator, rate collector, banker and marine insurer, employer of all dockworkers, bridge operator, and landlord. In addition, the company catalyzed the development of the adjacent massive complex at Trafford Park, the world's first industrial park. Trafford Park became one of the most important centers in Britain for foreign direct investment (FDI) and for the development of mass production: Westinghouse opened in 1902, Ford's first U.K. factory opened in 1911, Harley Davidson arrived in 1916, Kellogg's in the 1920s, and Procter and Gamble in the 1930s. At its peak during World War II, the canal company employed 75,000 people. Significantly, Trafford Park's dozens of firms had almost no connection to the cotton industry, thus guaranteeing the realization of the canal backers' original desire for economic diversification. The canal extended Manchester's manufacturing economy for at least five decades, at precisely the time—although few realized it until later—when the city's traditional cotton economy was passing its prime and beginning to decline.[25]

These two projects—the Manchester Ship Canal and the Pennsylvania Railroad—served as functional equivalents for one another. Gigantic in scope, they entailed similar mobilizations of the local state in alliance with manufacturing interests. Backers of both projects successfully built broad political coalitions of support—quintessential growth machines—on the basis of claims that intercity competition needed combating. Indeed, one of the notable features of these projects is that the strongest resistance to them came from other, competing cities rather than from disgruntled local residents worried about the potential impact on their own livelihoods or neighborhoods. They were important, medium-term successes for their regional economies, fostering economic growth and diversification while at the same time furthering each city's participation in international trade.[26] Also, each project had the effect of reinforcing second city position by emphasizing the shortage of finance capital in Philadelphia and Manchester, necessitating a turn to New York and to London for investors. Such global transport infrastructure projects may vary in terms of how much directive authority the local state exercises, but the projects' public-private character is not merely of historical interest. It continues into the present day as a major aspect of MFP—the main tool city governments have to bolster their integration with the world economy and to pursue their own global interests.

Taking Off: New Transport Connections
in the Twentieth Century

After World War II, the global transport infrastructures of both cities suffered from relative decline. Both cities were far inland and were negatively affected by containerization in the 1960s. Manchester's share of U.K. foreign trade peaked in 1956 (7.2 percent of imports, and 4.1 percent of exports) at just a little more than £406 million. The port and the Manchester Ship Canal went into steep decline in the later 1970s, and closed for good in 1987. Although tonnage and value continued to increase, Philadelphia lost ground to sunbelt ports in particular. In 1990 the Delaware River ports ranked fifth in foreign trade tonnage, behind New Orleans, Houston/Galveston, New York and Norfolk/Newport News, and just ahead of Los Angeles/Long Beach. Although the city maintained its lead over Baltimore and pulled ahead of Boston for the first time since the early nineteenth century, this slippage in the rankings was a sign of deeper economic shifts.[27]

In addition, the Pennsylvania Railroad underwent a catastrophic bankruptcy that threw Philadelphia's significance as a major trading node into doubt. The Pennsy, like other railroads, had suffered as both its freight and passenger businesses lost out to competition from other modes of transportation (road and air) that were more highly subsidized by government. The Pennsy's ill-conceived merger with the New York Central in 1968 became, in 1970, the largest bankruptcy in the history of the United States, and forced the separation of freight from passenger service nationwide. In the early 1970s, the federal government effectively nationalized nearly all railroading in the Northeastern United States and created two public for-profit corporations—Amtrak for passenger service and Conrail for freight.[28] Conrail was headquartered in Philadelphia and during the 1980s transformed the shell of the Penn Central into a successful, profitable freight line. By 2000, Conrail had been broken up and sold to two railroads headquartered elsewhere, and Philadelphia's rail era was essentially over. While trains would continue to pick up and offload cargo at the port and passengers at Thirtieth Street Station, they would no longer bear any deeper connection to the city itself.

The decline of older modes of transport negatively affected both cities' larger industrial sectors. Employment at Trafford Park, for example, fell to a low of 24,500 in 1985, and one-third of the estate's buildings emptied out. Ship and locomotive building industries in Philadelphia laid off workers; Baldwin ceased locomotive production in 1956. The most dramatic example was the final closure in the early 1990s of the Philadelphia Naval Yard, the U.S. Navy's two-hundred-year-old shipbuilding and repair facility. These changes forced both cities to rethink their global transport infrastructure strategies. Philadelphia's response was to consolidate and modernize its port facilities while concentrating on a few niche roles in international trade; Manchester closed its port altogether and redeveloped the canal and the waterfront for postindustrial uses, primarily office space and leisure.[29] In addition, both cities, at slightly varying times, generated a new focus on airports and air transit. And once again, agencies of local government have played the leading roles.

During the past two decades, Philadelphia's port, with its steady if threadbare approach to revitalization, has increasingly tried to modernize and develop a limited number of specialized, niche roles. In addition to its important crude oil importation facilities, it has added specialties in lumber and wood products, steel and other metals, and winter fruit from South America. (Figure 6.5 shows a contemporary freighter on the Delaware River.) The port containerized in the late 1960s, constructed new piers and terminals, and built intermodal connections. In the 1990s Philadelphia Mayor Edward Rendell struggled to redevelop the Navy Yard, the city's most symbolic vacant industrial site. After one deal with German shipbuilder Meyer Werft collapsed in late 1994, the city and state inked a deal with Norwegian shipbuilder Kvaerner in 1997 to open a state-of-the-art facility, primarily for building cruise ships. Now called the Aker Philadelphia Shipyard, it is perhaps the most technologically advanced

Figure 6.5: Ship on the Delaware River.

shipbuilding facility on its side of the Atlantic. The port has done a better job of maintaining its relative position than has either Baltimore or Boston, its old rivals, suffering approximately the same relative decline in foreign trade position as New York.[30]

Yet the port, spread out along one hundred miles of waterfront in several localities and on both sides of the river, under the jurisdiction of three states—Pennsylvania, Delaware, and New Jersey—has historically been governed by no comprehensive planning and with control divided among competing players and interests. Despite the creation in 1952 of the Delaware River Port Authority (DRPA), which manages the river channel and the bridges, the Pennsylvania and New Jersey sides of the river continue to be run by separate organizations. In 1994 the two states concluded an agreement to create a united entity called the Ports of Philadelphia and Camden, which would function as a subsidiary of DRPA and control port operations on both sides of the river, but consolidation has not yet happened.[31] Divided control over the Philadelphia and Delaware River ports has caused a political weakness that strongly recalls Philadelphia's 1820s and 1830s problems with rail transit and the Main Line. Disputes among different government agencies have surfaced most recently in the plan to dredge the Delaware River shipping channel to a depth of forty-five feet; the plan is supported by the U.S. Army Corps of Engineers and the state of Pennsylvania but opposed by New Jersey and many environmental groups. As growth machine theory argues, the controversy over the dredging plan shows that global transport infrastructure projects are the object of conflict; different local constituencies often have divergent interests, and the rhetoric of international competition is not always persuasive. Given that the structural shifts in global patterns of waterborne trade during the past fifty years tended to marginalize ports with Philadelphia's characteristics—specifically, inland ports with modest channel depths—the port's future is not assured despite its importance to Philadelphia's overall global integration.

As their ports have struggled, both Philadelphia and Manchester have increasingly come to rely on a new global connector—air travel. Investment in airport infrastructure is the functional equivalent of the investments in railroads and ports that the cities made more than a century ago. The two cities first began planning for air travel early, between the world wars; Manchester even "lays claim to the world's first scheduled air service, to Blackpool and Southport in 1919." Both cities built their airports in the late 1930s and initiated transatlantic service soon after World War II—1945 for Philadelphia and the early 1950s for Manchester. Since that time, however, developments at Manchester have consistently led those at Philadelphia by about two decades. This gap arose in part because Manchester's water port was failing while Philadelphia's continued to grow and in part because the regulatory structure of the American air industry inhibited Philadelphia's growth. Manchester's airport grew in a neatly inverse relation to the shrinkage of its port; it embarked upon a major upgrade and expansion, for example, in the late 1970s, just as the Manchester Ship Canal was entering its final decline.[32]

In that decade, Manchester city government argued that central government funding should be put into developing air facilities in the north of England rather than in the already overcrowded southeast. In 1978 Manchester Airport was designated a Category A Gateway International Airport, along with Heathrow and Gatwick—the only one outside the southeast. Since then, the airport has boomed. Expansion has included new access roads, two new terminals in the 1990s (one for passengers and one for freight) and in 2001 a second runway. Traffic at Manchester grew swiftly, making the airport among the world's top twenty for international passengers in the late 1990s, "with more international passengers than Chicago"; passenger totals surpassed 22 million in 2005, with international travelers accounting for more than 18 million.[33]

Growth at Philadelphia International Airport, by contrast, was slow until the late 1980s. Deregulation of the airlines in 1978 prompted two changes that helped Philadelphia expand: it led to the establishment of the hub-and-spoke system, in which large airlines would control a majority of slots at their hub airports; and it led to a wave of airline mergers that included the formation of U.S. Airways out of the smaller Piedmont, Mohawk, and Allegheny airlines. A new international terminal opened in 1991, and the airport and the airline jointly engaged in a massive expansion plan in the late 1990s, including the construction of an additional international terminal (which opened in 2003), at a cost of more than $500 million. The airport's fortunes, however, have depended heavily on the fortunes of its major airline, U.S. Airways. Even today, U.S. Airways still accounts for more than 60 percent of the airport's flights. U.S. Airways declared bankruptcy twice in the early 2000s; in the process, the company was forced to lay off more than one thousand local employees. When the company finally emerged from bankruptcy for good in 2005, it merged with America West. Still, expansion has been rapid. The airport has grown from 65 gates to 120 since 2001, and in 2005 it handled more than 4.1 million international passengers and 31 million total passengers.[34]

Both airports are directly city-owned, rather than structured as quasi-public authorities, but the form that ownership takes is different in each case. Philadelphia International Airport is a city entity, a subagency of the city's Department of Commerce. Philadelphia has entered into an extremely close partnership with U.S. Airways, with responsibility for terminal and construction improvements shared between the two entities. Indeed, U.S. Airways served as developer for the new international terminal rather than the city, although the city owns the airport and the bonds for the project were issued by the Philadelphia Authority for Industrial Development. Manchester Airport is a for-profit corporation with local governments as the sole shareholders. It is, as its Web site says, "proud to be publicly owned and privately managed." The city of Manchester owns 55 percent of the shares and the nine other local municipalities hold 5 percent each; the board is composed of nine Manchester councillors and one apiece from the other local governments, plus the airport's chief officers. Since 1999, Manchester Airport has transformed itself into Manchester Airports Group and has begun buying other British airports, which it now runs. Manchester's approach is truly an aggressive, mercantilist form of state enterprise conducted on behalf of local government.[35]

Airport expansion is essentially local government economic development planning. Investment in airports intentionally builds new international trade and economic linkages for freight, business, and leisure, thereby integrating the city more deeply into the world economy. One consultant called the expansion plans for Philadelphia International Airport, for example, "a larger project than the Naval Yard over the long haul, as far as income, employment and job creation for the city." Geographically, both Philadelphia and Manchester are located along the world's premier air corridor over the North Atlantic (Washington to New York to London-Paris-Milan) and are promoting themselves as alternatives to the incredibly overcrowded airports of nearby global cities. Their international route systems have expanded greatly during the past fifteen years. International passenger traffic has grown sixfold at Manchester since 1980, from 2.9 million to 18 million. Philadelphia handled more than 558,000 tons of cargo in 2005, including nearly 140,000 tons of international cargo and 535,000 takeoffs and landings—ninth most in the world.[36]

The airports have indeed become immense economic centers; in the late 1990s each airport and its airlines directly employed approximately ten thousand people, and despite post–September 11 layoffs, they have continued to grow since. They are perhaps the most dynamic growth poles in their regional economies, stimulating employment in hotels, shipping and freight, conference centers, and companies that see an airport location as good for business. A great percentage of these firms are business service firms that are at the core of recent global economic expansion and transformation—not simply freight handlers, car rental agencies or hotels, or even express delivery giants like UPS and Federal Express, but firms like German software giant SAP, which located its American headquarters in Philadelphia. Through transportation services and global networking, these airports are contributing to the economic diversification and industrial transformation of Manchester and Philadelphia. This combining of old and new can be seen readily in the takeoff-and-landing approaches at Philadelphia International Airport, where planes fly over the Navy Yard and the tank farms and oil refineries along the southern stretch of the Delaware River port facilities.

Conclusion: MFP, Transport, and Globalization

The worldwide economic transformation of the 1970s threatened the global position of both cities. Local states responded by trying explicitly to open new channels of trade and transport integration in the hope of maintaining their second city positions. The Philadelphia seaport and both airports show an intensive urban mercantilism at work—state-owned enterprises operating in the global political economy to benefit major cities and their regions. Furthermore, from a global perspective, these transportation projects are not simply forced adjustments by local states to macro-level economic shifts. By reinforcing their own roles as commercial and transit nodes, the city governments of Philadelphia and Manchester have been active participants in knitting together the world economy and thereby creating the process we call globalization.

Global transport infrastructure projects are the most important planning and MFP initiatives these cities have undertaken. These projects simultaneously serve three functions. First, they respond to the competitive dilemmas that the cities face. They help cities overcome competitive threats to their standing relative to other cities, as Philadelphia responded to Baltimore in the first half of the nineteenth century. Indeed, the expansion of Manchester Airport in recent years is intimately connected to the city's drive, as I discuss in Chapter 7, to be recognized as "capital of the North." Second, these projects deepen the city's integration with the world economy at large. Each project opened new channels of trade, business, and communication, allowing the city to institute new linkages with cities, companies, and individuals in other countries. The nature of these linkages is, of course, highly variable—migration, tourism, material goods, financial transactions, FDI, subsidiaries, friendship, cultural exchange. But in all instances, what results is an intensification of the city's involvement in the global economy. Finally, these projects foster diversification of the local industrial base, through several mechanisms. The infrastructure itself is a large employer. It stimulates growth in supplier firms like Baldwin Locomotive or charter travel companies. It facilitates the expansion (whether by export or FDI) of local firms, allowing them to tap new markets. And it increases the city's attractiveness to companies from outside the region. Significantly, a large proportion of this transport infrastructure–led growth occurs in industries that are new to the region, and therefore it also revitalizes and diversifies the local economy.

In revitalizing their economies and global roles, however, these projects have also had the unintended effect of reaffirming each city's "second" position. The Pennsy and other railroads, for example, were too expensive for family or partnership entrepreneurialism, and required larger sources of capital: European financiers and what historical sociologist William Roy calls the "socialization" of capital through dispersed share ownership. Both of these investment channels ran through Wall Street; American railroads created real trading volume on the New York Stock Exchange, centering the nation's financial market and international financial connections in New York. Philadelphia could compete with and eventually best Baltimore, but both were battling for the wedding bouquet; the gold ring had gone to New York.[37] Similarly, the inability or unwillingness of local capital to subscribe shares for the Manchester Ship Canal meant that canal backers had to turn to London's financial interests—the Barings and the Rothschilds—for resources. Between the canal and Trafford Park, Manchester recreated and reinvigorated its historic emphases on commerce and manufacturing, not on finance.

It is noteworthy that Philadelphia's efforts to use transport infrastructure to address competitive threats and revitalize the city's economy have been more fraught and halting than Manchester's. Philadelphia's "lateness" and difficulty in achieving transport infrastructure goals in recent decades bear a marked similarity to its fumbling response to interurban competition in the 1820s and 1830s. In the simplest terms, this is about power and intergovernmental relations: Philadelphia has had to negotiate with governments over which it could exert little or no influence. The Philadelphia seaport, for example, has required the not-always-forthcoming cooperation between two quasi-sovereign authorities—Pennsylvania and New Jersey. Another way to interpret Philadelphia's difficulties is to argue that local backers of growth-oriented projects in Philadelphia have faced greater resistance and have had more difficulty persuading other interest groups and constituencies to go along with their proposals. In most cases, Manchester's government has been more politically unified and effective than Philadelphia's, yet both have managed to succeed; they have successfully negotiated approval or subsidy from higher levels of government, and when necessary, the two cities have often been able to make stick their claims of hegemony over other local governments.

A word of caution is warranted, however, about the straightforward application of growth machine ideas to MFP in general or to these kinds of projects in particular. We should take care to disaggregate conflict or competition *within* these cities and their regions from competition or conflict *between* these cities and other places. Both kinds of conflict are important. Yet the strongest opposition to the Pennsy and to the Manchester Ship Canal came not from within but without—from other localities outside the region that felt threatened. Similarly, despite the last three decades (and in Manchester, even longer) of ideological emphasis on markets, there is hardly even a pretense in these cities of leaving the modern transport infrastructure projects to the market or private enterprise. Local state authorities have themselves usually believed that these projects are public goods that they are duty-bound to provide; they have been helped in this belief by the demands of their citizens. This has been true partly because many in the cities have desired economic revitalization or diversification, and partly because the rhetoric of urban competition has been powerful. In addition, city governments and politicians have seen themselves as struggling to win resources for the city either from other (also self-interested) local governments or from distant central governments. In other words, they felt tugged by the demands of conflict or competition among cities as much as they were tugged by competing demands within their cities.

As a result, although the city governments of Philadelphia and Manchester pursued these projects in coalition with private actors and the local economic elite, we should not overstate the importance of private actors' roles. Local states have played and continue to play multiple roles in the planning, funding, and management of global transport infrastructures; this quasi-governmental character is not unusual. What has changed over time is not the fact of state participation but its form—whether the state is owner, investor, planner, manager, or some combination of these roles, and whether elected officials are directly responsible for infrastructure decision making or not. There has been a notable increase in the importance and responsibility of government officials, such as mayors, for these projects and local state involvement may in fact have been smallest in the mid-nineteenth century. Along the way, in all cases, these global transport infrastructure projects have been defined and treated as public goods, although they are not always run directly by the local state and are not organized in ways that are directly democratically accountable to the citizenry. Whatever the ownership structure, the companies that build and run these facilities have been prominent examples of mixed public-private economic entities.

Municipal foreign policy operates, therefore, as a kind of urban mercantilism, in which city governments try to do what is best for the city as a whole no matter what people outside the region think or want—and no matter what the national interest might be. At times, it even seems that urban and national interests conflict with one another. An argument can be made that postwar national policy making in both countries played a major role in the economic decline and difficulty in both cities. National policies subsidized suburbanization, fostered the growth of competing transportation modes (especially car and truck travel), drew military contracting away from Philadelphia to the South and West, and denied Manchester assisted-area status in the early 1960s, thereby drawing employment away from the city. Local states see transport infrastructure as one of the main tools they have to pursue their own needs and interests in the face of both global and national challenges, including challenges from other governmental bodies. This urban mercantilism is most evident in the Manchester Airport Group's (MAG's) purchase and takeover of other cities' airports, with the profits from the enterprises distributed back to MAG's shareholders—who are, of course, Manchester and nearby local governments.

Municipal foreign policy as we have considered it thus far focuses on political economy, straightforwardly understood as local state planning that enhances a city's position as a node in a network of global economic flows. But matters are in reality more complicated, and the urban political economy interacts with the city as a symbolic construct. Chapter 7 shows how Philadelphia and Manchester consciously elaborated second city identities that helped them define their policy choices, desired outcomes, and places in the world. In crafting these identities, Mancunians and Philadelphians each narrated their city's place as a meaningful actor in a global society, and this public identity is reflected in all of the infrastructure projects discussed above. Their political cultures are, like their transportation infrastructure facilities, formulated with global objectives in mind.

7

Identity and Governance in the Second City

The previous chapters demonstrate the substantial similarities between Manchester and Philadelphia in their global structural positions over time. They do not touch upon, as this chapter does, whether people in the cities were really conscious of those global positions. Did people in the two cities develop any identifiable second city identity? Did these places become cultural objects that meant something to people, that embodied their own understanding of their place in the world as a whole? In a word, yes: people in each city elaborated a definition of the city's global position that, in various ways, referred explicitly to its "secondness."

The construction of an urban identity as a second city responded both to local needs, particularly to the attempt to overcome political conflict and fragmentation, and to global pressures of interurban competition and the desire for recognition. In this meeting of global and local, second city identities were "glocal," in Roland Robertson's phrase: what people considered "local" was designed and produced with explicit reference to distant or global concerns and exemplars.[1] The discourses of urban identity mobilized in Manchester and Philadelphia did not necessarily invoke the phrase "second city." Rather, the ways people talked about the city located it in a second-tier position relative to other cities. The elements of a second city identity included the following:

• Invocation of the city's "second" past to valorize present projects and reinvigorate a previous identity

- National comparisons—claims to a hegemonic, superior position over lesser cities in the national space
- International comparisons—contrasts with acknowledged global cities and claims to parity with other cities that are internationally integrated but not global cities
- Explicit definition of the city as "second" or status claims to its being a provincial center/capital

Comparisons with other cities lay at the heart of urban identity construction. The claim to being "second," for example, was inherently comparative—but people and city governments in Manchester and Philadelphia also went substantially further, naming specific examples of other cities. These comparisons explicitly positioned the cities above, below, and parallel to other urban centers, and such comparisons were the symbolic raw material for a second city identity. In various ways, the two cities were marked as not quite global but superior to any other nonglobal (national) city around, and on par with other (international) regional capitals. Manchester and Philadelphia were seen as combining a consciousness of global engagement with a sense of separateness from the global city, explicitly invoking the process of globalization as part of the explanation for their positions.[2]

Where Chapter 6 stresses the mobilization of resources by players in each city to reinforce the city's *material* position in a global economy, this chapter focuses on how political entrepreneurs mobilized resources to augment the city's *symbolic* position. They did this, above all, by pursuing massive cultural planning projects. I analyze four such projects: the 1857 Art Treasures Exhibition in Manchester; the 1876 Centennial Exhibition in Philadelphia; Mayor Ed Rendell's attempts to create an "Avenue of the Arts" in Philadelphia in the 1990s; and Manchester's bids for international sporting events in the 1980s and 1990s. More broadly, cultural planning intertwines the built environment, political power, and urban identity.[3] "Reconstruction" is a not entirely metaphorical concept that encompasses all three of these purposes: the *physical reconstruction* or redesign of part of the city; the *political reconstruction* of the city's governing coalition or regime; and the *symbolic reconstruction* of the city's public, global identity as in some way "second." I elaborate on each of the three core ideas as follows:

Physical reconstruction. Cultural projects took material form as massive interventions in the city's built environment. By dedicating space in the city for culture, political entrepreneurs aimed to demonstrate physically the value of the cultural approach. They colonized new neighborhoods, redeveloped old land uses into new ones, and integrated formerly separate spaces of the city. These new uses for land and buildings were the main tangible "deliverables" or outcomes that political entrepreneurs promised—and thus the chance that the new land uses might fail to generate excitement and commitment was one of the prime risks they ran. The most well-known selling point they used to win support for the city's physical transformation by culture was economic revitalization, but prestige and status—for example, the reliance on star architects—were at least as important.

Political reconstruction. The most important lesson of this "sales" effort by politicians and civic leaders is that cultural products or events themselves were viewed as secondary to other purposes, most particularly to the formation of durable political coalitions, commonly called regimes. According to regime theory, no single player in urban politics has enough power or authority to govern a city alone; thus, coalition building is a core concern for politicians and other interested parties. The cultural projects in this chapter arose in times of deep political fragmentation; political entrepreneurs in Philadelphia and Manchester used these projects as tools for overcoming that fragmentation and building new governing regimes. The collection of donations and investments for the projects played an important role in developing commitment and building consensus among the fragmented elite and political actors. Precisely because they were cultural rather than political (i.e., partisan), these projects had the potential to bridge divides between old money and new money, classes, ethnic groups, generations, parties, and other political factions.[4] Although this potential was never fully realized—resistance and exclusion were always part of these governing regimes—politicians used culture to bypass conflict and resistance and to build relatively broad political coalitions that attracted wide support.

Symbolic reconstruction. Cultural projects were not simply instruments for political coalition building. They were also vehicles for the generation of local identity. People and groups bought into a regime in part because they were persuaded that it spoke to and for them; they saw themselves and their concerns reflected in the regime, and it afforded them recognition. Political entrepreneurs used cultural projects to express their definitions of the city to both locals and outsiders. These definitions of urban identity invariably made claims about the city's role in a global society—as part of an international network of cities, home of a "world class" activity, or the embodiment of progress. In this way the construction of a second city identity helped locals navigate globalization as a framework for interpreting the world. It helped them define their place within and relative to the global system, and it is in particular via these projects that concerns about the global position of the city relative to other cities consciously entered into urban life.

Although both Philadelphia and Manchester used cultural projects to build public identities as second cities, each filled this identity with different contents. Those contents responded to and mobilized the legacies of their divergent pathways to second city status. Manchester's power and wealth in the Victorian decades fostered a political and ideological hubris that was visible to commentators at the time. This sense of proud arrival has colored the city's image of itself ever since. Manchester was a city that thought more highly of itself than it really ought to, that strove to do more with less—a classic overachiever. This identity is still clear today in the city's two bids for the Olympics and in its downtown redevelopment campaign. Philadelphia, on the other hand, is best described as a classic underachiever. Its loss of the competition for global city status had enduring effects on local life and political culture. The city has struggled ever since with an "inferiority complex deeper than the Delaware." Its acceptance of "second" position has always been ambivalent, and the city had a curious way of developing and becoming modern against its will. This theme repeats itself again and again in characterizations of the city, in E. Digby Baltzell's works, the writings of contemporary journalists, and in the words of Nathaniel Burt several decades ago: "In fact, negativeness itself is typical. What Owen Wister called the 'instinct of disparagement' that makes Philadelphians habitually run everything down, especially things Philadelphian, is a form of this negative. This has the advantage of modesty; it also is a blight on creative effort, on reform, on any new enthusiasm. . . . It is, for example, *not* like New York."[5]

Culture, Power, and Identity in the Nineteenth Century

From the 1830s through the 1860s, both cities experienced immense social and political upheaval: rapid population growth, industrialization, pollution and disease, working-class agitation for political participation and the establishment of unions, racial and religious riots, nativist activism, and even (in the United States) civil war. This upheaval was an outcome of social changes that were of global, not just local, significance; these cities, like others, were the sites for a vast array of global changes in population, economy, and consciousness, which posed difficult problems of both political and symbolic order. How was a person, a group, or a city to derive meaning from this unstable situation and out of his, her, or its own evolving place in the world?

Politicians, the elite, and civic leaders turned to two strategies to cope with the crisis: growing the institutional power of the local state and establishing a new cultural identity for the city that would unite contending factions and shore up elite power. City governments radically transformed themselves and expanded by an order of magnitude between 1840 and 1870. Manchester won incorporation in 1838 and reformed its municipal government in the 1840s, acquiring control of the police, the courts, the gas corporation, and local taxation. From the 1850s on, the town corporation started to buy and municipalize the private companies that had previously provided services like water and transit. Similarly, Philadelphia's efforts to administer itself were growing through the provision of clean water, parkland, fire protection, and more. Perhaps most important, Philadelphia annexed all the outlying, independent districts in Philadelphia County in 1854; one of the primary reasons for the consolidation was to provide more effective policing.[6]

In terms of identity, the manufacturing elite in particular promoted an instrumental, utilitarian approach to culture that fit its background and ethos. Manufacturers believed in the manipulation and transformation of the world around them by the application of diligence, ingenuity, and (increasingly expert) skill. They viewed industrial design as a kind of art, bolstered the prominence of their cities as progenitors of this art, and claimed to respect creativity in labor so as to win over artisans and mechanics. Art was distinctly not for art's sake but for its utility in serving other agendas. They valorized the industrial city as the native home of a new, modern culture. Expressed and elaborated in each city's world's fair or exposition, Philadelphia and Manchester directly contrasted their newfound role and identity with New York and London, the global cities closest to them geographically.

But this industrial culture took on a distinct cast in each city. In Philadelphia, the new industrial culture was alloyed with regret and a sense of possibilities lost. Industrialization was perceived as a loss imposed from without, or a consolation prize, and this presented difficult cultural and identity problems for the city. Elite Philadelphians, powerfully affected by the eighteenth-century Quaker legacies of quietism and withdrawal from leadership, struggled with their loss of status. Old Philadelphian Sidney George Fisher—admittedly a curmudgeon, but still one of the great diarists of his era—bemoaned the victory of President Andrew Jackson over the Second Bank of the United States and fretted about his own social class' declining moral and cultural authority: "The good, respectable, old-family society for which Philadelphia was once so celebrated is fast disappearing, & persons of low origin & vulgar habits, manners & feelings are introduced, because they are rich, who a few years ago were never heard of."[7]

Manchester's identity, by contrast, was celebratory, even triumphalist. The city's "dark Satanic mills" were widely seen as *the* symbol of the new industrial era and a harbinger of the future. Travelers from many countries journeyed there in hopes of discerning the outlines of the days and years to come. Part of the city's challenge, therefore, was to define itself rather than be defined by others. Charles Dickens, for example, described Coketown, his fictionalized Manchester, as smoky, loud and joyless: "It was a town of red brick, or of brick that would have been red if the smoke and ashes had allowed it. . . . It contained several large streets all very like one another . . . inhabited by people equally like one another, who all went in and out at the same hours . . . to do the same work, and to whom every day was the same as yesterday and tomorrow. . . . You saw nothing in Coketown but what was severely workful."[8] Thomas Carlyle, on the other hand, while decrying the march of "Mechanism," marveled at "the rushing-off of [Manchester's] thousand mills, like the boom of an Atlantic tide, ten-thousand times ten-thousand spools and spindles all set humming there . . . sublime as a Niagara." Local industrialists picked up on this more grandiose interpretation of the manufacturing city; men like Richard Cobden portrayed Manchester as glorious, powerful, and cosmopolitan—and as generative of a new, modern culture.[9]

"As Great a Human Exploit as Athens"

Manchester's incorporation as a city represented the political triumph of the bourgeois, middle-class Liberals over what passed for England's ancien régime. Liberal control of the new polity was fragile, however, because it was achieved primarily through the withdrawal, from the political field, of opposing factions—upper-class Conservatives, who resisted change, and working-class Chartists, who organized unsuccessfully for the right to vote. There were, for example, no Conservative MPs or local elected officials in Manchester until 1868. Three core dividing lines characterized Lancashire politics at the time. The first was respect for and adherence to tradition, especially religious tradition. The polity was split between Anglicans, who tended to support the Tories, and Dissenters; there was an additional division between Catholics and Protestants. Religious dissent, especially among Unitarians and Quakers, provided a strong social basis for Liberal leadership.[10]

The second dividing line was class: Lancashire was split between landowners, manufacturers (the middle class), and workers. Class, however, would not become the primary basis for party affiliation until the end of the nineteenth century. In large part this was because class determined whether or not you could vote at all; questions of party were thus secondary to the larger issue of suffrage. The 1832 reforms, which enfranchised the lower-middle-class clerks and shop owners, only expanded Manchester's electorate to about five thousand people; workers did not get the vote until 1867. Struggles over suffrage in turn drove those who were excluded, especially workers, toward the call for the Charter (the founding meeting of the National Charter Association was in Manchester in 1840). After 1843, however, the Chartist movement faded and the working class did not reemerge as a political force until the 1870s.[11]

The third dividing line was between class fractions within the middleclass or bourgeois manufacturers. Radicals and Liberals wanted to expand the franchise and pushed strongly for repeal of the Corn Laws, while more "complacent" Whiggish manufacturers (the Whigs sought to limit royal authority) preferred to improve their position within the existing social order rather than overturn it. This political split became institutionalized in 1845 during the fight over the Corn Laws. In that year the Manchester Commercial Association (MCA) broke off from the Manchester Chamber of Commerce (MCC); the two groups disagreed over how involved merchant organizations should be in matters of state and foreign policy. The radicals who had formed the Anti–Corn Law League (ACLL), like John Bright, George Wilson, and Cobden, pushed the MCC into taking increasingly strident lobbying positions on foreign, trade, and imperial policy. Members of the breakaway MCA were notably more conservative; they disagreed with the close alliance between the MCC and the ACLL, and lobbying on "political" questions not directly related to industrial matters was prohibited in the MCA's bylaws.[12]

For nearly twenty years after 1838, therefore, Manchester was ruled by an exclusive, fragmented regime rather than an inclusive, incorporating one. The politically engaged Liberals and Radicals had succeeded in driving both the landed elite and the more conservative manufacturers out of politics, and workers were wholly excluded. The division among Liberals, Tories and Whigs was not as deep as it appeared, however; by 1850, the increasing wealth of many Liberal manufacturers had tempered their reformist zeal. Thus, when the rapprochement between different wings of the elite came in the late 1850s, neither side had to travel particularly far. Two events of 1857 marked a significant reconfiguration of the local political regime and brought the city's factions back together. First, in elections at the end of March, the radical former-ACLL members were turned out of Parliament in Lancashire, including Cobden, Bright, and Milner Gibson, to be replaced by more centrist figures like John Potter, the son of Manchester's first mayor, and James Aspinall Turner, president of the MCA. This result signaled a definitive move toward a more established and comfortable liberalism; it was not yet conservatism, but to a certain extent, the reforming fire had gone out of Lancashire politics.[13]

Second, from May through October of that year, the city hosted an international exposition, the Art Treasures Exhibition. The exhibition was the world's largest collection of art ever assembled in one place, gathering sixteen thousand works, and was visited by 1.3 million people. The idea for such an exhibition at Manchester was first floated in the winter of 1856. J. C. Deane, organizer of the 1853 Dublin exposition, proposed the concept in a letter to Manchester engineer Thomas Fairbairn. In March, Fairbairn held a planning meeting in the mayor's offices. Within three weeks Manchester citizens and merchants had subscribed £62,000 to begin planning the event and to insure the artworks. The executive committee included both the mayor and the politically powerful town clerk, as well as Fairbairn, Edmund Potter (brother of MP John Potter), and Thomas Ashton (ACLL veteran and, later, head of the capital campaign for Owens

College). The general plan was decided before the end of June 1856, and the guarantee fund increased to £75,000.[14]

The Art Treasures Palace, located at Old Trafford, to the southwest of Manchester proper and reachable by an exhibition-specific railway station, covered three acres. While dominated by English artworks, especially a large portrait gallery, the Art Treasures Exhibition also displayed a vast collection of Renaissance-era paintings and sculptures from Belgium, France, Holland, and Italy, and included exhibits of armor, pottery, glass, textiles, and furniture. Belgium, Haiti, and the United States sent envoys to the opening ceremonies; foreign visitors included Emperor Louis-Napoléon, Queen Sophie of Holland, Nathaniel Hawthorne, and several Russian nobles, although visitors from France and Germany were the most common.[15]

Politically, the Art Treasures Exhibition of 1857 was a mechanism for the construction of a new regime and galvanized an elite consensus within the city. The Art Treasures executive committee sat at the apex of this regime, but one can get an idea of its breadth from the list of people who were given seats on the dais at the opening ceremonies. These included the members of the executive committee and local MPs (such as James Turner of the breakaway MCA). Also on the dais were representatives of the pre-1838 ancien régime, such as James Prince Lee, the city's Lord Bishop. There were radical cotton merchants who had supported the ACLL, such as the Heywoods, the chemist Lyon Playfair, and prominent cotton manufacturers, merchants, and engineers, such as Edward Tootal, Joseph Whitworth, and Thomas Bazley. The boards of certain locally based educational and cultural organizations also played a role in an expanding circle of cultural institutions that helped hold a governing coalition together: the Manchester Literary and Philosophical Society (Lit&Phil), the Athenaeum, the Manchester Statistical Society, the Royal Manchester Institution, the Manchester Mechanics' Institute, and the Owens College board of trustees. Cross-matching the names on these boards with other lists, such as the heads of large manufacturing firms and the general membership of the Lit&Phil, reveals that the exhibition served to integrate a wider, more disparate network.[16] The MCC and the MCA, separate organizations since 1845, even united again in 1858, and from then on the moderates had a numerical superiority and a growing hegemony in Manchester politics and opinion, including among labor leaders.

Culturally, Mancunians used the exhibition to help them lay claim to a new international status and prestige that combined an appreciation for "culture" with respect for the city's industrial prowess. Many, including both Thomas Fairbairn and Prince Albert, royal consort to Queen Victoria, hoped that the exhibition would contribute effectively to educating the working classes in the aesthetics of industrial design. To further this end, several people suggested reducing the admission price on Saturdays, when mill hands worked only a half day. The *Manchester Guardian*'s reviewers wrote that the exhibition "furnishes to the intelligent manufacturer and workman, the most valuable store of examples, suggestions, and warnings, that can teach him in what spirit to work, what to aim at, and what to avoid." (Of course, workers were the objects rather than the subjects of these exhortations; they had little role in and received little benefit from the Exhibition.)[17] Furthermore, the reviewers made an intimate connection between the two cultural purposes of workingmen's education and the elevation of the city's profile:

As society grows more cultivated, it demands more and more as much beauty in things of daily use as can be infused into them. Superiority in design may often be the determining element in deciding between rival centres of manufacturing industry. If to cheapness of production England can add beauty of design, she is doubly armed against all competitors. This Exhibition has wisely been planned with a recognition of this double service of art.[18]

In fact, it was precisely this melding of art with design in the service of a more cultured commerce that made cities like Manchester noteworthy. The *Manchester Guardian*'s reviewers extolled the fame of those cities that in the past had been associated with particular craft styles, and it noted that excellence in industrial design was one way to earn a place in history. Cities like Cordoba, the reviewers wrote, along with "Milan, Rome, Venice, Florence, Augsburg, Nuremburg, and Paris will for ever be noteworthy in history as the great workshops from whence emanated some of the most beautiful productions of industrial art." Industrial culture and product design were viewed as pathways to civilization in its loftier connotations, as well as to broader public esteem and status for the city.[19]

This vision of themselves as cultural leaders assisted the city's elite in cementing Manchester's undisputed status as England's second city. The *Manchester Guardian* crowed, saying, "A collection so vast and various, so rich and rare, was never before brought together in this country; and we may safely hazard the assertion that the great and triumphantly successful experiment and achievement can never be repeated." Contemporary commentators, including writers for the *London Times*, were astonished that such a huge exhibition should occur in Manchester rather than London and recognized that the city had achieved a prestigious coup. The city even had some advantages over London because it was less dominated by the pomp and sycophancy of the royal court and its traditions. Also, the exhibition lured Charles Hallé to establish a full-time orchestra in the city, helping Manchester escape "the fate of Leeds, Birmingham and Sheffield" and allowing the city to assert its cultural superiority over the other provincial centers for decades.[20]

Backers also used the exhibition to catapult the city into parity with the great continental cultural centers. The leadership of the Anti–Corn Law League had purposefully chosen to call itself a "league" in order to draw attention to this historical resonance. The ACLL's founders believed they were re-creating the great systems of city-states that had existed in history: ancient Greece, Carthage, and Phoenicia, medieval Italian cities like Florence and Venice, and of course the Hanseatic League. International expositions had rapidly become the "new thing" after London's Crystal Palace in 1851, and Manchester merchants wanted to best, or at least equal, the Paris Exhibition of 1855 and the Dublin Exhibition of 1853. The exhibition guide published by the *Manchester Examiner and Times*, for example, compared the city to Renaissance Florence, and the sense of communion with cultural centers on the Continent and with the great cities of history was spectacularly embodied in Manchester's new architecture. The new civic leaders rebuilt much of the downtown in their own image and in the service of their own myths (see, for example, the city's gothic town hall, pictured in Figure 7.1). Manchester developed a distinctive architectural style, as cotton magnates erected the city's signature yellow-and-red stone-and-brick warehouses. This "palazzo" style deliberately imitated the cities of the Italian Renaissance; the Renaissance symbolism fit perfectly with civic leaders' own self-conception and garnered praise in architectural periodicals like *The Builder*. As the *Building News* opined in 1861, "Manchester is a more interesting city to walk over than London. One can

Figure 7.1: Manchester's massive gothic town hall, completed in 1877.

scarcely walk about Manchester without coming across examples of the *grand* in architecture. There has been nothing to equal it since the building of Venice."[21]

Victorian Mancunians were proud of their city and its achievements. Civic leaders openly used the Art Treasures Exhibition to imagine a connection to a global network of cities, and they bolstered Manchester's place in that network by appealing to a productive, industrial culture of design and innovation that was supposedly urban based. They used these aspects of the city as tools to proclaim their exclusive hold on second position behind London. This state of mind reveals itself repeatedly in the histories and memoirs of the time, which increasingly noted that Manchester led "the way among provincial cities."[22] Regional hegemony, combining a relatively secure status as capital of the North with pride of place among provincial cities, was the logical counterpart of municipal internationalism and inter-urban competition.

Philadelphia in "the Year of the Century"

In contrast to Manchester, where the Art Treasures Exhibition served as a sort of triumphal procession for a city still on an upward trajectory, Philadelphia struggled for decades with both the symbolic and the political consequences of its loss of "first" status. Even as it grew into the country's second city, and its most powerful, diversified manufacturing center, no one group was able to persuade enough people to follow it to establish hegemony, and durable governance or political authority was absent. A new governing regime and a new urban identity would only fully emerge in the mid-1870s through planning for the nation's Centennial Exhibition, which was held in Philadelphia in 1876.[23] Politically, the Centennial Exhibition enabled a rapprochement between elite good-government reformers and the city's professional politicians. But because the politics of corruption and reform were themselves so divisive, the coalition among these constituencies was achieved through cultural means. Symbolically, the Centennial Exhibition served as a mechanism for reconstructing the city's identity by transforming protectionist ideology into a broader, more wide-ranging self-conception as a world-class industrial metropolis. Philadelphia's new urban identity possessed many of the same elements as Manchester's: a manufacturing or productive ethos that connected "high" culture with manufacturing design, a comparison to other great cities around the world, and a negative contrast with the country's main global city, New York.

The Centennial Exhibition was a fantastic success and dramatically displayed Philadelphia's wealth and industrial might. More than 186,000 people gathered on opening day on May 10, and between nine and ten million—nearly one-fifth of the country's population—had attended by its close in November. At noon, on the exhibition's first day, President

Figure 7.2: Philadelphia's Memorial Hall, one of the only Centennial Exhibition buildings left standing.

Ulysses S. Grant along with Emperor Dom Pedro I of Brazil opened the festivities. Items on display included the huge Corliss steam engine that powered all of the other machinery exhibits, the Remington typewriter (the first QWERTY-style machine), root beer from Hires, the Statue of Liberty's torch, the Westinghouse air brake, Fleischmann's yeast, cable from the Brooklyn Bridge, the Bell telephone, and the Otis elevator. The main exhibition building was the largest in the world, more than a third of a mile long.[24]

Physically, the Centennial Exhibition helped knit together the far-flung city, connecting West and Northwest Philadelphia more firmly to the existing core. Located in the newly established Fairmount Park, the exhibition drew millions to the park, spurred park improvements (including Memorial Hall, pictured in Figure 7.2), and firmly established it as one of the city's core attractions. The Pennsylvania Railroad opened its West Philadelphia Station at Thirty-second and Market streets in May 1876, just in time to handle exhibition traffic, and another at Forty-eighth Street. The Reading Railroad's nearby station "handled 247 trains per day and a total of 3,295,120 passengers" that year. The celebration also offered a myriad of opportunities for hoteliers, restaurateurs, and other retailers; John Wanamaker, for example, opened his new store at Thirteenth Street that year. The exhibition finally made Philadelphia into a *metropolitan* center, the cosmopolitan heart of a great region.[25]

Politically, the exhibition effort became the chief vehicle for the rapprochement among the city's feuding constituencies and interest groups, especially the accommodation of elite reformers with the corrupt or "regular" Republican party bosses and machine. The city's politicians, of course, saw the Centennial Exhibition as a cow fit for milking; historian Howard Gillette's data indicate that city expenditures for streets and highways, fire, and water boomed in the mid-1870s, and the police budget nearly doubled. Elite reformers, on the other hand, turned to the exhibition effort after the political frustration of losing to the Republican machine repeatedly in the 1860s and early 1870s. The key organization for the accommodation and incorporation of elite, reformist elements was the Centennial Board of Finance, established by Congress in June 1872, which oversaw fundraising and budgeting for the exhibition. Playing more junior roles were the Franklin Institute and the Union League, both of which had relatively exclusive boards with significantly larger total memberships; the Franklin Institute had approximately two thousand members, and the Union League nearly one thousand. These organizations and others like them mixed the city's elite with up-and-coming clerks, engineers, and other members of the middle classes. Given the native backgrounds of most reformers and middle class participants, however, the line between inclusion and exclusion broke down along entirely predictable ethnic, racial, and religious lines. The Republican coalition made little effort to include African Americans, even though they had recently reclaimed the right to vote in Pennsylvania, and Catholic immigrants were also largely left out.[26] Still, the exhibition brought a wide range of people and groups to the table via donations, collective spirit, volunteerism, the prospect of personal profit, and the desire to do well for the city. Cultural planning thus became an avenue for building public agreement at a time when politics itself was too divisive.

The exhibition furthermore played an important role in the process of political and cultural unification by helping to transform Republicanism from a relatively narrow political economic ideology into a broader worldview about the city's place in the world and in history. Protectionism became a more comprehensive part of the political culture; its supporters began emphasizing the aesthetic and civilizing value of manufacturing by associating industrial with artistic production. The Centennial Exhibition tightly melded culture with commerce and industry; art works and machines were often displayed next to one another. By raising industry to the level of "culture," the exhibition's backers worked out an accommodation with the more vulgar elements of Horatio Alger–style—and corrupt—modernity. This producer-oriented industrial ethos was subscribed to by most of the elite, a majority of the city's middle classes, and even many workers.[27]

Also, the Centennial Exhibition gave Philadelphia a chance to show itself off to the world and inaugurated mass tourism to the United States as foreigners flocked to see it. Dozens of foreign governments contributed exhibits; Austrian, Brazilian, Japanese, and Turkish officials, among others, attended the opening ceremony. In fact, it was precisely the international component of the Centennial Exposition that had been most difficult for Congress and other cities to swallow. At an 1878 fete for Congressman Daniel Morrell, who had been an early supporter of the exhibition, one speaker remarked: "A large number of the commissioners, as well as many of our leading citizens, were opposed to its international feature. . . . The bitter jealousies of rival cities still sought to destroy it rather than to allow Philadelphia to have the glory of the location." Just as in the case of Manchester's Art Treasures Exhibition, Philadelphia had scored a coup that others begrudged it. The city was widely recognized as being of international stature, both by others and by its own residents, "the Centennial was altogether a lesson in self-respect for the city; it showed its present greatness and its potentialities. . . . The *Chicago Tribune* [reported] that staid old Philadelphia was gone, and that the city was 'as cosmopolitan as Paris and as lively as Chicago.'"[28]

The exhibition resolved Philadelphia's ambiguous post-1840 position as the city that should have been global but did not quite make it by melding Old World high culture and New World industrial design. Philadelphians had long attempted to distance themselves from New York by complaining about that city's vulgarity. Sidney George Fisher had written as long ago as 1837 that "in N. York, there is all the vulgarity, meanness, & ostentatious parade of parvenuism. . . . [M]oney there is the only test, the society is composed of people from every rank in life, even the lowest." By lionizing Paris instead, Philadelphians could disparage New York implicitly and adopt an alternate path for themselves, one that appeared to have more status. And at the same time as it flattered the elite, the Parisian model, at least symbolically—by claiming that industrial design could be beautiful—valorized the skilled craftwork that was at the heart of the city's economy. Making this comparison on such a prominent international stage allowed the city simultaneously to assert its difference from New York, its old foe, and to stake out an accommodation with its own difficult history.[29]

At the conclusions of both the 1857 Art Treasures Exhibition and the 1876 Centennial Exhibition, the artworks were packed up, the machines disassembled, and the buildings torn down. Nothing remains of the Manchester site, and only two buildings out of several dozen are left standing in Philadelphia's Fairmount Park. The transience of the physical structures, however, is a poor measure of the political and symbolic impacts of the expositions. During the course of the 1800s, Manchester and Philadelphia achieved much more than simple placement on the world map as industrial powerhouses. They also both used massive cultural events as tools to win international cultural status. Each city played host to hundreds of thousands of visitors; they took part in an ongoing program of world festivals that gave citizens and residents a sense of local pride and worth. Through these events, they renarrated distinctive local identities as second cities— one triumphal, another ambivalent—with critical roles to play in defining and shaping an international, cosmopolitan, urbane modernity.

Political Realignment in the Late Twentieth Century

The global identities Manchester and Philadelphia forged in the nineteenth century were substantially transformed by the growing institutional power of the nation-state. This national frame devalued the cities' nineteenth-century global connections and identities but offered them something in return: a powerful and seemingly stable position in a national urban hierarchy. In recent decades, however, under the pressures of deindustrialization, economic restructuring, and suburbanization, the material referents of Manchester's and Philadelphia's second city identities disintegrated. Simultaneously, immigration and other aspects of globalization eroded the significance of the national institutional frame, leading not just to economic distress but also to what one might call "identity decay"—the loss of a sense of the city's place in a larger cultural and symbolic system. The most visible consequence of this identity decay, in both cities, was profound political division and fragmentation in the 1970s and 1980s.

The new challenge for Philadelphia and Manchester was to invent diagnoses and solutions that could overcome this decline, and reassert or revitalize their urban identities given the new contours of globalization. Both cities have engaged during the past two decades in a process of once again "learning to be global."[30] Yet their attempts to reinvigorate themselves at the end of the twentieth century also reinscribed historic identities and patterns of political action. Manchester's claim to be a "European regional capital" reinvoked the city's glorious past and the city was systematically more self-conscious about choosing to affiliate with a global urban system rather than the nation. Manchester's strategy for building a new global identity, true to historical form, relied again on new, "vulgar" cultural elements; the city quite openly adopted pop-culture industries—music and sport in particular—as incubators of its new claim to prestige.

Philadelphia's search for a renewed second city identity was more ambivalent. The city was slow to think internationally or globally, and city leaders adopted a conservative, high-culture approach from the top down that focused on the professional middle classes who worked in the city's biggest industries (hospitals and universities), re-created the city's legendary stodginess, and kept its distance from the city's grassroots. The city's hesitation reinscribed its past insecurity over its global role, yet in the 1990s the city began to speak explicitly about itself as a "second city."

Philadelphia's Avenue of the Arts

Philadelphia reached its nadir in the years between 1976 and 1985. The population dropped by nearly one-fourth between 1950 and 1990, and factory employment declined by more than three-fourths; the nation's first manufacturing powerhouse lost almost all its manufacturing jobs. The film

Rocky portrayed the city, like Sylvester Stallone's character, as a gruff but lovable loser who could take the punishment but could not win the fight, condemned always to be runner-up. The film gave shape to the city's ongoing identity crisis, and did so in ways that re-created rather than challenged its old identity as the great loser for a new era. Just as it had lost out 150 years earlier in the battle for global city status and had turned to manufacturing as a kind of consolation, so now it was losing its manufacturing status. But what would be the consolation this time?

Alongside the Rocky image was the Rizzo reality. The reform movement of the 1950s and 1960s that had ushered in Democratic control of city government collapsed as a result of its struggles with the new Democratic machine over control of city government. As the reformers faltered, Frank Rizzo's election as mayor in 1971 broke the Democratic coalition in two; he won even though the majority of African Americans crossed parties to vote Republican against him. Rizzo, chief of police in the 1960s, had developed a rowdy reputation either as a bigoted bully or as a strict law-and-order enforcer, depending on which neighborhood you solicited an opinion from. He took personal control of nearly four thousand public jobs during his first term as mayor, spent freely on contracts with city unions, and designated a squad of police to investigate his political enemies, including former mayors Joseph Clark, Richardson Dilworth, and James Tate. As a result, after his reelection in 1975, the city found itself $80 million in the hole; real estate and wage taxes, along with water and sewer rates, were all increased by 30 percent.[31]

But Rizzo's divisive mayoralty was simply the most obvious manifestation of a wider disarray that reached deep into city politics. Conflicts over housing led to repeated demonstrations and the takeover of city offices, and a fistfight between councillors even broke out on the floor of city council in 1982. The ineptly managed bicentennial celebration of 1976 nearly collapsed after Rizzo publicly requested fifteen thousand troops, claiming the threat of riots or terrorism; the bicentennial's fate was sealed by the outbreak of what came to be called Legionnaires' disease, which killed thirty-four visiting conventioneers that summer at the landmark Bellevue Hotel. The capstone was undoubtedly the firebombing and destruction of two city blocks by the police in 1985 during Mayor Wilson Goode's confrontation with the black radical organization MOVE. Flashed around the world, the story made Philadelphia infamous as the only city to have bombed itself. The tragedy of the fire was followed by farce: in 1986 a ship called the *Khian Sea*, filled with fifteen thousand tons of Philadelphia's incinerator waste, wandered the globe from port to port, looking for a country that would allow it to dump the trash (none agreed).[32]

Despite a changing skyline—several new skyscrapers in the mid-1980s towered over the symbolically important statue of William Penn atop city hall—Philadelphia lacked both a functioning polity and a powerful or directive business community. Indeed, corporate interests were widely regarded as having little pull and even less vision. This was true despite corporate leaders having established a CEO-only organization called Greater Philadelphia First (GPF) to provide greater civic oversight and input. GPF's successes were modest at best, and one journalist even argued that "the city's business community . . . could perhaps best be described as supine."[33]

Only in 1991 did a series of events begin to overcome the city's disarray. First, the state legislature passed legislation establishing the Center City District (CCD), a business improvement district that relied for its funding on mandatory extra property tax collections from landowners within its boundaries. In addition to providing street sweeping, streetscape improvements like new lighting fixtures, and uniformed employees who roamed the streets assisting travelers and business professionals, the CCD issued a plan to transform the Benjamin Franklin Parkway, a wide boulevard that leads from city hall to the Philadelphia Museum of Art. For better or worse, by the year 2000, the CCD and its executive director, Paul Levy, had effectively replaced the City Planning Commission as the planning authority for downtown.[34]

Second, the Central Philadelphia Development Corporation (CPDC) published a plan for turning South Broad Street into "Avenue of the Arts." Several organizations, such as the University of the Arts and the Philadelphia Orchestra, had long had separate ideas for building new spaces for their own institutions, but no overall plan tied them together. Avenue of the Arts combined these separate projects while adding several new ones to the list. The CPDC plan foresaw a South Broad Street that in 2002 would be "one of America's grandest urban boulevards," and would include neighboring spin-off developments, like a multiplex cinema and ethnic restaurants along South Street. The centerpiece would be the new Regional Performing Arts Center (RPAC) that would showcase the orchestra, dance troupes, the American Music Theater Festival, and other performing arts organizations. Designed by architect Rafael Viñoly, the center is shown in Figure 7.3.[35]

Third, in 1991 Edward Rendell was elected mayor on a platform promising to confront the city's deepening fiscal crisis (the deficit during his first year in office amounted to approximately $250 million, or 10 percent of the city's budget). Rendell won cuts in city union contracts and actively pursued hotel development and riverboat gambling in attempt to spur the hospitality industry. In addition to these programs, Rendell touted the Avenue of the Arts, and culture more generally, as an economic development tool. Adopting CPDC's plan for the Avenue of the Arts (AA), Rendell became the chief fund-raiser and cheerleader for the project; he expanded the number of venues, tying the plan into a tourism and convention development agenda. The total public cost of the enlarged project was estimated at $300 million.[36]

Figure 7.3: Philadelphia's Kimmel Center for the Performing Arts, on South Broad Street's Avenue of the Arts.

For Rendell, the AA was not primarily about the arts. On one hand, the construction of new venues for the performing arts was pressed into the service of local economic development goals. Ellen Solms, the executive director of the AA, stated openly that arts organizations were not viewed as ends in themselves but as tools in urban revitalization: "This project is not just a cultural development project. . . . It's an economic-development project. The case for support for the Avenue of the Arts is not based on [the health of the arts organizations] but on the impact the project will have on the city as a whole." On the other hand, Rendell's solution to political fragmentation was to utilize the AA as the vehicle for building a new political coalition. Rendell took it upon himself to bring together the region's disparate, feuding constituencies—business and labor, white people and African Americans, city residents and suburbanites, downtown and the neighborhoods. Broadening the AA plans to include more buildings and more constituencies was the sine qua non of success for this strategy. According to orchestra executive director Joseph Kluger: "I am hopeful that if it's repositioned as a community based project, some of the larger funding sources will be persuaded to invest in it. CPDC is doing it so it doesn't look like it's just us."[37]

Rendell focused immense personal effort on convincing people of all backgrounds to "buy into" the project. The list of donors that gave significant amounts of money to various AA projects included both of the main opponents of the RPAC—Walter Annenberg and the Pew Charitable Trusts—as well as Sidney Kimmel of the Jones New York clothing business (as the largest individual donor, the RPAC was named after him). In Kimmel's role one can see the importance cultural projects can have for integrating new money into established society. In addition, Rendell galvanized significant funding from various levels of government, including city, state, federal, and school district. Most of the corporate donations were from companies that were dependent on the regional economy—banks, newspapers, utilities—or that were headquartered in the region (e.g., Unisys); still, some of the money came from branch plants (e.g., Boeing).[38]

The AA board was filled with politically connected members of the community. Ellen Solms had worked for the Convention and Visitors Bureau during the bicentennial, served on the board of the Pennsylvania Ballet, and raised $1.9 million for Rendell's previous mayoral campaign, in 1987. Ron Rubin owned the Bellevue—situated on South Broad Street between city hall and the AA proper—as well as other valuable downtown properties. Joseph Neubauer was the CEO of Aramark, one of the city's largest corporations, and a longtime supporter of the Philadelphia Orchestra. William Hankowsky was the head of the Philadelphia Industrial Development Corporation (PIDC), city government's primary economic development arm. Walter Dallas headed Freedom Theater, one of the city's premier African American arts groups. Cultural producers were thus offered a seat at the table in planning and organizing the Avenue. Dallas and Naomi Street, wife of then–city council President (and later mayor) John Street, signaled Rendell's intention to include African Americans in decision making and in the distribution of federal and state dollars that would be necessary for the projects to succeed. The presence of Alice Lipscomb, a longtime housing activist, helped reassure people that nearby neighborhoods would be dealt with in good faith.[39]

This nucleus was broadened by the incorporation of other elite organizations, the Democratic Party, labor unions, and community organizations. The boards of organizations such as the CPDC, CCD, GPF, and PIDC included a wide cross-section of the local elite, from downtown property interests to manufacturing firms to telecommunications. In addition, the allegiance among them was cemented by overlapping memberships; for example, in 1991 twelve companies were represented on the boards of both GPF and the CPDC. African Americans and the arts community were incorporated directly through representatives on the AA board. Labor unions were less centrally involved, primarily through their ties to the Democratic Party (Mayor Rendell, although he had a rocky relationship with the public-employee unions, got along warmly with the building trades because projects like the RPAC generated increases in construction payrolls). The Orchestra Association and other arts organizations incorporated not simply arts producers but also the suburban upper-middle classes, giving them a stake in the regime's success; suburban acquiescence, or even enthusiasm, was aided by the fact that Rendell was Philadelphia's most popular mayor across the region in decades.

Still, the renarration of the city's identity was slow and difficult. There existed substantively different visions of how the city should develop, both among politicians and within the arts community. Many questioned the emphasis on downtown cultural consumption over other priorities. Some wondered whether it was wise to subsidize (well-off people's) cultural consumption by building new performance venues rather than to subsidize (artists' and city residents') cultural production by providing studio spaces, fellowships, and programming support. In fact, several potential tenants pulled out of the RPAC because of concerns over whether they could shoulder the high maintenance costs. Also, many donors were doubtful of the plans for the new performing arts center; Walter Annenberg, for example, gave $20 million to the Avenue of the Arts but refused to allow any of it to go toward the new hall. Neighborhood-based cultural organizations were also skeptical. Johnny Irizarry of the North Philadelphia cultural organization Taller Puertorriqueño, for example, questioned the focus on large downtown institutions: "I do believe the downtown will definitely benefit. . . . People will come from the suburbs and eat in restaurants. But it won't be our community or our restaurants that benefit."[40] Of all city residents, the insecurely housed probably suffered the most. The emphasis on tourism and cultural consumption led to a campaign to reduce the public presence of the homeless on downtown streets. It was also combined with an effort to demolish nearby public housing projects and move their residents elsewhere, further contributing to the gentrification of the neighborhoods closest to the AA and the downtown.

In addition to these political disputes, the early phases of AA planning and of Philadelphia's efforts at identity reconstruction were striking for their parochialism. In part this was due to the city's legendary sleepiness and its staid and unadventurous character; "withdrawal" has been a part of the city's character at least since the mid-eighteenth century. City residents were notoriously ambivalent about their city's charms, and around the region people were even less enthusiastic. But in particular, a global consciousness was almost entirely absent, and when it existed was generally unfavorable. The City Planning Commission's 1988 *Plan for Center City*, the first major planning document for downtown in twenty-five years, contained only two references to international concerns and they were not a centerpiece of any of the plan's recommendations. In 1989 a *Philadelphia* magazine article chose national models over international ones: "So maybe it's worth the risk of being mistaken for Cleveland. Anyhow, it beats being mistaken for Beirut." Or, as *Inquirer* columnist David Boldt wrote, "There is the feeling that the city is getting increasingly out of control; that maps of it could be made like the old maps of Vietnam, showing shaded areas that are either 'not under government control' or 'not under government control at night.'"[41] In contrast to older comparisons to foreign models like Paris, the city set its sights much lower and closer to home.

Beginning in the mid-1990s, however, no longer was Cleveland the model and no longer were international images to be avoided. Compared to Philadelphia's centennial identity, the key shift in the 1990s was a turn away from Paris, and the category of the global city in general, toward cosmopolitan but second-tier metropolises. In this process, the city began explicitly to conceive of a second city identity in positive terms. In 1993 a "Philadelphia-Paris Forum" brought together architects and planners from both cities to consider whether there were lessons in Paris's *Grand Projets* redevelopment strategy that could be applied to Avenue of the Arts. John Higgins of the Foundation for Architecture captured the spirit of the conversation: "Philadelphia will never be Paris. But it can become a great second city. It will be a Florence, a Seville, a Lyon, cities that are great because they are provincial."[42] Philadelphians reconfigured the image of the second city in positive terms as provincial: in essence, cosmopolitan but livable. Indeed, the City Planning Commission even decided to market the city internationally as a "second city" destination for investment and tourism: "Like Florence (Italy), St. Petersburg (Russia), Kyoto (Japan) or even Barcelona, Philadelphia can be a classic second city—a center of national historical importance, large and sophisticated enough to be interesting, but more intimate in scale and, thus, better able to display its culture and character."[43]

Several subsidiary elements of the city's renarration also showed a renewed consciousness of globalization and the city's global role. The most significant was the burgeoning discourse around regionalism. The corporate elite signed on to the ideological project of building a consciousness of the "Delaware Valley" as a united region, with Philadelphia as primus inter pares. Philadelphia Newspapers, publisher of both local dailies and a member of GPF, even went so far as to commission a report on the Philadelphia "citistate" from noted regionalist writer Neal Peirce. Crucially, the report defined regionalism and regional unity as the necessary local counterpoints to globalization. As Rosemarie Greco, CEO of CoreStates Bank and later chairwoman of GPF, said: "Regionalism is not about inner-city guilt, or helping the poor. It's about being able to compete in the world. It's not about correcting the past, but rather optimizing for the future. We need to develop the idea of globalization for people to understand regionalism."[44]

Philadelphia's strategy for developing a new identity, however, was largely a forced march, directed from the top down. It is difficult to determine how far this new awareness of globalization, or of Philadelphia's global role and position, has penetrated most people's everyday consciousness. Rendell's coalition did have striking success in changing both local and suburban attitudes toward the city, making it more positive. And cultural consumption was an important part of that change. The annual Philadelphia Festival of World Cinema, which has been successful in bringing films from dozens of countries to the United States, is now more than twenty years old. Explicitly global themes and concerns clearly began to shift the thinking not just of the elite, but of sectors of the middle classes, particularly the intelligentsia and cultural producers. But it was unclear how much deeper Philadelphia's new urban identity really ran, or what it offered to the native, nonimmigrant poor in particular; it was also unclear whether Rendell would be able to hand off a fully functioning regime to his successor, black city council President John Street. The regime seems to have survived: after winning the closest mayoral election in a century in 1999, Street was reelected in 2003 by a landslide, and Rendell's popularity propelled him into the governorship of Pennsylvania. To a certain extent, the handing of the regime's reins over to a black politician with a deep neighborhood base answered concerns about working-class and poor residents' inclusion. These questions about a new urban identity's depth or penetration and about a regime's durability can serve as yardsticks for assessing Manchester's late-twentieth-century transformation as well.

Twenty-Four-Hour Party People

As in Philadelphia, the 1970s and early 1980s were not a good time for Manchester. The city was hemorrhaging jobs as factories moved out of town or shut down. Unemployment climbed to 20 percent for the city as a whole and reached 30 percent in the racially mixed working-class neighborhood of Moss Side. There was public discontent over the city's slum clearance program—reputedly the largest in Europe—in Hulme and Moss Side, including protests at the ugly and deplorable Hulme Crescents, the concrete *banlieue* that had replaced the earlier slums. In July 1981, Moss Side erupted in three days of rioting, centered on black residents' perceptions of police violence, disrespect, and excessive force. Rioters destroyed a police station, attacked and were attacked by police, and looted dozens of neighborhood shops along Princess Road. During the course of the 1980s, Moss Side was increasingly identified with crime, violence, drugs, and gangs; eventually this association took over the city as a whole and Manchester became known as "Gunchester."[45]

The conflict and disorganization on Manchester's streets characterized the city council as well. Suburbanization, deindustrialization, and redevelopment exacerbated the problems by eroding the city's working-class voter base, disrupting Labour's political support and contributing to a split between the moderate and left wings of the local Labour Party. The left wing opposed increases in local tax rates, cuts in the local housing budget, and plans for layoffs of government employees—whereas the moderates were prepared to compromise with Prime Minister Margaret Thatcher's demands for reduced central government support of local service provision. Disputes became so rancorous that Labour's national office had to step in to broker a compromise after the moderates expelled left-wing councillors from city council's Labour caucus and the left wing in return deleted moderates from the party's slate of candidates for the next election.[46]

In the 1983 local elections the left wing won enough seats to become the dominant faction on the council. Their leader was Graham Stringer, who remained head of the city council until 1997, when he moved to Parliament. During those years, he led the transformation of Manchester's politics toward partnership and engagement with global forces; he reconceived the object of local politics to be the growth-oriented development of a competitive European city-region. Symbolically, he led a reinvigoration of Manchester's historic urban identity as a vanguard participant in a cosmopolitan, internationalist league of cities. Physically, the vehicle for reconstructing urban politics and identity was a massive downtown redevelopment campaign focused on leisure, sports, and culture; at its heart were nightlife and the city's two bids to host the Olympic Games.[47]

Stringer took advantage of the shifts in other people's thinking to build a powerful pro-development regime. It was organized into a web of planning and development bodies, such as the Central Manchester Development Corporation (CMDC) and the Trafford Park Development Corporation (TPDC). Stringer used the rhetoric of "partnership" to influence the activities and plans of others, maintaining personal control over most projects, directly deciding personnel, running the committees that handled the flagship projects, and even turning the CMDC into an instrument of his will. But the organizations that really forged a new consensus between the political and business elite and indigenous or grassroots transformations in the city's culture and economy were the Olympics and Commonwealth Games bid committees. The city twice became the United Kingdom's official bid city for the Olympics—for the 1996 and 2000 games; although it lost both bids, it used the experience to win the 2002 Commonwealth Games. The committee for the 1996 Olympics bid, organized in 1985 and chaired by Robert Scott, a local theater producer, included representatives from the Manchester City Council, both of the development corporations, the Northwest Business Leadership Team, Manchester United Football Club, the University of Salford, textile maker Coats Viyella, and the television production company Granada. The bid committees were deeply interwoven with other key public and private elite organizations. Overlapping memberships included both individuals like Bob Scott and Gerald Cavendish Grosvenor, the Duke of Westminster, and organizations like Manchester Airport, Amec (a construction conglomerate), Granada, Kellogg, and Ciba-Geigy (a pharmaceuticals firm).[48]

The new regime was made more inclusive partly because of a deliberate strategy of inclusion and incorporation by local politicians and partly by the coincidence of its elite elements with independently generated cultural, social, economic, and political shifts at the grassroots. Youth, gays, cultural producers, and ethnic minorities all found reasons to sign on; there was little to nothing in the way of a jobs program for the urban poor, however. Young professionals moved downtown. Musicians, graphic and fashion designers, and textile makers reopened abandoned factory sites in the "Northern Quarter," and student enrollments at the universities doubled. "Every one of the city's major civic institutions signed up to the Games bid. In 1991, a local poll revealed that three-quarters of local residents were in favour"; the electronic dance band 808 State even contributed a single, "Olympic State," to support the first bid. Local government's strategy of cultural promotion definitively favored popular or mass over high culture; some councillors were even photographed inside the Hacienda dance club late at night.[49]

On the physical side, an immense redevelopment campaign pumped more than £2 billion worth of new investment in land and buildings into the downtown area between 1987 and 2002. The redevelopment was originally fertilized by bottom-up investments in nightclubs, record shops, recording studios, and other establishments related to the nightlife and cultural industries: "Clubs took over old buildings in rundown areas . . . and thus achieved a trailblazing position at the forefront of city centre regeneration." With the founding of the development corporations, Stringer's rise to power and the Olympics bids, however, planning became much more ambitious (Figure 7.4 shows Manchester's new performing arts hall, for example). The city used its sports bids to galvanize several hundred million pounds worth of central government and European Union investment in transport infrastructure, athletes' housing (later turned into university dormitories), and sports centers, including a £90 million stadium that afterward became home to the Manchester City Football Club. Additionally, approximately £500 million in public investment was part of a rescue package for two downtown shopping-district blocks destroyed in 1996 by an IRA bomb, the most powerful explosion in England since World War II.[50]

The emphasis on sports, music, nightlife, and consumption was perhaps the central feature in a thoroughgoing reconstruction of Manchester's identity that included multiple elements: a redefinition of the city's industrial past, the explicit invocation of globalization as a theme, a multicultural celebration of the city's diversity, and an emphasis on cosmopolitan urbanity that allowed the city simultaneously to claim regional leadership and a renewed status as a "European regional capital." The 1995 Manchester Plan, for example, explicitly invoked global urbanization as a justification: "The City Council wishes to see Manchester plugged in to the network of world cities."[51] Moreover, city government quite openly recognized its turn

Figure 7.4: Downtown Manchester's Bridgewater Hall.

toward sports and culture activities as a tool for raising the city's international prestige: "Cities and their regions operate in increasingly global markets. Competition is fierce, and the key to success for many cities has been to differentiate themselves by demonstrating a distinctive culture and image. . . . Manchester has attracted a range and quality of cultural and sporting facilities and events which are having a measurable beneficial impact on the City's image and status."[52]

Simultaneously, Manchester's cultural planning effectively redefined the city's historic identity away from its industrial past. The rhetoric of development was suffused with images and references to the city's past, but this rhetoric was given a new spin, describing Manchester as "a cosmopolitan City with a great tradition of welcoming visitors of all nations." Local government consciously adopted a multicultural strategy that praised and incorporated the city's diverse populations, particularly if they had money to spend on downtown property development. For example, the city council supported the growth of the Gay Village along Canal Street in the early 1990s, centrally located on valuable land in the middle of downtown; it also partnered with Chinatown in 1987 to build a Chinese imperial arch, and Manchester's tourist pamphlets routinely trumpeted the city's Chinatown as "the largest outside London." These policies of support were simultaneously an attempt to incorporate minorities, migrants, and new interest groups politically and a global marketing tool for the new regime.[53]

Indeed, the emphasis on tolerance, diversity, and multiculturalism was a critical feature of Manchester's attempts to renew its position in the global urban hierarchy. The Olympics bids and the Stringer regime defined an identity for Manchester by juxtaposing the city simultaneously with two sets of reference cities: a set of cosmopolitan European cities toward which Manchester aspired, and another set of northern English cities that Manchester dominated. On one hand, Manchester thought of itself as "capital of the North." In contrast to Liverpool for example, Manchester articulated the entire region and helped bind it together. On the other hand, "Europeanness" and "cosmopolitanism" were the key signifiers that distanced Manchester from places like Sheffield, Blackburn, Preston, and Bradford. In Ian Taylor, Karen Evans, and Penny Fraser's interviews with residents of Manchester's Gay Village, the authors identified the city's embrace of multiculturalism and a range of personal identities or lifestyle communities as a critical aspect of its cosmopolitanism: "The discourses we heard in the Village involved a very clear emotional investment in the idea that Manchester, having become the location of the Gay Village, was essentially a 'progressive' place, and specifically, a kind of vanguard European city unlike, therefore, other irretrievably 'English' cities in the North. This kind of definition of Manchester is very much shared by the local Council and Development Corporation."[54]

The city's ultimate goal was to be recognized as a "European regional capital," like Barcelona, Florence, and Lisbon. Other potential competitors or models, identified through a variety of studies, included Copenhagen, Geneva, Hamburg, Lyon, Rotterdam, Stuttgart, Turin, and Zurich—a veritable inventory of Europe's second-tier cities. Barcelona in particular was the obvious inspiration for the city's 1996 and 2000 Olympics bids. The name was different, but the substance was nearly identical with Philadelphia's repositioning of itself: Manchester wanted to be thought of as a city that was wealthy and cosmopolitan but not necessarily a global city.[55]

Conclusion: The Construction of Hegemony

At various times, in multiple ways, political entrepreneurs in Manchester and Philadelphia turned to cultural planning that explicitly invoked global concerns as well as local ones. These cultural extravaganzas or projects simultaneously reconstructed the physical, political, and symbolic aspects of the city. Politically, each of the regimes discussed in this chapter was more inclusive than the one immediately preceding it. In each case the preexisting political conflict was deep and the sense of cooperation or agreement the projects built was real. Precisely because the issue was how to unite people and groups who disagreed about politics and the distribution of power, cultural projects became important. Each regime explicitly sought to include contending elite factions in its chief associations, and each sought and won the sponsorship of higher levels of government for its projects, which in turn helped stimulate local participation and investment. Because the projects the new regime promoted were cultural—and typically involved a great deal of bricks-and-mortar construction—its promoters had tools with which to win the assent of people for whom the benefits of the regime were unclear. To some extent, these claims of inclusiveness were tenuous—in the nineteenth century because many residents could not vote and in recent decades because the projects offered little to the poor. Yet the appeal of these projects was often substantial and their support more widespread than one might at first think, not least because many residents had wearied of the preexisting political conflict and disarray in each case. Regime builders could make at least prima facie claims (regardless of whether they were true in a deeper sense) that these cultural projects were universal in their appeal to the region's contending factions, and that they lay outside the brutal sphere of partisan politics. Cultural projects were thus viewed instrumentally by the political entrepreneurs and coalition leaders who pursued them.

Symbolically, the declaration of an urban identity as a second city not only defined a common ground that brought people and constituencies together but also gave clearer shape to the term "globalization" and helped people in the city and region orient themselves to the forces that were affecting their lives. A consciously elaborated second city identity generally contained three elements: an explicit declaration of "secondness," the conscious use of comparisons to other cities and the attempt to delineate an urban "peer group," and the commitment to specializing in certain kinds of middle-class cultural endeavors. First, although the declarations did not necessarily involve explicit use of the term "second city," these places claimed to be, in one way or another, provincial capitals—places that were simultaneously cosmopolitan yet smaller, slower, or more relaxed than global cities. In Manchester in the 1990s, for example, the city's self-proclaimed goal was to be a "European regional capital." The status of provincial capital also included a claim of dominance over a large hinterland, as in Manchester's claim to be "capital of the North" of England.

Second, this identity was constructed or defined through comparisons with other cities. Through comparison, the city attempted to find a "peer group" of similar cities or a "league" in which to play. In the nineteenth century, both Philadelphia and Manchester tried to differentiate themselves from their co-national global cities, New York and London. Mancunians did this by asserting their superiority and modernity over the pretentiousness and stuffiness of the capital, whereas Philadelphians chose to affiliate with Paris in order to emphasize civility and culture over brashness. More recently, the two cities have staked out similar peer groups of internationally prominent, thriving regional capitals, like Barcelona, Kyoto, Florence,

Lyon, Turin, and Vancouver. The search for an international peer group usually included a claim to superiority over similar national cities as well. Manchester in particular has durably seen itself as superior to other English cities like Liverpool or Leeds; Philadelphia's vision of itself in comparison to national rivals like Baltimore, Cleveland, and Pittsburgh has been more fraught.

The final shared characteristic of these second city urban identities was a noticeable "middlebrow" character to their plans and discourses. This is not to say that high culture was absent; indeed, it was often trumpeted loudly by political entrepreneurs and leaders, as in the case of the Avenue of the Arts. But the degree to which high culture took a backseat is surprising. This middlebrow character was most obvious in contemporary Manchester's emphasis on pop music, sports, and nightlife, but it was also visible in both cities in the nineteenth century; the Centennial and the Art Treasures exhibitions used "art" as a tool to raise each city's own status by claiming that higher aesthetic purposes and effects could be realized in industrial design and manufacturing. This middlebrow inflection was connected to the cities' class composition, their histories of cultural production, and a felt sense of their own global role as cosmopolitan but distinct from true global cities.

These similarities, however, should not obscure the ways in which the two cities' identities were different from one another. The emotional valences of their identities reflected the different legacies of their pathways into second city status nearly two centuries before, demarcated by Manchester's legacy of *rise* into second city position and Philadelphia's legacy of *decline*. It is striking, given the great historical distance from their entries into second city status, to see the continuing relevance of these political and symbolic legacies.

In turning to cultural projects as tools for revitalizing a second city identity, participants in these cultural planning efforts sought to reframe the city. Both Rendell and Stringer, for example, wanted to reinforce the power and importance of the city center on a regional scale, hopefully counteracting its decline. They also attempted to shift the two cities' identities beyond national frames of reference toward more cosmopolitan, less parochial conceptions. In so doing, in claiming a globally relevant identity for themselves, Philadelphia and Manchester helped to construct a global cultural system that fostered new connections across people and places and increased their own and others' global awareness. The ultimate impact of these attempts is the topic of Chapter 8.

8

A World of Cities?

Philadelphia and Manchester have been able, with great effort, to maintain their positions as second cities for more than 150 years, despite numerous serious challenges. They have been fully integrated participants in global society, not just as recipients of global social forces but as progenitors and sustainers of globalization in their own right. Their ongoing occupation of this position illuminates, in turn, several critical features of globalization as a process. In this final chapter I consider the broader implications of Manchester's and Philadelphia's particular histories: the potential of the second city as a theoretical concept, the significance of city agency, and the ultimate impact that urban action, on a global scale, may have on the long-term course of globalization as a whole.

Manchester and Philadelphia as Second Cities

The process of globalization is organized and perpetuated, in large part, through a global network of cities. The urban network *is* the infrastructure of globalization; it provides the nodes that not only concentrate people, capital, and ideas, but that also facilitate the flow of these items around the world. Chapters 3, 4, and 5 detail Philadelphia's and Manchester's positions within this architecture. Contrary to much of the scholarship and popular literature on globalization, they have not been marginalized by globalization's progress. Instead, during the course of nearly two centuries, they have persisted as globally important centers, fully integrated into global flows.

Economically, Philadelphia and Manchester were centers of production for the leading industries of each era, particularly but not solely in manufacturing. Chapter 3 emphasizes four aspects of their regional economies that demonstrated their distinctiveness relative to global cities: their importance in industrial production for world markets, their role as headquarter locations, the nature of their developing "professional service" sectors, and their lack of international financial sectors. Manchester and Philadelphia were integrated into international networks of trade and production as both originators and recipients of foreign direct investment; they housed the headquarters of globally important firms and they exported substantial portions of their total products. As the chapter's database of corporate hierarchies shows, they have not become economically marginalized in the most recent phase of globalization, despite not being financial centers. While they have shed a majority of their manufacturing jobs, they have developed new, globally significant concentrations in a handful of service industries, especially in education and health care. They continue to be the economic powerhouses of their regions, performing central-place functions for wide hinterlands, and their regional economic hegemony has helped give substance to their claims of being globally important.

Chapter 4 demonstrates that migration to Manchester and Philadelphia followed a common pattern that clearly differentiated them from global cities. Where global cities were magnets for international migration in vast numbers from many source countries, Philadelphia and Manchester developed global niche roles, receiving international migrants in large numbers from only a few source countries. In addition, internal migration, particularly by ethnically distinct, socially subordinate groups, such as the Irish in Manchester and African Americans in Philadelphia, played an important role. This configuration of migrant groups made these two cities socially diverse and cosmopolitan, although not as polyglot as global cities. It also gave a distinctive character to inequality and politics within the two cities. Politics tended to revolve around a conflict between majority and minority-group natives, with immigrants relatively sidelined, while patterns of social inequality stressed race and ethnicity (and, in the nineteenth century, religion) at least as much as class. The result was a highly exclusive local political culture and a very slow process of inclusion for all minority groups.

Chapter 5 analyzes the roles of Manchester and Philadelphia as producers and innovators of global culture. Cultural production in the two cities emphasized middle-class endeavors like political ideologies, professions, and scientific disciplines. Laissez-faire liberalism was so closely identified with Manchester that it was even called the Manchester School, and Philadelphia's contrasting commitment to economic protectionism served as the political bedrock of the developing Republican Party. They also were centers for the development of new professions and claims to expert knowledge: a wide range of medical schools, organizations, and societies; the Wharton School's management training and Frederick Taylor's detailed division of labor program for industrial efficiency; and advances in chemistry, physics, and engineering. Each of these innovations sprouted from a tightly knit social network of cultural producers and supporting institutions that was highly localized and that also possessed a common class or ethnic identity. Such efforts were often justified explicitly by references to their social utility in defeating foreign competition or in raising the city's profile, and the position of these cities relative to others in global networks interacted with internal class and ethnic dynamics to influence the types of cultural products the cities produced.

This cultural environment in Philadelphia and Manchester tended to develop separately from, or even in opposition to, patterns of cultural development and production in global cities. Philadelphia and Manchester tended not to focus on "high culture," and the approach elite patrons took toward high culture was typically instrumental: high culture, as in Manchester's Art Treasures Exhibition, was a tool for boosting the city's prestige. This instrumental attitude may have been due in part to the shortage of high-culture producers in both cities, because of the seductiveness of global city cultural institutions and networks. Similarly, pop innovators often had to rely on connections or moves to global cities in order to ensure popularity, distribution, and diffusion. Impermanence was thus a permanent feature of the second city cultural scene, at least from a global rather than local perspective, and pop-culture innovations in second cities were often temporary or generational; an essentially local "scene" was elevated to world visibility.[1]

Manchester's and Philadelphia's similar positions in global flows of goods, capital, migrants, and ideas constitute an enduring and distinctive pattern of global integration rather than marginalization. They were most certainly not global cities, yet they occupied different, distinctive positions in global affairs that did not consign them to marginality. Their experience contradicts some claims of the WCH (world city hypothesis) about the nature of inequality between cities, but it also vindicates and extends the general WCH approach of examining international connections across cities. Moreover, during the long haul, these two cities converged: their identities became more clearly defined, their economic specializations more crystallized, their use of transportation infrastructure more self-aware, their migration patterns more congruent. Their various crises and responses served as functional equivalents for one another, provoking a growing similarity in their economic, political, and cultural characteristics. In part because of the gradual development of a second city identity, Philadelphia and Manchester became more similar over time. This remarkable convergence, however, begs two further questions. First, how did this convergence come about—what produced it? Second, is the "second city" a structural position in the world urban system that is available to other cities besides Philadelphia and Manchester?

Municipal Foreign Policy and the Fates of Cities

Membership in the urban hierarchy is not static; the global urban system is dynamic, and cities can and do rise and fall. Philadelphia and Manchester, for example, both entered second city position in the early nineteenth century by developing as two of the world's earliest industrial manufacturing centers. Manchester and Philadelphia have engaged in functionally equivalent patterns of action to maintain their positions, both in material or political-economic terms (such as the use of infrastructure projects to capture global flows) and in cultural or symbolic terms (the development of a second city identity that defines the city's "place" in the world-system). I call these actions "municipal foreign policy" (MFP) because they are efforts designed to pursue the city's interests at a global rather than a local or national scale. Urban planning for global integration can and does alter the "pitch" of the world-system so that the spatial patterning of global flows (of people, capital, goods, and ideas) shifts.

Chapters 6 and 7 analyze the major strategies of MFP that the cities used to bolster their own positions. Chapter 6 examines how Manchester and Philadelphia responded to global competitive and restructuring crises with transportation projects that integrated them more deeply into the world economy and provided for decades of continued prosperity. The local state took a leading role in planning, funding, and managing immense transportation infrastructure projects that enhanced the city's position as a transit or exchange node, reinforced its dominance over its regional hinterland, stimulated economic diversification, and spread the city's economy into new leading sectors. These projects also had the effect of knitting the world more closely together by facilitating trade and transportation. The transport infrastructure project turns out to be the most important sphere of local decision making in terms of ability to connect with the rest of the world during the long haul.

In Chapter 7, political entrepreneurs devised massive cultural projects to simultaneously redevelop parts of the city, cement new political coalitions, and define a second city identity. These identities stressed the following characteristics: reinvigoration of a second city history; claims to superiority over other national cities; claims to parity with an international peer group of cities; and explicit naming of the city as "second." Such cultural projects were particularly useful in situations where local political capacity was in doubt because of deep conflict or fragmentation; they had the potential to build goodwill where it was lacking and to convince potential coalition partners to commit. By defining a narrative and a symbolic position for the city, these projects gave the city's activities and aspirations meaning for both residents and outsiders, showing that city government's actions were comprehensible and that the city occupied a legible place in the global system overall. Culture and politics thus mattered just as much as economics, if not more so, in overcoming crises and in maintaining global position.

Local identities are therefore only partly local. "Manchester," for example, came to be recognized in the nineteenth century—both by Mancunians themselves and by outsiders—as a collective actor identified with the city in general and with an industrial way of life, not just with a class interest. Globalization, by connecting us to other peoples and other cultures, increases our awareness of the world around us and pushes us to define ourselves more clearly relative to "others." In other words, "the expectation of identity declaration is built into the general process of globalization," and this emphasis on the crafting of identity is an inescapable part of globalization.[2] By bringing us into greater contact with people, discourses, symbols, and practices from all over the world, globalization relativizes our own standpoint. We are increasingly unable to assume our own identity or take it for granted—it must be made conscious. By defining the city's place in the world as a whole, a second city urban identity gives people a place in global processes, and so may provide a basis for agency—for realizing one's own power to act on a global scale.

What does it mean to speak of "the city" as an actor in this way or to say that cities carry out their own municipal foreign policy? Although I have at times referred to the city itself as an agent, the cities themselves are not living, breathing entities with their own free will. In the most straightforward terms, "city" means the city government: government officials represent and are chosen by the city's residents, speak for the city as a whole, and make local policy. The crucial point is that cities are states, just like other governments, although local states are clearly subordinate to their national governments and lack the full autonomy of nation-states. It is also true, however, that city governments, whether mayors or city councils or commissions, rarely act alone; they typically make policy in concert or coalition with other individuals and groups in the city, and so that coalition of people can also be a collective urban actor that makes decisions and creates policy.

The composition of urban political coalitions can vary but usually includes politicians, the urban elite, small business people, large property owners or developers, and some subset of the urban population at large—grouped by class, ethnicity, political party, or neighborhood. Growth machine theory and regime theory are the two main competing explanations of this process of coalition formation. Although I have nodded to both theories in the previous chapters, the conclusions of the comparative analysis lean toward regime theory. Growth machine theory, invented to explain the U.S. political system in particular, argues that urban politics is driven by conflicts over land use and that the major players are property owners and developers; coalitions are effectively capitalist, pro-growth alliances between the corporate elite and political leadership. Regime theory, on the other hand, specifies neither that land use conflicts must be the motor of politics nor that real estate interests must be in the driver's seat, but allows both the relevant issues and the composition of the coalition to vary more freely. Regime theory is thus broader and more flexible, particularly in comparative urban studies, because in many cities around the world (including Manchester in the 1990s) private capital has clearly *not* been the driving force in the political coalition.[3]

But one cannot conclude that these efforts were consensual or unanimous—neither were they beneficial for all city residents. There was always disagreement, and some people were always either left out or actively harmed by the decisions of the local state and the governing coalition to pursue deeper global integration. Once again, the WCH's emphasis on inequalities within cities is supported, but with a twist: where much of the WCH has emphasized that globalization exacerbates the economic inequalities in global cities, in Philadelphia and Manchester inequality was organized along axes of ethnicity, race, and politics at least as much as along lines of class. Workers and the Irish were excluded from Manchester's nineteenth-century regime, in large part through prejudice and disfranchisement, and African Americans were excluded from participation in the Centennial Exhibition. One must also note the political exclusion of women. The twentieth-century coalitions, however, were significantly more inclusive. Although many of the poor were excluded, labor and minorities both had seats at the table via parties and elected officials; overall, a much greater number of people were able to participate. In analyzing the process of exclusion that often coincides with the drive for global integration, moreover, we must remember that the regimes discussed in Chapter 7 *resolved* significant problems of conflict and exclusion—many people were already being harmed by the dysfunctional politics of the 1970s in both cities, for example.

The exercise of agency by the local state also has implications for the other half of the WCH's argument about globalization and inequality—inequalities between cities. The great effort that went into producing Philadelphia's and Manchester's continuity shows that local policy makers were keenly aware of the possibilities for movement up and down the urban hierarchy. City governments and their leaders are indeed under pressure to make choices, and they can make wrong ones, which have costs in terms of international position, reputation, and status. How they respond to crises of restructuring can determine a city's well-being for decades, and taking advantage of opportunities for economic diversification lies at the root of a city's continuing economic significance across historical eras. Occasionally, cities that make the right choices at the right time can become global cities—for example, early-nineteenth-century New York or post–World War II Toronto—but this is a very rare event.[4] Very few places have the option of becoming an international financial center in the way that New York, London, Hong Kong, or Paris is, and more generally, as the story of the United Nations in Chapter 1 suggests, global cities often possess the wherewithal to resist attempts by challengers to take global city roles away from them.

Instead, Philadelphia and Manchester engaged in strategies to try to remain second cities when that position or status was under threat; engaging in these efforts was not at all easy, and much could have gone wrong. Philadelphians, for example, very nearly made a serious mistake in the 1820s and 1830s with the inefficient, hopelessly multimodal Main Line, which helped the city drop from global to second. We can identify other places that have suffered similar losses in recent decades. Much has been written about these troubled places, like Cleveland, Marseille, Liverpool, and Saint Louis. The single clearest example of a declining city is Detroit, a one-industry town that failed to diversify its economy even as its core employers lost prestige and profits to foreign competitors.[5] Detroit rose to prominence in the early twentieth century as the home of the infant auto industry; it became an industrial powerhouse and a paradigmatic second city. Its major automakers were globally important, technologically sophisticated, and among the biggest firms in the world. The city's industrial might drew in eastern European immigrants (and later Arabs) and tens of thousands of black workers from the American South. Culturally, Detroit was the seeding ground for Fordist industrial organization, militant black radicalism and nationalism, and the distinctive pop sound of Motown, which also gave the city a globally recognizable identity. But Detroit's prolonged overemphasis on a single major industry was compounded by a political weakness that stemmed both from the diffidence of its major employers and from black-white conflict and fragmentation. The combination of rapid suburbanization with the hemorrhage of manufacturing jobs that began in the 1970s left Detroit a shadow of its former self.

Sheffield, England, suffered a similar fate. The Steel City built a global reputation in the nineteenth century based on an extraordinary concentration in high-skill, craft-based production of specialty steels by an immense number of small firms.[6] The city was an innovator in both production processes and in materials, including the invention of stainless steel. Its craft and small-firm orientation, however, despite the development of chemical testing labs, never resulted in the immigration of skilled workers, the rise of prominent educational facilities, or much investment in new industries. Sheffield largely failed to pursue diversification, and it never overcame its relative geographic isolation. The absence of transportation infrastructure projects harmed its ability to capture global flows, and its identity remained largely insular and parochial. Buffeted by deindustrialization and the severe rationalization of the steel industry, the city's redevelopment efforts since the 1980s have had only limited success.

Second Cities in the Global Urban System

To say that cities can rise or fall (or maintain position), however, implies that one has some broader conception of the context—the global system of cities—within which these terms might make sense. The very use of the term "second city" to describe Manchester and Philadelphia implies that there is some ranked set of positions. According to the WCH, a relatively small number of global cities sit at the top of the world urban system, perhaps three dozen. This system, however, is more inclusive than many scholars have generally believed; globalization proceeds by incorporating cities into distinct positions or roles, rather than by marginalizing them altogether. We should, therefore, be able to extend the reach of the WCH significantly by asking how other cities might be incorporated into globalization processes in different ways.

As a hypothesis for further investigation, it is worth examining whether the pattern of global integration characteristic of Philadelphia and Manchester might be available to other cities as well. This larger potential group of second cities would consist of what people often call the provincial capitals—the large, cosmopolitan regional cities. Although certainly less prominent than global cities, they would be many in number and would possess significant power and influence in their own right—certainly enough to act on a global scale. This pattern would involve four crucial characteristics, derived from the analysis in the prior chapters. First, second cities should be more focused on global production than on finance, with gradual growth in producer services, including some giant firms. Their major industries would be the leading industries of a given era, technologically advanced and characterized by high growth; their continuing vitality would depend upon their ability to shift into new leading industries as such industries develop. Second, these cities should have migration patterns that would include substantial internal migration by ethnic minorities combined with selective international migration from a limited number of source countries. Third, they should develop cultural specializations in ideological, pragmatic, and professional endeavors that would give the cities distinctly middle-class casts. Finally, over time they should develop a second city identity, visible in cultural projects, local discourse, and official comparisons of the city with other places.

If the current universe of global cities numbers a few dozen, the universe of such potential second cities is undoubtedly larger but still limited. While it is impossible to present a definitive list, existing research into "world city formation" offers a tentative set of candidates. In an article published elsewhere, based on economic and migration variables, I identified six likely candidates for second city status in the United States, in addition to Philadelphia: Atlanta, Denver, Phoenix, San Diego, San Jose, and Seattle. More comprehensively, research done by the Globalization and World Cities project categorized sixty-seven cities as showing some evidence of "world city formation." Project researchers classified both Manchester and Philadelphia in this group, and many of these cities might be better understood as second cities. Combining these various sources, a suggestive list of likely second cities includes, among developed countries other than the United States, Barcelona, Birmingham, Düsseldorf, Glasgow, Hamburg, Leeds, Lisbon, Lyon, Melbourne, Montreal, Osaka, Rotterdam, Stuttgart, Tel Aviv, Turin, and Vancouver. Barcelona is probably the most prominent second city in the late twentieth century, given its use of the 1992 Olympics to redefine itself and enhance its global position.[7] Since that time, Barcelona's revitalization planning has been studied and emulated by dozens of cities across the globe, Manchester not least among them.

It is worth noting, however, that successful integration into world society is not confined only to the "First World" or the "core." The United States was not a core country when Philadelphia became a second city in the 1830s, and cities in developing countries have been becoming second cities for as long as the urban hierarchy has existed. Monterrey, Mexico, for example, has long had a reputation as a provincial capital and as Mexico's premier industrial city, the "Pittsburgh of Mexico."[8] It exhibits nearly all the identifying traits of the second city. The city's growth began in the late nineteenth century after the arrival of international railway connections to the United States, and later to the Gulf of Mexico ports. In the succeeding decades, Monterrey became Mexico's first heavy industrial center, focused on steel, brewing, glass, and ceramics. It diversified over time and experienced another growth spurt after the building of the Pan-American Highway in the mid-twentieth century. The city has grown in large part through domestic migration from the surrounding region (although there has been some international migration of Americans and Germans, it departs from the usual second city pattern in that there has been little internal ethnic minority migration). The city is also culturally distinctive within Mexico, widely known for the leadership of its *regiomontano* elite and for a cross-class identity of conservatism and industriousness. The city's economic interests combined with this local conservative identity to produce a deeply antistate political culture that from a very early date challenged the Mexico City establishment and the hegemony of the Institutional Revolutionary Party. The city's elite even founded the conservative National Action Party in the 1930s. Monterrey is perhaps the premier embodiment in Latin America of a politically and culturally conservative, bourgeois provincial city.

The most spectacular contemporary example of a city rising into second position, however, is certainly Bangalore, India. Bangalore is the poster child for the influence of information technology and telecommunications on twenty-first-century development, and the "shock city" of the information age.[9] Situated near the border of several Indian states, it has long been ethnically and linguistically diverse; only a third of the population speaks Kannada, the main language of Karnataka State. In recent decades the city has grown spectacularly, from 991,000 in 1951 to 4,086,000 in 1991. Even here, however, second city status has deep roots. Bangalore became an administrative center under British control in the early 1800s; it developed a vast textile sector that is still the city's largest industry. Investment in engineering, science, and technology began, even before India's independence, with electronics firms, Hindustan Aircraft, and the Indian Institute of Science, which was founded in 1911. The region now has scores of colleges and universities, with more than 175,000 students, and a famous software export sector, including the headquarters of global firms like Infosys, despite the persistence of an extremely large informal sector. The development of transportation infrastructure has lagged behind, however, although there is a new international airport. The construction of an urban identity and global profile for the city is a work in progress as well, although the city is already well known as the home ground for India's new neoliberal middle class.

These are just a few examples of the possible applicability of the second city concept; other candidate cities from developing countries include Durban, Cape Town, Guadalajara, Guangzhou, Izmir, Kiev, Rio de Janeiro, and Medellin. Obviously, we cannot generalize on the basis of only two cases, or even four. But there is a great need for research that examines the broader urban network on a global scale, and the second city hypothesis suggests a range of important empirical phenomena that can guide the investigation.

Conclusion: Cities and the Long-Term Course of Globalization

There is a voluble debate on what globalization means for cities and regions. On one side, a variety of critics argue that globalization is profoundly disempowering; they view capitalist globalization as inherently exploitative and socially destructive, and they argue that local responses are inherently too weak to combat successfully the destabilization it produces. Structuralist urban scholars tend to view cities as powerless in the face of globalization, as tossed about on seas of global change and hanging on for dear life. From this view, city residents and their governments cope as best they can, but they are not in a position to exercise much control over their own fates. On the other side, some people claim that globaliza-tion is empowering, that it gives cities and regions an immense opportunity to forge their own destinies and pursue their own paths to growth and prosperity. It is possible, for example, to see globalization in this way in Chapters 6 and 7, as a boosterist account of how local states use MFP to secure their own prosperity.[10]

The debate between the structuralists and the boosterists presents an overly simplistic, dichotomous interpretation of what we might call "urban agency," however. On both sides, urban action by the local state is merely local, the endpoint or last stop in a one-way causal chain of adaptation that then goes no further. There is no return channel for local choices to rebound back on the trajectory of globalization as a whole. But the causal chain is really a circle, and local states are yet another globalizing force rather than simply on the receiving end. Their responses to globalization themselves become causes and help create and sustain globalization as a process. Urban agency, therefore, also constitutes the very process of glob-alization—it is the stuff of which globalization is made. This view of cities as powerful global actors contrasts not only with the structuralists but also with the boosterists.

Local state action in pursuit of global integration has important impli-cations for the course of globalization as a whole. Where Chapters 6 and 7 explore how city agency works within the existing limits of the system of globalization as a structure, this final chapter examines the potential for *structural change in the overall global system* as a result of urban agency. It closes the analytical circle by returning from agency back to the structure of the global urban hierarchy and the course of globalization in general. The issue, therefore, is precisely whether the limits of the structure really are set or whether the attempts of local states to exercise or increase their autonomy might have structure-changing impacts. Can the actions of cities rebound structurally on the nature and course of globalization as a whole?

Three kinds of structure-changing effects might be envisioned. First, local states help make globalization happen by facilitating international connectedness, pursuing cultural innovation, and promoting cosmopolitan visions. Cities' global transport plans, for example, knit the world together by providing globalization's infrastructure. The physical networks of trade and communication make global flows speedier and more efficient, increas-ing mobility and turnover. Naturally, what happens in one city is likely to have consequences for other cities. Sometimes there are zero sum, competi-tive decisions—for example, the story of how the United Nations ended up in New York rather than Philadelphia, or the way in which Manchester's rise as a center for cotton textiles in the eighteenth century meant Dhaka's decline. But it is mistaken to think of municipal foreign policies as simply zero sum. Instead, they are often complementary; global transportation infrastructure, for example, makes all kinds of transactions and flows easier, and so can contribute to the prosperity of multiple cities. It can even facilitate cooperative relationships with other cities that benefit both partners. This is also true of the cultural projects discussed in Chapter 7. These projects promote a cosmopolitan vision of cities as centers of world civilization and as part of a network of enlightened places committed to leisure, cultivation, and human fulfillment; this vision touches and benefits all cities. (Of course, cities do not typically live up to this ideal, but it is important to recognize that the ideal exists.)[11]

Second, therefore, cities are also the homes for an emerging global civil society. The main carriers or propagators of this global civil society are international nongovernmental organizations (INGOs), like Amnesty International, and modernizing, rationalizing professions, like planning, law, and the sciences. According to proponents of the "world polity" school, such as John Boli and John Meyer, a global or world culture, dedicated to values of rationality and progress, has gradually emerged during the past century and a half.[12] This is a dream of cultural rather than economic liberalism that harks back to the Enlightenment and echoes some of Richard Cobden's anti-imperialist beliefs. It is at heart a deeply cosmopolitan vision, focused on world (rather than national) citizenship, a cosmopolitan ethic, and the moral influence of public opinion. In its most utopian forms, it envisions a world without nation-states, but in most versions, nation-states simply have less power and in fact derive much of their legitimacy from following, rather than challenging, the principles and norms of the world culture, such as respect for human rights.

It is too rarely acknowledged, however, that cities are the most important sites for the production and dissemination of this global culture. Cities are the places where strangers meet, cultures mix, tolerance is a virtue, and cosmopolitanism thrives. Manchester, for instance, hosted the Pan-African Congress of 1945 (attendees included W.E.B. DuBois, Kwame Nkrumah, and Jomo Kenyatta), which ushered in the international movement for decolonization and independence. And Philadelphia is headquarters to one of the most prominent peace-related INGOs, the American Friends Service Committee (AFSC). Founded during World War I to pursue peaceful alternatives to America's military involvement, the AFSC has sponsored peace, development, and community programs in dozens of countries.[13] Cities' most important role, however, has been to foster the professional and technical cultures identified in Chapter 5, which are critical for the international spread of a rationalizing, modernizing, progressive world culture. Philadelphia's and Manchester's urban universities in particular have played a crucial role in innovating and fostering these cultural achievements. It is professionals above all who are carriers of global culture, both because they travel widely and because their occupational cultures stress the growth of rationality and modernity worldwide, beyond borders.

As Chapters 5 and 7 both demonstrate, second cities concentrate the personal networks, the media, and the organizational infrastructure of cultural innovation and propagation. Indeed, cities do not simply "participate" in the construction of a global civil society. They originated the voluntary organizations and scientific disciplines that constituted it in the mid-Victorian decades. The organizational headquarters, the annual meetings and conferences, the educational institutions that train professionals and propagate the tenets of a rationalizing world culture—all are housed in major cities.[14] This global civil society and second cities like Manchester and Philadelphia grew up together.

Finally, where the vision of a global civil society is utopian and idealistic, one can also envision a more straightforwardly political set of structural effects for local state agency. Urban agency is yet one more challenge to the authority of the nation-state brought about by globalization. Political pressures on the nation-state are building from below as well as from above, and many scholars have predicted its decline as cross-border economic transactions increasingly exceed its regulatory, taxation, and oversight capacities. These pressures are clearly evident in Europe, where the increasing institutionalization of the European Union as a supranational government has come in tandem with increasing power for subnational regions through E.U. structural funding, devolution (especially in the United Kingdom), and arrangements for greater autonomy for provinces like Catalonia. Cities and regions have a new freedom to determine their own economic and even their social policies. Officials in many European cities are seeking to take advantage of this opportunity by "delinking" themselves from their states— some in the hopes of achieving better economic performance and some in the desire for more political and cultural autonomy.[15]

Cities have historically had good reason to be dissatisfied with their subjection to national states. The era of strong national states has not always been good for them.[16] Cities lost power over taxation and budgets, over setting their own rules and laws, and even over movements across their own borders. In the middle of the twentieth century, extensive national intervention in economic and welfare matters did not do many cities much good, and may even have harmed them significantly. National policies emptied out the urban core, devastated the urban tax base, and promoted political conflict between cities and their suburbs. The explicit logic behind post–World War II planning, for example, was to decentralize the largest urban areas, and these planning initiatives harmed both Philadelphia and Manchester. By the early 1980s, these policies were overlain by a partisan conflict as well—city leaders and national leaders came from different political parties—but Philadelphia and Manchester were weakened by national policies long before the arrival of Reagan and Thatcher.

The point, however, is not about the welfare of individual cities or regions. Globalization raises the question of whether, as nation-states decline or lose power, new institutional space opens up for cities to reclaim some of their older prominence. Might we, at some point, transition to "a world of cities," in the words of Barcelona's former mayor, Pasqual Maragall?[17] Municipal foreign policy is where local states come closest to having their own independent interests vis-à-vis globalization, separate from and perhaps even contradictory to those of the national states of which they are members. One can find the beginnings of attempts by cities to define their own collective interests through multilateral and multinational organizations *of cities*. The most established of these efforts is the Eurocities organization, an association of over one hundred large cities in Europe. Founded in 1986, its charter looks forward to a future in which Europe's cities—not its nation-states—are the main locus of citizenship and policy making. Although associations of this type are often simply lobbying organizations dedicated to boosting local economic prospects, they could in time become something more. This is particularly the case with Eurocities, which is dedicated to winning greater political power and resources for cities and regions within the E.U. There is as yet little evidence of success; there is no group in North America equivalent to Eurocities for Philadelphia to join, and it is unclear whether much or even any of the political potential will be realized. But these organizations are the forums that allow city governments from many countries to become directly connected to one another.

The opportunity for city governments to elaborate their own collective interests, at least potentially in opposition to the nation-state, implies a more conflictual and directly political vision, in which cities are primarily seen as centers of power. A belief that city-regions are legitimate centers of power and authority in their own right, independent of their connection to a nation-state, thus leads to a form of competition very different from the one usually envisioned in the literature on globalization—one between levels of government rather than between units at the same level. As Max Weber noted, and as Manchester's partisans of free trade in the nineteenth century clearly recognized, the competition between city-states and nation-states as institutional forms is a very old one. The contest for supremacy between these two types of government in Europe lasted several centuries, but eventually the city-states succumbed to the territorial states; the Hanseatic League and the Italian city-states, like Venice, declined as territorial dynasties like the Bourbons and the Hapsburgs grew in power. Cities paid with their independence and autonomy for the privilege of being protected by the king's army; even the institution of citizenship passed out of their hands to the national level.[18] Only Singapore now remains as a city-state, despite a few rump European principalities like Monaco.

Contemporary patterns of globalization may signal the resurgence of this centuries-old power struggle between cities and states, and provide a new opportunity for cities to win back some of the political autonomy they have lost. Such a resurgence would constitute a momentous structural impact for MFP and a major shift in the course and significance of globalization. There is little direct evidence for this Weberian proposition—after all, nation-states remain the most important actors on the global stage, and they are unlikely to concede direct challenges to their authority by other territorial organizations. No nation-state has yet dissolved, no city-state has yet declared independence, and a wave of urban revolutions or secessions is certainly not in the cards. And of course, most cities, including second cities, simply do not have the leadership or the political capacity to agitate for such a world-historical shift. Only a handful of scholars have considered the competition between cities and nation-states seriously. One or two have suggested that we might be on the cusp of a "new medievalism"—a global-level institutional rearrangement in which state boundaries are much more porous and nation-states are just one among many kinds of actors and power centers.[19]

But the evidence for the first two global effects of urban action is much stronger. There is very clearly recognizable growth of a global civil society and movement toward the institutionalization of global civic actors. These actors are profoundly urban centered, despite promises of the irrelevance of space offered by computers, telecommunications, and other technological advances. Even more noticeable is the progressive knitting together of the world by the increase of transportation and communications infrastructure— and by our increasing awareness of the world as one place.

These global developments are all profoundly urbanized and urbanizing: globalization and urbanization are not opposed tendencies but in fact proceed in tandem. And second cities like Philadelphia and Manchester have been and continue to be crucial contributors to these processes. As they reach beyond their national borders to define and claim their own distinctive place in the world, their actions and ideas help knit the world together. In the process they are helping to make the world into that single place that some theorists of cultural globalization see taking shape. Globalization is therefore not simply an external or structural force out there in the world to which cities must mechanically and mercilessly adapt; in a crucial sense, globalization is *in* them, or *in us* as agents. Manchester, Philadelphia, and other second cities will shape the futures not only of their nation-states but of us all.

Notes

CHAPTER 1

1. Atwater 1976.
2. See Albrow 1997; Robertson 1992.
3. Giddens 1990. Neil Brenner uses the terms "deterritorialization" and "reterritorialization" to describe the same ideas (Brenner 1999, 2004).
4. Amin and Thrift 1994; Holston and Appadurai 1996; Sassen 1991.
5. Cohen 1981; Friedmann 1986; Friedmann and Wolff 1982; Knox 1995; D. R. Meyer 1991; Sassen 1991: 3, 1994; P. Taylor 2004. I borrow the term "world city hypothesis" from John Friedmann (1986), although there is a dispute in the literature over whether "world city" or "global city" is a more accurate name for the concept.
6. Some of the original proponents of the WCH focused on economic matters nearly to the exclusion of everything else; as John Friedmann wrote, "The economic variable . . . is likely to be decisive for all attempts at explanation" (1986: 317). This economism is not universal, however, as other scholars have paid significant attention to the cultural aspects of global city status (Abrahamson 2004; A. D. King 1990a).
7. The full list varies from author to author, but generally includes London, New York, Paris, and Tokyo at the apex, followed by (in no particular hierarchical order) Amsterdam, Chicago, Frankfurt, Hong Kong, Los Angeles, Madrid, Mexico City, Milan, Sao Paulo, Shanghai, Singapore, Sydney, Toronto, and Zurich. In some cases, analysts add Bangkok, Beijing, Buenos Aires, Johannesburg, Miami, Mumbai, Osaka, San Francisco, Seoul, Taipei, and Washington, D.C. See Abrahamson 2004; Alderson and Beckfield 2004; Friedmann 1995; Keeling 1995; Sassen 1994; Short et al. 1996; Smith and Timberlake 2002; P. Taylor 2004. On the GaWC, see P. Hall

2001; P. Taylor 2004; Taylor, Walker, and Beaverstock 2002. The GaWC Web site (http://www.lboro.ac.uk/gawc) contains a wealth of information, working papers, links, and other material about the project.

8. Arrighi 1999; Braudel 1984; Chase-Dunn 1989; A. D. King 1990a, 1990b; P. Taylor 1995; Wallerstein 1974.

9. Kresl 1992; Kresl and Gappert 1995; Markusen 1999; Markusen, Lee, and DiGiovanna 1999. For a different, more boosterish account of the diverse routes to economic success, see Rosabeth Moss Kanter's book *World Class* (1995).

10. Lever 1997; Lyons and Salmon 1995; Sassen 1996: 212.

11. For information on Chicago as a global city, see Abu-Lughod 1999; Cronon 1991; Koval et al. 2006; Madigan 2004; for Toronto and Sydney, see Sassen 1994.

12. Regarding all census data in this book, the United States conducts its census in "zero" years, such as 1850 and 1980, and Great Britain conducts its census in "one" years, such as 1851 and 1981. I treat the censuses of adjacent years—such as U.S. 1970 and U.K. 1971—as comparable.

13. Dickens 1854: 52, 65; Engels 1958; Kay 1832.

14. For a sampling of the current wave of critical interpretations, see Cochrane, Peck, and Tickell 1996; Dicken 1992; Mellor 1989, 1997; Mole 1996; Peck and Tickell 1995; Peck and Ward 2002; Quilley 1995, 1999, 2000; Tickell and Peck 1996; Tickell, Peck, and Dicken 1995.

15. Quilley 1995: 105.

16. Adams 1988, 1991; Adams et al. 1991; Baltzell 1958, 1979; Bartelt 1989; Gillette 1970; L. Steffens 1904; S. B. Warner 1968.

17. S. B. Warner 1968: 44–45.

18. Adams et al. 1991.

19. Adams 2003.

20. Amin and Thrift 1994: 2. See also Peck and Tickell 1995.

21. The position I adopt here shares similarities with the "structuration" approach of Anthony Giddens (1981, 1984, 1990).

CHAPTER 2

1. For details on the Panic of 1837 and the course of bank suspensions, see B. Hammond 1957: 457–480; McFaul 1972; McGrane 1965; Sharp 1970.

2. Fisher 1967: 134–135; McGrane 1965: 130–131; Redford 1964: 119.

3. The phrase is attributed to Asa Briggs (1963).

4. For early Manchester history, see Axon 1886; Chapman 1904; Kennedy 1970; Redford 1940; Wadsworth and Mann 1931.

5. Bridenbaugh 1938, 1955; N. Burt 1963: 71–72; Garvan 1963: 189–190; S. B. Warner 1968.

6. Tolles 1960: 3; S. B. Warner 1963. Quakerism has deep roots in both study sites; George Fox founded the sect in 1652 after a vision on Pendle Hill in Lancashire (Baltzell 1979).

7. Redford 1940.

8. Nash 1979; Tolles 1948: 142–143, 1960.

9. Braudel 1984; Wadsworth and Mann 1931: 17–22, 116.

10. O'Hearn 1994; Rose 2000; Wadsworth and Mann 1931: 103–105.

11. Chapman 1904; Farnie 1979; Rose 2000; Wadsworth and Mann 1931: 23–25.

12. Chapman 1904; Farnie 1979; Wadsworth and Mann 1931. The ban on textile imports was repealed in 1774.

13. Bridenbaugh 1938, 1955; Lemon 1967; Nash 1979: 178; S. B. Warner 1968.

14. S. Burt 1945; Wright 1986.

15. Briggs 1963; Chapman 1904: 149; Farnie 1979: 7; Spencer 1877.

16. Chapman 1904; Smelser 1959: 87–93; Wadsworth and Mann 1931: 178–179.

17. Barr 1991: 87; Chapman 1904: 58; Lloyd-Jones and Lewis 1988. Most firms were family proprietorships or partnerships and specialized in just one part of the textile production process: spinning, weaving, bleaching, or dyeing; together they constituted a densely networked web engaged in multiple transactions with other firms. Manchester thus became the original "Marshallian industrial district" (Amin and Thrift 1992).

18. Gunn 1992; Mills 1921: 75–76; Parsons 1904; G. Shaw 1989: 67–70.

19. Kaplan 2006; Wadsworth and Mann 1931.

20. Barr 1991; O'Hearn 1994; Smelser 1959: 53, 93–94; Wadsworth and Mann 1931: 161–163.

21. Alexander 1973: 13; Baltzell 1958: 81; S. Burt 1945: 110–112.

22. B. Hammond 1957: 42–49; Scharf and Westcott 1884.

23. Miller 1982.

24. Albion 1938: 17–47; Glaab and Brown 1983; Scharf and Westcott 1884: 2216.

25. Baltzell 1958: 90; B. Hammond 1957: 305.

26. There has been a dispute in the historiographic literature about the extent to which the bank's destruction was driven by rival capitalists and financiers in New York and Baltimore, who wanted to destroy Philadelphia's financial supremacy in the hope of winning it for themselves. The weight of evidence appears to make the battle more political than economic—the party and sectional interests at stake, in more detailed analyses, do not boil down to clear class or class-fraction positions—and to downplay as well the significance of any rivalry between cities for financial hegemony. The outcome, however, had clear implications for the economic standing of the country's major cities. For sources, see Gatell 1966; B. Hammond 1957; McFaul 1972; McGrane 1965; Meyers 1957; Schlesinger 1945; Sharp 1970; W. B. Smith 1953; Sumner 1896; Wilburn 1967; Zachary 1974. I have relied substantially on these sources in my account of the Bank's activities and history.

27. N. Burt 1963: 52; B. Hammond 1957: 329.

28. J. K. Brown 1995: 2; Freedley 1859; Scranton 1983; S. B. Warner 1968.

29. Ayerst 1971: 37–38; Chapman 1904; Howe 1984; Lemon 1967; Lindstrom 1978; G. Shaw 1989.

30. Bagwell and Lyth 2002: 11; Lindstrom 1978; Livingood 1947; Vigier 1970: 156–160. The cities took defensive measures as well; Pennsylvania even forbade by law the removal of obstructions in the lower Susquehanna River in order to prevent Baltimore from winning central Pennsylvania's agricultural export trade.

31. Burgess and Kennedy 1949: 7, 10; Glaab and Brown 1983; Goodrich 1960; Livingood 1947; Schotter 1927; G. R. Taylor 1951.

32. For sources on migration prior to 1840, see Chapman 1904; Frangopulo 1965; Kazal 1998: 25–38; Pooley and D'Cruze 1994; Redford 1964; B. Roberts 1978a, 1978b; Wadsworth and Mann 1931; S. B. Warner 1968; Wolf 1976; Wright 1986: 30–33.

33. Neal 1990: 13; Redford 1964.

34. Crawford 1962; Scholes 1871; Wadsworth and Mann 1931: 235–236; B. Williams 1976.

35. Hershberg 1981: 379–380; Morais 1894; Nash 1988; Scharf and Westcott 1884; Wright 1986: 31.

36. Baltzell 1979: 169; Tolles 1948: 206, 1960: 69. Franklin's letter of 1738 quoted in Wright 1986: 48.

37. Franklin quoted in Wright 1986: 70–71. For more information on Franklin's life and role in Philadelphia, see Bridenbaugh and Bridenbaugh 1942; Franklin 1986; Scharf and Westcott 1884.

38. Roscoe 1895: 9–10. For further information on John Dalton's scientific career and its relationship to Manchester science, see Cardwell 1968, 1976; Clow 1968; Kargon 1977; Patterson 1970; Scott 1968; Thackray 1972.

39. Kargon 1977; Thackray 1974.

40. Baker et al. 1999; Brockbank 1952; Scharf and Westcott 1884.

41. Dalton for long even "firmly declined to be put up for membership in the Royal Society of London" (Bridenbaugh and Bridenbaugh 1942: 305; Thackray 1972: 22–23).

42. Allinson and Penrose 1887; Sumner 1896; Wright 1986.

43. Baltzell 1979: 43–44.

44. Gatrell 1982; Howe 1984; Redford 1940; Vigier 1970.

45. Ayerst 1971; Gatrell 1982: 32–35; Mills 1921: 9–12; Redford 1940. For research on the geographic variation across Lancashire in middle class social backgrounds, see Gunn 1992; Howe 1984; B. Lewis 2001. Gatrell notes the astonishing significance of the Unitarian social network in particular: "In the course of the nineteenth century as a whole, the trustees of the Cross Street Unitarian chapel alone were to provide Liberal Manchester with seven of its Mayors, and the nation at large with a dozen MPs [members of Parliament]" (Gatrell 1982: 23–24). The related story of early-nineteenth-century working-class agitation, including the Peterloo massacre in 1819, has been told in detail by E. P. Thompson (1963). On August 16, more than fifty thousand workers gathered for a protest at St. Peter's Field in Manchester. The alarmed local magistrates summoned the military, who charged the crowd, killing fifteen people and injuring hundreds. Proletarian uprisings like the St. Peter's Field protest and the Luddites occasionally won real, if temporary, relief and benefits for workers, and invariably caused anxiety among landowners and employers. But for most middle- and upper-class people, there was no thought of granting equality or the vote, and the real political struggles of the day lay elsewhere (Read 1958, 1959; Smelser 1959: 132–133).

46. Gatrell 1982: 19; Howe 1984: 94–98. But Manchester's electorate only increased to 4,293 registered voters, out of a total population of approximately 150,000.

47. Gatrell 1982: 38; Cobden quoted in Redford 1940: ii, 16.

48. Gatrell 1982; Medcalf 1854; Cobden quoted in Morley 1890: 83–84; Redford 1940: ii, 24–28. The final demise of ancien régime rule occurred when the city government bought the manorial rights from Mosley for £200,000 in 1846 (Gunn 1992).

49. Gatrell 1982: 50.

CHAPTER 3

1. Watts 1866: 404–405 (the "dire calamity" quote is from the CSA's fifth annual report [p. 402]); see also Farnie 1979; Harnetty 1972; Henderson 1934; Redford 1956; Silver 1966.

2. Henderson 1934. S. G. Checkland (1964) argues that the Famine was actually a boon to manufacturers because by raising prices they increased their profits.

3. Ross 1992: 114; see also Hall 2001 and Storper 1997. The NIDL theory is explained in Barnet and Muller 1974; Cohen 1981; Dicken 1986; Frobel, Heinrichs, and Kreye 1980; Hymer 1979; Sklair 1998.

4. Noyelle and Dutka 1988; Noyelle and Stanback 1984; Sassen 1991: 3, 1994: 4, 2001a; Stanback and Noyelle 1982; P. Taylor 2004; Taylor, Walker, and Beaverstock 2002.

5. Kindleberger 2000: chapter 11; D. R. Meyer 1986; Reed 1981; Sassen 1991: tables 6.22 and 6.15, 2001a. See also the revised second edition of Saskia Sassen's *The Global City* (2001b).

6. Directory of Corporate Affiliations 1999; International Directory of Corporate Affiliations 1981, 1991; Who Owns Whom 1974, 1980, 1991, 1998; Who Owns Whom: North American Edition 1973. In assembling these databases, I have also consulted other sources—such as newspapers and banking directories—when appropriate. I have not located a comprehensive data source for privately held firms; thus, my information on them is limited.

7. Farnie 1979: 7; Laurie and Schmitz 1981; Lindstrom 1978: 23; U.S. Bureau of the Census 1854; Wainwright 1982.

8. Binzen 1970: 92; Laurie and Schmitz 1981; Spencer 1877.

9. Baltzell 1979; J. K. Brown 1995; Burt and Davies 1982; Chapman 1904; Parsons 1904; S. B. Warner 1968.

10. Gunn 1992: 74–75; Nicholls 1996; B. Rodgers 1986: 42–43.

11. Laurie and Schmitz 1981; Wainwright 1982; S. B. Warner 1963; Weigley 1982.

12. Some clerical employment probably should be counted as part of the financial industries, and much of it was probably employed in professional service firms. In New York City's employment profile in 1910, manufacturing accounted for 41 percent of the workforce, finance 2 percent, and professional services 5 percent. These numbers are modestly different from those of Philadelphia and Manchester, but in directions that correspond to the global city/second city divergence. Moreover, while the overall ratio of jobs in New York to jobs in Philadelphia was 3:1, the ratio of bankers between the two cities was 5:1 in New York's favor.

13. Abernethy 1982: 533; Adams et al. 1991; Bowker 1928; Fowler 2003; Hobsbawm 1968: 174–175; Mole 1996; Singleton 1991.

14. Engels 1958; Haines 1981; Licht 1992.

15. Fowler 2003; Joyce 1980; Licht 1992.

16. Greater Manchester Council 1975; Manchester and Salford Inner Area Partnership Research Group 1978; Manchester City Planning Department 1982, 1986; Nicholls 1996; H. B. Rodgers 1980; Stull and Madden 1990; Warner and Borowski 1994.

17. Adams 2003; D. E. Fletcher 1992; Luce and Summers 1987; Madden and Stull 1991; B. Rodgers 1986; H. B. Rodgers 1980. Growth in Manchester's FIRE employment is to some degree an artifact of the data: the "clerical" sector from

1951 should be distributed across all of the other sectors, and in 1951 the FIRE category only counted bankers and insurance agents, not the majority of financial sector office staff.

18. Adams et al. 1991: 44–45; Giordano and Twomey 2002; Herd and Patterson 2002; U.S. Department of Commerce 2000: table P159, "Poverty Status in 1999."

19. Ayerst 1971: 335; J. K. Brown 1995; Chapman 1904; Farnie 1979; Laurie and Schmitz 1981; Redford 1956; Rose 2000; Scholes 1871; Spencer 1877.

20. Information about foreign investors in the Pennsylvania Railroad drawn from Burgess and Kennedy 1949; Roy 1997; Schotter 1927. Information on foreign property ownership in Philadelphia taken from Adams et al. 1991; Hodos 2002.

21. Appel 1970; Baltzell 1979: 234; Checkland 1964: 112; Rottenberg 2001; Scholes 1871; Wanamaker 1911; Whitfield 1988.

22. My account is based on Hochheiser 1986.

23. I. Clarke 1985; Dicken 1986: 55; Sklair 1998; S. Warner 2000; Wendt 1993: 11. A large literature on the "theory of the firm" tries to explain the conditions under which companies choose to internationalize; Dicken gives a comprehensive overview. The account of SmithKline is based primarily on Wendt 1993.

24. Recently, others have analyzed the geographic distribution of different sets of large TNCs (Alderson and Beckfield 2004; P. Taylor 2004; Taylor, Walker, and Beaverstock 2002). My database sacrifices the breadth in these analyses—I cannot make any statements about the NIDL across all cities—but I believe this is compensated by greater depth. Where Alderson and Beckfield focus only on Fortune Global 500 firms, and Taylor, Walker, and Beaverstock focus only on producer service firms, my database includes *all* publicly owned companies (and some privately owned ones as well) in Philadelphia and Manchester that have a foreign "link," or tie, regardless of size or industry. The data is regional—drawn from the eight-county PMSA for Philadelphia and the three-county region (GMC, Cheshire, and Lancashire) for Manchester. The database almost certainly underestimates the true number of linkages: the directories are probably conservatively biased in their listings, missing many small firms, and they do not cover privately held companies.

25. Arpan and Ricks 1993; Dicken 1986; Graham and Krugman 1993, 1995; Swenson 1993. For an interesting discussion of FDI's role in different regions of England, including greater Manchester, see Dicken and Lloyd 1979.

26. Sassen 1994: tables 4.2 and 5.3, 2001a.

27. D. E. Fletcher 1992.

28. The failure of Cooke's banking house, however, drained to the point of collapse by his quest to build the Northern Pacific Railroad, initiated the Panic of 1873 and inaugurated a four-year depression (Lubetkin 2006; Oberholtzer 1907: 207; Rottenberg 2001; Roy 1997; Wainwright 1953).

29. DiStefano 1998a, 1998b; Guthrie 2007; Philadelphia Stock Exchange 1992: 3; V. Silver 1998; D. Smith 1989; Vitiello and Thomas 2010. Peter J. Taylor (2004: 85) argues that, in most cases, insurance is an important industry for connecting to the global economy only for "lower-connected" cities, among which group he includes Philadelphia. For league tables that include Philadelphia, see Sassen 2001b: tables 7.3, 7.4, and 7.9. Of all the cities listed in Sassen's tables, however, Philadelphia's institutional equity holdings were the least internationalized—only 2 percent of institutional equity holdings were overseas (calculated from tables 7.3 and 7.4). Some of the information here gathered thanks to Nasdaq OMX: "PHLX"

(2010); London Stock Exchange (2010). In 2000, 2.2 billion shares traded hands on the exchange, and it also carried currency options and about 10 percent of the nation's volume in stock options trading; by contrast, on the New York Stock Exchange, more than 1 billion shares routinely trade hands each day.

30. This data was originally published in Hodos 2001; data on national-level sectoral patterns is from Sassen 1994: table 4.5.

31. Adams 2003; Dechert LLC 2010 (Dechert foreign offices are in Beijing, Brussels, Dublin, Hong Kong, London, Luxembourg, Moscow, Munich, and Paris); Devine et al. 2000; Fazey 1995; Sassen 1991, 2001b; Summers and Luce 1985.

32. Adams 2003; George 1997; Temple University 2010; University of Manchester 2010; University of Salford 2010. Drexel University planned to open a campus in Warsaw in 2001 but pulled back.

33. Herd and Patterson 2002; Mollenkopf and Castells 1991.

34. See Markusen, Lee, and DiGiovanna 1999; Sassen 1994.

35. Dicken 1992, 2002; Mole 1996; Quilley 1995: 173.

CHAPTER 4

1. For newspaper accounts of the stadium struggle, see Burton and Benson 2000; Jennifer Lin 2000a, 2000b; Rhor 2001; Ung and Bruch 2000; Ung and Harris 2000 (the "boisterous" quote is from this article).

2. Gammage 2004.

3. Quoted in Ung and Bruch 2000; Ung and Harris 2000.

4. For analyses of the various pathways by which migrants can become incorporated, particularly in a more or less explicitly subordinate social and political position, see Katznelson 1973; Light and Bonacich 1988; Portes 1998; Portes and Manning 1986; Waldinger 1996; Wilson and Portes 1980; Zhou 1992.

5. Winant 2001.

6. N. Foner 2005: table 8.2; Great Britain 2004; Waldinger and Lee 2001; note that Scotland and Ireland are excluded from the United Kingdom total in this paragraph.

7. The conventional distinction between internal and international migrants—international migrants, or immigrants, have to cross a national border to reach their destination, while internal migrants stay within one country—is complicated by difficulties in drawing the borders of a "country," especially one with an imperial past, like Great Britain. I classify Puerto Ricans in the United States and Irish in the United Kingdom as internal migrants. Additionally, before 1962, migrants to Britain born in Commonwealth countries were unrestricted; migration and citizenship rules have been substantially tightened since then. My practice is to classify non-Irish Commonwealth migrants as international because of the change in the citizenship status over time (Baines 1994; Layton-Henry 1994). The notion of a gateway city is discussed in Jan Lin 1998; Muller 1993.

8. The 0.5 percent cutoff is an arbitrary threshold, but note that it means an immigrant group need only have about 2,000 members in Manchester and 7,500 members in Philadelphia to be included.

9. The numbers of internal migrants in Manchester and London are underestimates because they do not include migrants from elsewhere in England, like Birmingham; I suspect that with the full numbers, the British pattern would look more like the American one.

10. Data on 1995 residence for Philadelphia and New York taken from the U.S. Department of Commerce (2000b: table PCT049, "Residence in 1995"); it is based on the number living in a different state or in Puerto Rico.

11. Great Britain 1982; Great Britain 1991; U.S. Department of Commerce 1984; U.S. Department of Commerce 1992; Waldinger 2001a; Waldinger and Lee 2001.

12. Baines 1994; Golab 1977; Great Britain 1854, 1913; Layton-Henry 1994; Roberts 1978a; U.S. Census Office 1872, 1883.

13. On labor markets, see B. Roberts 1978a, 1978b; Sassen 1991, 1994; Waldinger 1996, 2001b; Whalen 2001. A large literature in the United States has tried to assess whether African Americans and immigrants compete in the labor market; for examples, see Lieberson 1980; Lim 2001. This literature has largely focused, however, on global cities, especially New York.

14. Burt and Davies 1982; Crawford 1962; Frangopulo 1965; Golab 1977; Morais 1894; B. Williams 1976, 1985.

15. Owen 1996; Zecker 1998.

16. Golab 1977; Infield 1986; Shaffer 2000; Singer et al. 2008.

17. Immigrant passenger landings in Philadelphia most years were less than 10 percent of those landing at New York (Burt and Davies 1982; Golab 1977: 168–169, 210–211 [I am here comparing Golab's appendixes A and H]; Juliani 1980, 1998; Owen 1996; U.S. Treasury Department 1895; Ward 1975).

18. Of course, any individual stream of immigrants is internally diverse. For example, according to Pnina Werbner, there were three mini-waves of Pakistanis who came to Manchester: a "trader" wave in the 1930s and 1940s, a student wave in the 1940s and 1950s, and a worker wave from the late 1950s to the early 1960s. Over time, the migrant stream widened to include Gujarati Muslims from India, which lowered the class composition of the migrant group so that later arrivals often had fewer skills and opportunities (Golab 1977; Werbner 1990: 17).

19. Clark 1973a; Laurie, Hershberg, and Alter 1981: table 13.

20. Golab 1973, 1977; Juliani 1980, 1998.

21. Kadaba 1998; Kazal 1998: 39; Lee 2002; Lounsberry 1998; Power 1988; Scranton 1983: 10, 129–133; Werbner 1990.

22. Scholes 1871.

23. Chapman 1904; Kelly 1990; Redford 1964; Rees and Phillips 1996; Scranton 1983: 10, 129–133, 1989; Werbner 1990; B. Williams 1985.

24. Anwar 1979; Golab 1973, 1977; Juliani 1980, 1998; Kelly 1990; Lounsberry 1998; Power 1988; Sassen 1998; Waldinger 1996; Werbner 1990.

25. Manchester City Planning Department 1981b; Kadaba 1998; Kelly 1990; Laurie, Hershberg, and Alter 1981; Lee 2002.

26. Manchester City Planning Department 1981b; Ward 1975.

27. Kazal 1998; Redford 1964.

28. Redford 1964; Werly 1973.

29. DuBois 1996; Golab 1977; Goode and Schneider 1994; Koss 1965; Whalen 2001; numbers of African American migrants and Puerto Rican ethnics derived from U.S. Department of Commerce (various years).

30. DuBois 1996: 99–105; Hershberg 1981; Hershberg et al. 1981; Lane 1986; Licht 1992; Nash 1988; Winch 2000.

31. The poverty and deprivation of the Irish in Manchester were legendary; they formed the substance of a number of early theoretical and statistical investigations in

the Victorian decades (Engels 1958; Kay 1832; Thompson 1963: 434; Werly 1973). On Philadelphia's Puerto Rican population, see Koss 1965; Whalen 2001: 137. For data on employment and poverty for all three groups, see NOMIS (National Online Manpower Information System) 2007: table S109; U.S. Department of Commerce 2000c: table PCT075B and PCT075H, "Poverty Status in 1999 by Sex by Age."

32. Bonacich 1972; DuBois 1996; Lieberson 1980; Massey et al. 1998; Portes and Manning 1986; Waldinger 1996. Jennifer Lee's (2002) data on black-Korean conflicts in Philadelphia and New York support this interpretation.

33. Charles 2003; Massey and Denton 1993.

34. Joyce 1980; Kirk 1985; Millward 1985; Neal 1990; Scharf and Westcott 1884: 638. The intergroup violence in Philadelphia in the 1830s and 1840s was not solely between blacks and whites; some also occurred between white native Protestants and white (primarily Irish) Catholics.

35. Koss 1965; Jennifer Lin 1993; Morris et al. 1981; R. Roberts 1971: 170; Whalen 2001.

36. Baltzell 1958; Clark 1973a: 141–142, 1973b; DuBois 1996.

37. Hoge 2001; Lyall 2001a, 2001b. The quotation is from Lyall 2001a; there are parallels here to the generational profile of many of the anti-stadium activists in Philadelphia's Chinatown.

38. Clark 1973a; Gillette 1970; Strange 1973. For examples of studies of migrant political incorporation, see Erie 1988; Katznelson 1973, 1981.

39. Breton 1964; Clark 1973b; Feldberg 1973; Fielding 1988, 1992; Hershberg 1981; Hilton 1994; Johnson 1973; Nash 1988; Wainwright 1982; Werly 1973; Winch 2000: 40.

40. Goode and Schneider 1994.

41. Harris 2000; Shaffer 2000; Werbner 1990: 13.

CHAPTER 5

1. For theoretical accounts of global culture, see Boli and Thomas 1999a; Hannerz 1997; A. D. King 1997, 2004; Robertson 1992: 83, 1997.

2. Hertz 1912; Messinger 1985. There is, of course, a substantial historical literature on the culture of Victorian England and the Victorian middle class. I do not intend to engage this entire literature here; rather, I focus on some aspects of it in Manchester in particular. For more information, the reader may consult Archer 1985b; Bizup 2003; Briggs 1963; Carlyle 1971; Gunn 1992; Hewitt 1996; Heyck 1982; Hobsbawm 1968, 1984; Kidd and Roberts 1985; B. Lewis 2001; Wahrman 1995; Wiener 1981; R. Williams 1973.

3. Gatrell 1982; Gunn 1992; McCord 1958; Messinger 1985; Mills 1921; Robbins 1979; Silver 1966.

4. Other key members included Archibald Prentice, who ran the *Manchester Times*, George Wilson (league president for many years), Thomas Potter (manufacturer and the city's first mayor), and cotton merchants and manufacturers, such as Elkanah Armitage and Henry Tootal.

5. Manchester Chamber of Commerce President George Wood, quoted in Manchester Chamber of Commerce 1839 (1996): 165; Mills 1922: 45; Smith and Chapman 1838: 3; Cobden quoted in Morley 1890: 154–155.

6. Bourne 1877: 174.

7. Kaiser 1939; Rowe 1933.

8. E. Foner 1970; Geffen 1982; Green 1951; Kaiser 1939; Lippincott 1909; Richardson 1982; Rowe 1933; Yates 1987.

9. Lippincott 1909; Patten 1890; Sass 1982; R. E. Thompson 1875; Yates 1987.

10. Carey 1963: iii, 447; R. E. Thompson 1875; Wharton 1875: 305.

11. Dawson 2000; Ruggie 1982; R. E. Thompson 1875; Wharton 1875: 298.

12. Kidd 1985. For attempts to theorize this general argument, see Fischer 1975; Lloyd 2004.

13. The account given here relies particularly on Baker 1999; Baker et al. 1999; Berlant 1975; Geffen 1982; Warner 1999. I am grateful to Howard Kaye for pointing me toward these sources. The list of Philadelphia medical institutions included the University of Pennsylvania's medical school, the American College of Physicians (1786), Philadelphia College of Pharmacy (1821), Jefferson Medical College (1826), Hahnemann Medical College (organized in 1848 as the Homeopathic Medical College of Philadelphia), Women's Medical College (founded in 1850 and recognized as the first institution in the world dedicated to training women in medicine), and the American Pharmaceutical Association (1852) (Scharf and Westcott 1884).

14. Baker 1999: 36. Innovation in medical ethics was one endeavor that Philadelphia and Manchester shared. At Manchester, Thomas Percival, a founding member of the Manchester Infirmary and an officer of the Lit&Phil, wrote the first-ever code of medical ethics. In Philadelphia in the 1820s, John Bell and Isaac Hays had edited the American version of Percival's code, and Bell relied on it heavily in writing the new 1847 American Medical Association code (Baker et al. 1999: xvii–xviii; see also Brockbank 1952).

15. Baker et al. 1999: xiii.

16. A. D. King 1990b: 38–42; Larson 1977.

17. Copley 1923; Nelson 1980; F. W. Taylor 1911: 16.

18. Chandler 1977; Frederick Taylor's 1912 testimony before Congress, quoted in Copley 1923: 12; Larson 1977; F. W. Taylor 1911: 36–37.

19. Copley 1923; Haber 1964; Nelson 1980.

20. Cooke 1919; Copley 1923; Haber 1964: 64; Larson 1977; Licht 1992.

21. DuBois 1996; Lippincott 1909; Sass 1982; Yates 1987.

22. This discussion of scientific disciplines in Manchester relies on Heyck 1982; Kargon 1977; Thackray 1974. Robert Kargon's definitive account traces in particular detail not just the development of scientific activity in the city but also the changing self-definitions of those who supported and conducted research, from (in his terms) amateurs through devotees, civic scientists, and professionals.

23. Archer 1985; Kargon 1977; Roscoe 1895.

24. Kargon 1977: 44–45, 60; Platt 2005: 448–451; H. J. Steffens 1979.

25. Heyck 1982: 183; Kargon 1977: 168; Thackray 1974: 678.

26. Thackray 1972: 59.

27. Roscoe 1895: 11.

28. Heyck 1982: 93–94; Kargon 1977.

29. Briggs 1963; J. L. Hammond 1934; Kargon 1977; Messinger 1985.

30. Birks 1962; Heyck 1982; Kargon 1977: 176; Roscoe 1895; Thackray 1972: 32.

31. Heyck 1982: 120; Kargon 1977: 146.

32. Licht 1992: 86–87. According to T. W. Heyck (1982: 88), however, the new professionals did not always want to be considered purely middle class; the social status associated with the older gentlemanly model of science attracted them too.

33. But workers did not always volunteer in great numbers to be educated, and science was not popular enough all by itself to hold their interest. Many institutions for the improvement of workers failed after a few years (Hewitt 1996). For histories of some of these institutes, see Archer 1985; Cruickshank 1974; Kirk 1985; Richardson 1982; Scharf and Westcott 1884; Walls 1993; Whiffen 1985.

34. Archer 1985: 20–21; Cruickshank 1974; Fowler and Wyke 1993. On the Franklin Institute and affiliated organizations, see Licht 1992; MacDonald 1985: 41; Wahl 1895; Walls 1993: 178.

35. The combination of physics, engineering, and electronics at the University of Manchester continued into the 1940s, when researchers developed the first stored-program computer, the Mark I (IBM licensed the original patent from the university). Spin-offs from the school produced some of England's first high-tech firms, like Ferranti. As a school of not simply business management, but also social science and public administration, Wharton faculty and researchers in Philadelphia, especially Lawrence Klein, pioneered econometric methods in the 1950s and 1960s (D. E. Fletcher 1992; Large 1982; Sass 1982).

36. The issue of the cultural specializations of cities, and whether there are characteristic variations, was important several decades ago (Mumford 1938, 1961; Redfield and Singer 1969). Recently, there has been more interest in discussing cities as cultural centers, inspired particularly by Sharon Zukin's work on symbolic economies, European research on "festivalization," and analysis of the historic preservation and heritage movements (Hannigan 1998; Roth and Frank 2000; Zukin 1995).

37. A. King 1998; Mason 1980; M. Taylor 1997.

38. Haslam 1999: 268. As David Schuyler pointed out to me, Dick Clark's *American Bandstand* in Philadelphia is an exception to this point.

39. Champion 1990; Haslam 1999; Milestone 1996.

40. Haslam 1999: 117.

41. Champion 1990: 11; Haslam 1999: 115, 188–189; Schlosser 1998: 24.

42. Moon 2000; Nisenson 1993, 1997. Also see the liner notes to the Philly Sound CD box set (Gamble and Huff 1997).

CHAPTER 6

1. Morley 1890; Redford 1956.

2. Hobson 1919; Howe 1997.

3. Farnie 1979: 109–114; Redford 1934, 1956: 14–16; A. W. Silver 1966.

4. That the city's leaders simultaneously preached free trade and minimal government to others while looking for capital subsidies that would benefit their own interests at others' expense struck many as self-serving. Manchester became famous for a sort of "free trade imperialism" that opened the city's merchants and politicians to charges of rank hypocrisy (Arrighi 1999:47–58; Harnetty 1972: 77–78; Semmel 1970; Wharton 1875: 305).

5. Harnetty 1972: 34.

6. My use of the term MFP is similar to but broader than that of Kirby, Marston, and Seasholes (1995). See also Hobbs 1994; Kresl and Gappert 1995.

7. For material on growth machines, see Bassett 1996; Jonas and Wilson 1999; Lauria 1996; Logan and Molotch 1987; Mollenkopf 1978; Molotch 1976. I am not claiming that there were no local costs to these projects, only that these

costs were successfully downplayed by supporters. For example, it is quite clear that landowners and residents displaced by the transport facilities themselves suffered.

8. Albion 1970: 46, and appendices; Livingood 1947: appendices 1 and 3, pp. 24–26; G. R. Taylor 1951: 197; S. B. Warner 1968: 88.

9. Maritime historian Edward Albion (1970: 374) argues that "Philadelphia fell behind relatively not so much from lack of effort, but because its effort was not well-timed" (G. R. Taylor 1951). For Baltimore's story, see Browne 1980.

10. Burgess and Kennedy 1949: appendix G, pp. 807–808; Davis 1978; Schotter 1927. My account of the Pennsylvania Railroad's formation and growth relies on Burgess and Kennedy 1949; Goodrich 1960; Scharf and Westcott 1884; Schotter 1927; G. R. Taylor 1951. Additional sources include the *Dictionary of American Biography* and Albion 1970; Beers 1982; Browne 1980; Burt and Davies 1982; Chandler 1977; Daughen and Binzen 1971; Davis 1978; Fisher 1967; Hartz 1948; McClure 1905; Roy 1997; Schlegel 1947; S. B. Warner 1968; Weigley 1982.

11. Alexander McClure (1905) claims that the tonnage tax was inserted by backers of the B&O in order to hobble the Pennsy intentionally. Pennsy officials eventually got rid of the tax, but the price they had to pay was $7.5 million in cash to buy out the obsolete carriers (Goodrich 1960; Schotter 1927).

12. This was before the 1854 consolidation of the city and county of Philadelphia; therefore, Spring Garden and Northern Liberties were still independent jurisdictions.

13. President Roberts quoted in Schotter 1927: 229–235.

14. Burt 1963: 188.

15. J. K. Brown 1995: 31; Copley 1923; Freedley 1867; Tweedale 1986.

16. J. K. Brown 1995; U.S. Treasury Department 1892, 1912.

17. Browne 1980: 169–170; Burgess and Kennedy 1949: 441; Roy 1997: chap. 5; Schlegel 1947; G. R. Taylor 1951.

18. Albion 1970; Burt 1963: 195; U.S. Treasury Department 1862, 1892, 1912. The "historians' consensus" to which I refer is drawn from Albion 1970; Browne 1980; Duncan and Lieberson 1970; Glaab and Brown 1983; G. R. Taylor 1951.

19. *Manchester Guardian* 1882: 6. The history of the Manchester Ship Canal's genesis, construction, and early success has been told in detail elsewhere, so I provide only the most relevant highlights here. The key sources, from which much of this account is drawn, are Farnie 1980; Harford 1994; Leech 1907; Owen 1983; other useful sources include Quilley 1995; Redford 1940; W. A. Shaw 1912.

20. Leech 1907; Sharpless 1978; G. Shaw 1989. For a sampling of nineteenth-century expressions of concern about foreign competition, see A. W. Fletcher 1897; Fogg 1893; Manchester Chamber of Commerce 1839 (1996); Merttens 1901; Smith and Chapman 1838; Spencer 1877.

21. *Manchester Guardian* 1882. The occupational composition of the Provisional Committee is detailed in Harford 1994: 22–24; Leech 1907. Bosdin Leech also provides lists of donors to the approval campaign, and Ian Harford analyzes labor's support for the Canal in great detail.

22. Jacob Bright quoted in Leech 1907: 191.

23. Harford 1994: 53. For more on the history of attempts to organize a Liberal-Labour political alliance, see P. F. Clarke 1971; Quilley 1995.

24. Farnie 1980; *Manchester Guardian* 1894a, 1894b, 1894c, 1894d; Port of Manchester 1901, 1902; Redford 1940; B. Rodgers 1986.

25. For material on diversification and Trafford Park, see Farnie 1980: 8–9, 45; A. W. Fletcher 1897, 1899; Nicholls 1996; B. Rodgers 1986. These economic developments are said by some analysts to coincide with Britain's transition to "Fordist" economic patterns; see Elbaum and Lazonick 1986; Mellor 1989; Mole 1996; Quilley 1995; Zeitlin 1983; Zeitlin and Totterdill 1989.

26. In the early years of the past century, for example, Manchester housed thirty-four and Philadelphia thirty-seven consulates (Port of Manchester 1902; B. Rodgers 1986; Taylor and Schoff 1912).

27. Delaware River Port Authority 1971; Farnie 1980: table 1; Law and Grime 1993; Owen 1983: 118–119; U.S. Army Corps of Engineers 1990: table 5-2. For Philadelphia, the ranking is based on total tonnage for all Delaware River ports, including Marcus Hook, Wilmington, and Camden.

28. On the transformation of the U.S. rail system and the failure of the Penn Central, see Daughen and Binzen 1971; Dilger 2003; Gartner 1971; Itzkoff 1985; Salsbury 1982; Saunders 1978, 2003; U.S. Department of Transportation 1973.

29. The Ship Canal Company and local state agencies—the Trafford Park Development Corporation (TPDC) and Manchester and Salford city councils—have developed Trafford Centre, a gigantic two-million-square-foot suburban shopping mall on the outer edge of Trafford Park, and also generated more than five million square feet of office and commercial space (Law and Grime 1993; Parkinson-Bailey 2000).

30. For 2001 seaport data, see U.S. Army Corps of Engineers 2006. There was widespread unhappiness at the level of public subsidy—$400 million from the city, state, and federal governments. Philadelphia state Senator Vince Fumo, for example, claimed that the deal "was like the *Emperor's New Clothes* . . . [a] dumb deal from day one." See Bissinger 1997: chap. 18; Gorenstein 1997; Warner and Dilanian 1999: A1–A21.

31. For detail on the port's history, see Taylor and Schoff 1912. The Web site for the Philadelphia Regional Port Authority (http://philaport.com) contains substantial information about the organization's history and activities; see also Delaware River Port Authority 1994; McGurty 1994; and the Web sites for DRPA (http://drpa.org) and the South Jersey Port Corporation (http://www.southjerseyport.com).

32. Bagwell and Lyth 2002; Bednarek 2001; Fairhill 1980: 11; Quilley 1995; Redford 1940; B. Rodgers 1986. Steve Quilley's account of Manchester Airport's history is particularly informative.

33. Fairhill 1980; Manchester City Planning Department 1981a, 1987; Update Manchester 1997: 1. Passenger numbers quoted from Manchester Airport n.d.

34. For information on the U.S. airline industry and deregulation in general, see Bailey, Graham, and Kaplan 1985; Dilger 2003; Morrison and Winston 1995; Petzinger 1995; G. Williams 1994. For post-1990 airport expansion and material on U.S. Airways, see Belden 1997; Gelbart 2001; Lowe 2001; Maynard 2005, and the wealth of material available at Philadelphia International Airport (2007), including traffic statistics, expansion planning, and other reports.

35. Gelbart 2001; Manchester Airport 1991. Information on airport governance and ownership structures from Manchester Airport (2007) and Philadelphia International Airport (2007).

36. Caruana and Simmons 1996; Manchester International Airport Authority 1982; Shapiro 1997: A10; additional information from Manchester Airport 2007; Philadelphia International Airport 2007.

37. See Roy 1997 for a subtle, well-developed argument about how changing patterns of state involvement in infrastructure across the nineteenth-century United States redefined the meaning of property.

CHAPTER 7

1. Robertson 1992: 173–175.

2. Thus, they are closely related to what one writer recently called "scalar narratives:" "those stories that actors tell about the changes in the scalar localization of socio-political processes" (González 2006: 839).

3. Such projects constitute what the cultural sociologist Diana Crane (2002) has called cultural policy. Scholarly attention to cultural planning has become much more widespread since the early 1990s; the cultural sociologist Sharon Zukin's work is perhaps the most prominent (Bianchini and Parkinson 1994; Levine 1989a; Roth and Frank 2000; Zukin 1989, 1991, 1995). On the Olympics, see Hill 1996; Levine 1989b; McNeill 1999; Rutheiser 1996. Because Philadelphia's Centennial Exhibition and Manchester's Olympics bid have been discussed elsewhere (citations to those works are provided below), I give them only brief treatment here, but the analysis and conclusions are based on all four cases.

4. I do not deny that in other instances, cultural projects have generated conflict. This happened to some degree in the Avenue of the Arts, but to a lesser extent in the other cases; for an example of a cultural project which provoked political conflict, see de Frantz 2005. In all four cases considered here, however, high levels of political conflict *preceded* the regime, and declined significantly after the regime's establishment. On regime theory, see Stone 1989; for comparative examples, see Barnekov, Boyle, and Rich 1989; Bassett 1996; DiGaetano and Klemanski 1999; DiGaetano and Lawless 1999; Haughton and While 1999; Henry and Paramio-Salcines 1999; Lauria 1996.

5. Baltzell 1958, 1979; N. Burt 1963: 17. For the inferiority quote, see Harris 2001.

6. Beers 1982; Medcalf 1854; Redford 1940; Vigier 1970; S. B. Warner 1968.

7. Fisher 1967: 18.

8. Dickens 1854: 65.

9. Carlyle 1971: 211; Gunn 2000; Wiener 1981: 28.

10. The quotation about Manchester in the subheading is from the novel *Coningsby*, by Benjamin Disraeli (1948: 148) first published in 1844. On middle-class Dissent, see Gadian 1993; Gunn 1992; Parkinson-Bailey 2000: 96–97.

11. On workers, Chartists, and class antagonism, see Briggs 1959; L. Brown 1959; Joyce 1980; Kirk 1985; Pickering 1995; Read 1959; E. P. Thompson 1963; Webb 1891.

12. Ayerst 1971; Hammond 1934; Howe 1984; Redford 1934; A. W. Silver 1966.

13. Gunn 1992; Mills 1921; Robbins 1979; A. W. Silver 1966. Some have argued that politics in Manchester were always less radical than in the surrounding mill towns (Gadian 1993; Garrard 1983: 26; Gunn 1992; Joyce 1980).

14. Archer 1985b; Finke 1985; Gunn 1992; Kargon 1977; *Manchester Guardian* 1857b, 1857e. Some architectural and cultural historians have viewed the magnificent, gothic town hall of 1877 as the culmination of local Liberal rule, "the high point of civic patriotism" (Archer 1985a; Gunn 1992: 319; Messinger 1985;

Parkinson-Bailey 2000; Treuherz 1985; Walter 1976); obviously, my assessment differs.

15. Finke 1985; *Manchester Guardian* 1857e; Parkinson-Bailey 2000. The *Manchester Guardian* (1857b) printed an extensive series of critical notices, and eventually published them as a collection of handbooks; it also printed detailed articles about foreign attendees.

16. Howe 1984; Kirk 1985; A. W. Silver 1966. Although I have not been able to find a list of the donors to the guarantee fund, the *Guardian* reported that most of them had seats on the dais; sources for cross-matching regime members include Charlton 1951; Cruickshank 1974; Manchester Chamber of Commerce 1883; *Manchester Guardian* 1857a, 1857b, 1857e; Manchester Literary and Philosophical Society 1852; Mills 1922; Sanderson 1972.

17. Finke 1985; *Manchester Guardian* 1857b, 1857e: 3. For a skeptical take on elite attitudes and their effects on the working classes, see Hewitt 1996.

18. *Manchester Guardian* 1857c: 4–5.

19. *Manchester Guardian* 1857d: 4–5.

20. Archer 1985b; Finke 1985: 122; Gunn 1992: 129; Messinger 1985; Morris 1984; Parkinson-Bailey 2000; Russell 2000; Ryan 1937.

21. Archer 1985b: 5, 14–16; Briggs 1963: 93–94; Gunn 2000; Messinger 1985; *Building News* quoted in Parkinson-Bailey 2000: 103; Redford 1940; Whiffen 1985.

22. Gunn 2000: 14; Ryan 1937: 8.

23. The phrase "the year of the century" in the subheading is taken from Dee Brown's (1966) eponymous history of America in the year 1876. Some of the material contained here, and additional details, has been previously published in Hodos 2006.

24. Beers 1982; D. Brown 1966; Citizens of Pennsylvania 1878; Cordato 1983; Potter 1876; Randel 1969; Rydell 1984; Scharf and Westcott 1884: 1700. For a contrasting interpretation of public events and festivals like the Centennial Exhibition, see Glassberg 1983.

25. Appel 1970; J. P. Roberts 1980: 43; Schotter 1927. For more on the expansion of Fairmount Park, see Contosta and Franklin 2006. For material on the growth of the city's infrastructure and metropolitan characteristics, see Gillette 1980.

26. Adams 1988; Baltzell 1979; Beers 1982; Burt and Davies 1982; Gillette 1970: 174, 177 (table ii); McCaffery 1993; McClure 1905; on black people's exclusion from the Centennial Exhibition, see Rydell 1984: 28. I examined lists of the governing boards of multiple civic institutions in order to determine their overlapping memberships; sources include D. Brown 1966; Burgess and Kennedy 1949; Gibbons 1926; Gillette 1970; Scharf and Westcott 1884; Schotter 1927; Union League of Philadelphia 1866, 1876; Wahl 1895; Whiteman 1975. See Hodos 2006 for more details.

27. Beers 1982; Green 1951; Randel 1969; Rydell 1984; Weigley 1982.

28. Beers 1982: 470; D. Brown 1966; Lewis Smith, quoted in Citizens of Pennsylvania 1878: 10; Potter 1876; Scharf and Westcott 1884; Weigley 1982.

29. Fisher 1967: 21–22; "Or Should It Be Avenue?" 1993; see also Baltzell 1979; N. Burt 1963; Gillette 1980.

30. I am grateful to Darren O'Byrne for the phrasing.

31. Adams 1988, 1991; Adams et al. 1991; Bartelt 1989; Beauregard 1996; Daughen and Binzen 1977; Ekstrom 1973; Kleniewski 1984; Petshek 1973.

32. Adams 1988, 1991; Adams et al. 1991; Daughen and Binzen 1977; Feffer 2003; Reeves 2001.

33. Adams et al. 1991; Beauregard 1989, 1990; Greater Philadelphia First Corporation 1986. The "supine" quote is from Boldt 1989: C7.

34. The CCD was primarily the offspring of the Central Philadelphia Development Corporation (CPDC), discussed in the following paragraph. The CCD now staffs and runs CPDC, and the two organizations have combined their Web sites. Information obtained from the CCD Web site (http://centercityphila.org), accessed 17 April 2001. See Bartelt (1989) for a critique of the privatization of city planning in Philadelphia that predates the CCD's establishment.

35. Boasberg 1991, 1992; Central Philadelphia Development Corporation 1992: 4; Hall 1991; Oestreich 2001; Ravenscroft 1994; Valdes and Hine 1991.

36. Other estimates of the cost ranged as high as $750 million, and the price tag for the Regional Performing Arts Center ballooned from $140 million to more than $265 million (Oestreich 2001).

37. Solms quoted in Salisbury 1993b: A1; Kluger quoted in Valdes and Hine 1991: B1.

38. Donors and lists of boards of directors for organizations related to the AA regime were compiled from Bruch 1994; Central Philadelphia Development Corporation 1991; Greater Philadelphia First 1999; Oestreich 2001; Philadelphia Orchestra Association 1992; Salisbury 1992a, 1992b, 1993a, 1994, 1995.

39. Salisbury 1993a.

40. Bruch 1994; Hine 1992; Oestreich 2001; Irizarry quoted in Saffron 1992: N1; Salisbury 1995; Sokolove and Dobrin 1994.

41. Boldt 1989: C7; Huler 1989: 107; Philadelphia City Planning Commission 1988. See also Boasberg 1991: D1.

42. "Or Should It Be Avenue?" 1993; Saffron 1993: E1.

43. Quoted in Belden 1993: F1. See also the Delaware Valley Regional Planning Council's (1993) report, *Rating the Region*, which included comparisons to eight cities around the world, from Vancouver to Kyoto to Glasgow to Marseille.

44. Greater Philadelphia First Corporation 1986: 3; Hershberg 1994; Peirce and Johnson 1995. Greco quoted in Peirce and Johnson 1995: 12.

45. Haslam 1999; Manchester and Salford Inner Area Partnership Research Group 1978; Manchester City Planning Department 1981b, 1982. The subheading is borrowed from Michael Winterbottom's 2002 movie about Factory Records' Tony Wilson and the city's 1980s music scene. For material on the riots, see Hytner Commission 1981; J. Lewis 1981, 1982d; Morris 1981; Morris et al. 1981; Thornber 1981. Other scholars have published excellent research on Manchester's Olympics bids and redevelopment strategies; for more detailed information see Cochrane, Peck, and Tickell 1996; Peck and Tickell 1995; Peck and Ward 2002; Quilley 1995, 1999, 2000.

46. In the early 1980s, in opposition to Prime Minister Margaret Thatcher's deep cuts in aid to local governments and demands for service cutbacks and higher rates, nearly all British cities made sharp turns to the political left (Hetherington 1984; Labour Rebellion 1983; J. Lewis 1982a, 1982b, 1982c, 1983; Sharratt 1984).

47. Cochrane, Peck, and Tickell 1996; Quilley 1999, 2000, 2002; Robson 2002; Tickell and Peck 1996; Tickell, Peck, and Dicken 1995.

48. British Olympic Bid Committee n.d.; Cochrane, Peck, and Tickell 1996; Hill 1996; Peck and Tickell 1995. The development corporations were agencies of central government specifically designed to bypass local authorities; even more

than was the case in Philadelphia, the private sector was really the junior partner (Holden 2002; Quilley 1999, 2000; Robson 2002; Tickell, Peck, and Dicken 1995). Information about overlapping board memberships derived from these sources and from Central Manchester Development Corporation 1996; D. E. Fletcher 1992; Manchester City Pride 1997; Manchester Millennium 1997; Trafford Park Development Corporation 1997.

49. Cochrane, Peck, and Tickell 2002: 108–109; Mellor 1997; Wynne and O'Connor 1998. Some analysts, however, dispute the regime's inclusiveness; see above and O'Connor and Wynne 1996; Quilley 2000.

50. Haslam 1999: 188–189; Hetherington 1993; Hill 1996; Holden 2002; Manchester City Council 1995a, 1995b; Manchester City Planning Department 1986; Manchester City Pride 1997.

51. Manchester City Council 1995b: 94.

52. Manchester City Pride 1997: 50.

53. D. E. Fletcher 1992; Manchester City Council 1994: 7, 1995b.

54. Pieda plc 1993: 139; Quilley 2000; Taylor, Evans, and Fraser 1996: 197; Tickell, Peck, and Dicken 1995: 248.

55. Association of Greater Manchester Authorities 1993; Manchester City Council 1993, 1994; Manchester City Pride 1997; the list of cities is from D. E. Fletcher 1992: 5.

CHAPTER 8

1. Haslam 1999: 268; Lloyd 2004; Milestone 1996. Other intriguing examples include Motown in Detroit and grunge in Seattle.

2. Appadurai 1996; Robertson 1992: 46, 173–175.

3. The classic statement of growth machine theory is Logan and Molotch 1987. For discussions of regime theory that particularly point to its utility in comparative analyses, see Bassett 1996; DiGaetano and Lawless 1999; Henry and Paramio-Salcines 1999; Lauria 1996; Savitch and Kantor 2002.

4. For Toronto, see Sassen 1994.

5. The discussion of Detroit is based on Darden et al. 1987; Orr and Stoker 1994; Schopmeyer 2000; S. E. Smith 1999; Sugrue 1996; H. A. Thompson 2001; Zunz 1982.

6. This account draws on Brown, O'Connor, and Cohen 2000; Taylor, Evans, and Fraser 1996; Tweedale 1995.

7. Hodos 2007; Taylor, Walker, and Beaverstock 2002. See also Delaware Valley Regional Planning Council 1993. McNeill 1999 examines not just the Olympics, but Barcelona politics more broadly, uncovering the ambiguity and the price of the city's success.

8. This account is based on Balan, Browning, and Jelin 1973; Bennett 1995; Saragoza 1988.

9. For sources on Bangalore, see Basant and Chandra 2007; Dasgupta 2008; Friedman 2007; Heitzman 2004; Radakrishnan 2008; Srinivas 2001.

10. The list of analyses on both sides grows ever longer; for a sampling, see Amin and Thrift 1992; Barnes and Ledebur 1998; Clarke and Gaile 1997; Hambleton, Savitch, and Stewart 2003; Jessop 1996; Judd and Parkinson 1990; Kanter 1995; Peck and Tickell 1994; Peirce 1993; Peirce and Johnson 1995; Rhodes 1996; Sallez and Verot 1991; Savitch and Kantor 2002; Storper 1997.

11. The argument I make in this paragraph has also been advanced by Peter Taylor (2004).

12. This vision is largely Durkheimian, in which cities become the newly resurgent homes of a (peaceful) world civilization; see Boli and Thomas 1999a, 1999b; J. Meyer 1980; Robertson 1992, 1997; Thomas et al. 1987.

13. Beers 1982; Haslam 1999: 225–226; Scharf and Westcott 1884. The American Friends Service Committee (2010) Web site lists programs in seventeen foreign countries on five continents.

14. A. D. King 1990b.

15. Lever 1997.

16. See the two final chapters of P. Taylor (2004) for a similar argument.

17. Pasqual Maragall quoted in McNeill 1999: 103.

18. Tilly 1990; Weber 1958.

19. The number of scholars who have explicitly considered this possibility is small, but growing; see Brenner 1999, 2004; Häussermann and Haila 2004; Holston and Appadurai 1996; Lever 1997; Spruyt 1994; P. Taylor 2004; Tilly 1990.

References

Abernethy, Lloyd M. 1982. "Progressivism, 1905–1919." In *Philadelphia: A 300-Year History*, edited by Russell F. Weigley, 524–565. New York: W. W. Norton.

Abrahamson, Mark. 2004. *Global Cities*. New York: Oxford University Press.

Abu-Lughod, Janet L. 1999. *New York, Chicago, Los Angeles: America's Global Cities*. Minneapolis: University of Minnesota Press.

Adams, Carolyn. 1988. *The Politics of Capital Investment*. Albany: State University of New York Press.

———. 1991. "Philadelphia: The Slide toward Municipal Bankruptcy." In *Big City Politics in Transition*, edited by H. V. Savitch and John Clayton Thomas, 29–46. Newbury Park, CA: Sage.

———. 2003. "The Meds and Eds in Urban Economic Development." *Journal of Urban Affairs* 25:571–588.

Adams, Carolyn, David Bartelt, David Elesh, Ira Goldstein, Nancy Kleniewski, and William Yancey. 1991. *Philadelphia: Neighborhoods, Division, and Conflict in a Postindustrial City*. Philadelphia: Temple University Press.

Albion, Robert G. 1938. *Square-Riggers on Schedule*. Princeton, NJ: Princeton University Press.

———. 1970. *The Rise of New York Port, 1815–1860*. New York: Charles Scribner's Sons.

Albrow, Martin. 1997. *The Global Age*. Stanford, CA: Stanford University Press.

Alderson, Arthur S., and Jason Beckfield. 2004. "Power and Position in the World City System." *American Journal of Sociology* 109:811–851.

Alexander, John K. 1973. "Poverty, Fear, and Continuity: An Analysis of the Poor in Late Eighteenth-Century Philadelphia." In *The Peoples of Philadelphia*, edited by Allen F. Davis and Mark H. Haller, 13–36. Philadelphia: Temple University Press.

Allinson, Edward P., and Boies Penrose. 1887. *The City Government of Philadelphia.* Baltimore: Johns Hopkins University.

American Friends Service Committee (AFSC). 2010. "Where We Work." American Friends Service Committee. http://afsc.org/where-we-work.

Amin, Ash, and Nigel Thrift. 1992. "Neo-Marshallian Nodes in Global Networks." *International Journal of Urban and Regional Research* 16:571–587.

———. 1994. "Living in the Global." In *Globalization, Institutions, and Regional Development in Europe,* edited by Ash Amin and Nigel Thrift, 1–22. New York: Oxford University Press.

Anwar, Muhammad. 1979. *The Myth of Return: Pakistanis in Britain.* London: Heinemann.

Appadurai, Arjun. 1996. *Modernity at Large.* Minneapolis: University of Minnesota Press.

Appel, Joseph H. 1970. *The Business Biography of John Wanamaker.* New York: AMS Press.

Archer, John H. G. 1985a. "A Classic of Its Age." In *Art and Architecture in Victorian Manchester,* edited by John H. G. Archer, 127–161. Manchester: Manchester University Press.

———. 1985b. "Introduction." In *Art and Architecture in Victorian Manchester,* edited by John H. G. Archer, 1–27. Manchester: Manchester University Press.

Arpan, Jeffrey S., and David A. Ricks. 1993. *Directory of Foreign Manufacturers in the United States.* Atlanta: Georgia State University Business Press.

Arrighi, Giovanni. 1999. *The Long Twentieth Century.* London: Verso.

Association of Greater Manchester Authorities. 1993. "Greater Manchester Economic Strategy and Operational Programme." Manchester: Association of Greater Manchester Authorities.

Atwater, Elton. 1976. "Philadelphia's Quest to Become the Permanent Headquarters of the United Nations." *Pennsylvania Magazine of History and Biography* 100:243–286.

Axon, W.E.A. 1886. *Annals of Manchester.* Manchester: John Heywood.

Ayerst, David. 1971. Guardian, *Biography of a Newspaper.* London: Collins.

Bagwell, Philip, and Peter Lyth. 2002. *Transport in Britain.* London: Hambledon and London.

Bailey, Elizabeth E., David R. Graham, and Daniel P. Kaplan. 1985. *Deregulating the Airlines.* Cambridge, MA: MIT Press.

Baines, Dudley. 1994. "European Labor Markets, Emigration, and Internal Migration, 1850–1913." In *Migration and the International Labor Market, 1850–1939,* edited by Timothy J. Hatton and Jeffrey G. Williamson, 35–54. London: Routledge.

Baker, Robert B. 1999. "The American Medical Ethics Revolution." In *The American Medical Ethics Revolution,* edited by Robert B. Baker, Arthur L. Caplan, Linda L. Emanuel, and Stephen R. Latham, 17–51. Baltimore: Johns Hopkins University Press.

Baker, Robert B., Arthur L. Caplan, Linda L. Emanuel, and Stephen R. Latham, eds. 1999. *The American Medical Ethics Revolution.* Baltimore: Johns Hopkins University Press.

Balan, Jorge, Harley L. Browning, and Elizabeth Jelin. 1973. *Men in a Developing Society.* Austin: University of Texas Press.

Baltzell, E. Digby. 1958. *Philadelphia Gentlemen*. New Brunswick, NJ: Transaction.
———. 1979. *Puritan Boston and Quaker Philadelphia*. New York: Free Press.
Barnekov, Timothy, Robin Boyle, and Daniel Rich. 1989. *Privatism and Urban Policy in Britain and the United States*. New York: Oxford University Press.
Barnes, William R., and Larry C. Ledebur. 1998. *The New Regional Economies*. Thousand Oaks, CA: Sage.
Barnet, Richard J., and Ronald E. Muller. 1974. *Global Reach*. New York: Simon and Schuster.
Barr, Kenneth. 1991. "From Dhaka to Manchester: Factories, Cities, and the World-Economy, 1600–1900." In *Cities in the World-System*, edited by Resat Kasaba, 81–96. New York: Greenwood Press.
Bartelt, David. 1989. "Renewing Center City Philadelphia: Whose City? Which Public's Interests?" In *Unequal Partnerships*, edited by Gregory D. Squires, 80–102. New Brunswick, NJ: Rutgers University Press.
Basant, Rakesh, and Pankaj Chandra. 2007. "Role of Educational and R&D Institutions in City Clusters: An Exploratory Study of Bangalore and Pune Regions in India." *World Development* 35:1037–1055.
Bassett, Keith. 1996. "Partnerships, Business Elites, and Urban Politics: New Forms of Governance in an English City?" *Urban Studies* 33:539–555.
Beauregard, Robert A. 1989. "The Spatial Transformation of Postwar Philadelphia." In *Atop the Urban Hierarchy*, edited by Robert A. Beauregard, 195–238. Totowa, NJ: Rowman and Littlefield.
———. 1990. "Tenacious Inequalities: Politics and Race in Philadelphia." *Urban Affairs Quarterly* 25:420–434.
———. 1996. "City Planning and the Postwar Regime in Philadelphia." In *Reconstructing Urban Regime Theory*, edited by Mickey Lauria, 171–188. Thousand Oaks, CA: Sage.
Bednarek, Janet R. Daly. 2001. *America's Airports*. College Station: Texas A&M University Press.
Beers, Dorothy G. 1982. "The Centennial City, 1865–1876." In *Philadelphia: A 300-Year History*, edited by Russell F. Weigley, 417–470. New York: W. W. Norton.
Belden, Bob. 1993. "One Plan for Selling the 'City." *Philadelphia Inquirer*, 17 February, p. F1.
Belden, Tom. 1997. "US Airways Maps Airport Expansion." *Philadelphia Inquirer*, 4 November, p. A1, A10.
Bennett, Vivienne. 1995. *The Politics of Water*. Pittsburgh: University of Pittsburgh Press.
Berlant, Jeffrey L. 1975. *Profession and Monopoly*. Berkeley: University of California Press.
Bianchini, Franco, and Michael Parkinson, eds. 1994. *Cultural Policy and Urban Regeneration*. New York: Manchester University Press.
Binzen, Peter. 1970. *Whitetown USA*. New York: Vintage.
Birks, J. B., ed. 1962. *Rutherford at Manchester*. London: Heywood.
Bissinger, Buzz. 1997. *A Prayer for the City*. New York: Random House.
Bizup, Joseph. 2003. *Manufacturing Culture*. Charlottesville: University of Virginia Press.
Boasberg, Leonard W. 1991. "Culture Shock." *Philadelphia Inquirer*, 22 November, p. D1.

———. 1992. "Outlook for a New Concert Hall: Bleak." *Philadelphia Inquirer*, 16 February, p. F1.

Boldt, David R. 1989. "If Cleveland Can Come Back, Why Not Philadelphia?" *Philadelphia Inquirer*, 17 September, p. C7.

Boli, John, and George M. Thomas, eds. 1999a. *Constructing World Culture*. Stanford, CA: Stanford University Press.

———. 1999b. "INGOs and the Organization of World Culture." In *Constructing World Culture*, edited by John Boli and George M. Thomas, 13–49. Stanford, CA: Stanford University Press.

Bonacich, Edna. 1972. "A Theory of Ethnic Antagonism: The Split Labor Market." *American Sociological Review* 37:547–559.

Bourne, Stephen. 1877. "On the Increasing Dependence of This Country upon Foreign Supplies for Food." *Transactions of the Manchester Statistical Society* 1876–1877:156–181.

Bowker, B. 1928. *Lancashire Under the Hammer*. London: Leonard and Virginia Woolf.

Braudel, Fernand. 1984. *The Perspective of the World*. Berkeley: University of California Press.

Brenner, Neil. 1999. "Beyond State-Centrism? Space, Territoriality, and Geographical Scale in Globalization Studies." *Theory and Society* 28:39–78.

———. 2004. *New State Spaces*. New York: Oxford University Press.

Breton, Raymond. 1964. "Institutional Completeness of Ethnic Communities and the Personal Relations of Immigrants." *American Journal of Sociology* 70:193–205.

Bridenbaugh, Carl. 1938. *Cities in the Wilderness*. New York: Ronald Press.

———. 1955. *Cities in Revolt*. New York: Alfred A. Knopf.

Bridenbaugh, Carl, and Jessica Bridenbaugh. 1942. *Rebels and Gentlemen*. New York: Reynal and Hitchcock.

Briggs, Asa. 1959. "The Local Background of Chartism." In *Chartist Studies*, edited by Asa Briggs, 1–28. London: Macmillan.

———. 1963. *Victorian Cities*. New York: Harper Colophon.

British Olympic Bid Committee. n.d. "Manchester 96: Driving the Dream." Manchester: British Olympic Bid Committee.

Brockbank, William. 1952. *Portrait of a Hospital*. London: William Heinemann.

Brown, Adam, Justin O'Connor, and Sara Cohen. 2000. "Local Music Policies within a Global Music Industry: Cultural Quarters in Manchester and Sheffield." *Geoforum* 31:437–451.

Brown, Dee. 1966. *The Year of the Century: 1876*. New York: Charles Scribner's Sons.

Brown, John K. 1995. *The Baldwin Locomotive Works, 1831–1915*. Baltimore: Johns Hopkins University Press.

Brown, Lucy. 1959. "The Chartists and the Anti–Corn Law League." In *Chartist Studies*, edited by Asa Briggs, 342–371. London: Macmillan.

Browne, Gary L. 1980. *Baltimore in the Nation, 1789–1861*. Chapel Hill: University of North Carolina Press.

Bruch, Laura J. 1994. "City Art School Lands Major Patron." *Philadelphia Inquirer*, 15 March, p. B1.

Burgess, George H., and Miles C. Kennedy. 1949. *Centennial History of the Pennsylvania Railroad Company*. Philadelphia: Pennsylvania Railroad.

Burt, Nathaniel. 1963. *The Perennial Philadelphians*. Boston: Little, Brown.

Burt, Nathaniel, and Wallace E. Davies. 1982. "The Iron Age, 1876–1905." In *Philadelphia: A 300-Year History*, edited by Russell F. Weigley, 471–523. New York: W. W. Norton.

Burt, Struthers. 1945. *Philadelphia, Holy Experiment*. Garden City, NY: Doubleday, Doran.

Burton, Cynthia, and Clea Benson. 2000. "Ballpark Site Choice May Bring a Suit." *Philadelphia Inquirer*, 6 May, p. A1.

Cardwell, D.S.L. 1968. "John Dalton and the Manchester School of Science." In *John Dalton and the Progress of Science*, edited by D.S.L. Cardwell, 1–9. Manchester: Manchester University Press.

———. 1976. "Science and Technology: The Work of James Prescott Joule." *Technology and Culture* 17:674–687.

Carey, Henry C. 1963. *Principles of Social Science*. New York: Augustus M. Kelley.

Carlyle, Thomas. 1971. *Selected Writings*. Harmondsworth, UK: Penguin.

Caruana, Viv, and Colin Simmons. 1996. "Municipal Enterprise in Pursuit of Profit: Manchester Airport, 1945–78." *Manchester Region History Review* 10:62–69.

"Census Lost 25,000 People." 2003. BBC News, 4 November. Available at http://news.bbc.co.uk/2/hi/uk_news/england/manchester/3240307.stm (accessed 5 November 2003).

Central Manchester Development Corporation. 1996. "Eight Years of Achievement, 1988–1996." Manchester: Central Manchester Development Corporation.

Central Philadelphia Development Corporation. 1991. "Annual Report 1991: 35 Years." Philadelphia: CPDC.

———. 1992. "South Broad Street Economic and Cultural Development Plan." Philadelphia: CPDC.

Champion, Sarah. 1990. *And God Created Manchester*. Manchester: Wordsmith.

Chandler, Alfred D., Jr. 1977. *The Visible Hand*. Cambridge, MA: Harvard University Press.

Chapman, Sydney J. 1904. *The Lancashire Cotton Industry*. Manchester: Manchester University Press.

Charles, Camille Zubrinsky. 2003. "The Dynamics of Racial Residential Segregation." *Annual Review of Sociology* 29:167–207.

Charlton, H. B. 1951. *Portrait of a University, 1851–1951*. Manchester: Manchester University Press.

Chase-Dunn, Christopher. 1989. *Global Formation*. Oxford: Blackwell.

Checkland, S. G. 1964. *The Rise of Industrial Society in England, 1815–1885*. London: Longmans.

Citizens of Pennsylvania. 1878. *Testimonial to Daniel J. Morrell*. Philadelphia: Allen, Lane and Scott.

Clark, Dennis. 1973a. *The Irish in Philadelphia: Ten Generations of Urban Experience*. Philadelphia: Temple University Press.

———. 1973b. "Urban Blacks and Irishmen: Brothers in Prejudice." In *Black Politics in Philadelphia*, edited by Miriam Ershkowitz and Joseph Zikmund, 15–30. New York: Basic.

Clarke, Iain. 1985. *The Spatial Organisation of Multinational Corporations*. New York: St. Martin's Press.

Clarke, P. F. 1971. *Lancashire and the New Liberalism*. Cambridge: Cambridge University Press.

Clarke, Susan E., and Gary L. Gaile. 1997. "Local Politics in a Global Era: Thinking Locally, Acting Globally." In *Globalization and the Changing U.S. City*, edited by David Wilson, 28–43. Thousand Oaks, CA: Sage.

Clow, Archie. 1968. "The Industrial Background to John Dalton." In *John Dalton and the Progress of Science*, edited by D.S.L. Cardwell, 125–139. Manchester: Manchester University Press.

Cochrane, Allan, Jamie Peck, and Adam Tickell. 1996. "Manchester Plays Games: Exploring the Local Politics of Globalisation." *Urban Studies* 33:1319–1336.

———. 2002. "Olympic Dreams: Visions of Partnership." In *City of Revolution*, edited by Jamie Peck and Kevin Ward, 95–115. Manchester: Manchester University Press.

Cohen, Robert B. 1981. "The New International Division of Labor, Multinational Corporations and Urban Hierarchy." In *Urbanization and Urban Planning in Capitalist Society*, edited by Michael Dear and Allen J. Scott, 287–315. New York: Methuen.

Contosta, David R., and Carol L. Franklin. 2006. "Community Advocacy and Volunteerism in Wissahickon Park, 1895–2005." In *Social Capital in the City*, edited by Richardson Dilworth, 56–78. Philadelphia: Temple University Press.

Cooke, Morris L. 1919. *Our Cities Awake*. Garden City, NY: Doubleday, Page.

Copley, Frank B. 1923. *Frederick W. Taylor: Father of Scientific Management*. New York: Taylor Society.

Cordato, Mary Francis. 1983. "Towards a New Century: Women and the Philadelphia Centennial Exhibition, 1876." *Pennsylvania Magazine of History and Biography* 107:113–136.

Crane, Diana. 2002. "Culture and Globalization." In *Global Culture: Media, Arts, Policy, and Globalization*, edited by Diana Crane, Nobuko Kawashima, and Ken'ichi Kawasaki, 1–25. New York: Routledge.

Crawford, W. H. 1962. "A Cosmopolitan City." In *Rich Inheritance*, edited by N. J. Frangopulo, 109–122. Manchester: Manchester Education Committee.

Cronon, William. 1991. *Nature's Metropolis*. New York: W. W. Norton.

Cruickshank, M. J. 1974. "From Mechanics' Institution to Technical School, 1850–92." In *Artisan to Graduate*, edited by D.S.L. Cardwell, 134–156. Manchester: Manchester University Press.

Darden, Joe T., Richard Child Hill, June Thomas, and Richard Thomas. 1987. *Detroit: Race and Uneven Development*. Philadelphia: Temple University Press.

Dasgupta, Simanti. 2008. "Success, Market, Ethics: Information Technology and the Shifting Politics of Governance and Citizenship in the Indian Silicon Plateau." *Cultural Dynamics* 20:213–244.

Daughen, Joseph R., and Peter Binzen. 1971. *The Wreck of the Penn Central*. Boston: Little, Brown.

———. 1977. *The Cop Who Would Be King*. Boston: Little, Brown.

Davis, Patricia T. 1978. *End of the Line*. New York: Neale Watson Academic Publications.

Dawson, Andrew. 2000. "Reassessing Henry Carey (1793–1879): The Problems of Writing Political Economy in Nineteenth-Century America." *Journal of American Studies* 34:465–485.

Dechert LLC. 2010. http://www.dechert.com/offices/offices.jsp?pg=home.

de Frantz, Monika. 2005. "From Cultural Regeneration to Discursive Governance: Constructing the Flagship of the 'Museumsquartier Vienna' as a Plural Symbol of Change." *International Journal of Urban and Regional Research* 29:50–66.

Delaware River Port Authority. 1971. "Report of Commissioners." Camden, NJ: DRPA.

———. 1994. "Comprehensive Annual Financial Report." Camden, NJ: DRPA.

Delaware Valley Regional Planning Council. 1993. "Rating the Region: The State of the Delaware Valley." Philadelphia: Delaware Valley Regional Planning Council.

Devine, Fiona, Nadia Joanne Britton, Rosemary Mellor, and Peter Halfpenny. 2000. "Work, Family, Space, and Time across the Life-Course." Paper presented at British Sociological Association Annual Conference, Leeds, 17–20 April.

Dicken, Peter. 1986. *Global Shift*. London: Harper and Row.

———. 1992. "Manchester's Economy in a Global Context." *Manchester Geographer* 13:3–18.

———. 2002. "Global Manchester: From Globaliser to Globalised." In *City of Revolution*, edited by Jamie Peck and Kevin Ward, 18–33. Manchester: Manchester University Press.

Dicken, Peter, and P. E. Lloyd. 1979. "The Contribution of Foreign Owned Forms to Regional Employment Change." Manchester: University of Manchester, North West Industry Research Unit.

Dickens, Charles. 1854. *Hard Times*. Harmondsworth, UK: Penguin.

DiGaetano, Alan, and John S. Klemanski. 1999. *Power and City Governance*. Minneapolis: University of Minnesota Press.

DiGaetano, Alan, and Paul Lawless. 1999. "Urban Governance and Industrial Decline: Governing Structures and Policy Agendas in Birmingham and Sheffield, England, and Detroit, Michigan, 1980–1997." *Urban Affairs Review* 34:546–577.

Dilger, Robert J. 2003. *American Transportation Policy*. Westport, CT: Praeger.

Directory of Corporate Affiliations. 1999. *Directory of Corporate Affiliations*. New Providence, NJ: National Register Publishing.

Disraeli, Benjamin. 1948. *Coningsby*. London: John Lehmann.

DiStefano, Joseph N. 1998a. "Mergers Aside, Area a Hub of Financial Services." *Philadelphia Inquirer*, 3 May, pp. D1–D2.

———. 1998b. "Some Find a Silver Lining in Pending Amex Merger." *Philadelphia Inquirer*, 11 June, pp. D1–D2.

DuBois, W.E.B. 1996. *The Philadelphia Negro*. Philadelphia: University of Pennsylvania Press.

Duncan, Beverly, and Stanley Lieberson. 1970. *Metropolis and Region in Transition*. Beverly Hills, CA: Sage.

Ekstrom, Charles A. 1973. "The Electoral Politics of Reform and Machine: The Political Behavior of Philadelphia's 'Black' Wards, 1943–1969." In *Black Politics in Philadelphia*, edited by Miriam Ershkowitz and Joseph Zikmund, 84–108. New York: Basic Books.

Elbaum, Bernard, and William Lazonick. 1986. "An Institutional Perspective on British Decline." In *The Decline of the British Economy*, edited by Bernard Elbaum and William Lazonick, 1–17. Oxford: Clarendon Press.

Engels, Friedrich. 1958. *The Condition of the Working Class in England*. Oxford: Basil Blackwell.

Erie, Steven P. 1988. *Rainbow's End*. Berkeley: University of California Press.

Fairhill, David. 1980. "Northern Gateway." *Manchester Guardian*, 18 February, p. 11.

Farnie, D. A. 1979. *The English Cotton Industry and the World Market, 1815–1896*. Oxford: Clarendon Press.

———. 1980. *The Manchester Ship Canal and the Rise of the Port of Manchester, 1894–1975*. Manchester: Manchester University Press.

Fazey, Ian Hamilton. 1995. "Half Mile Bubbles Over." *Financial Times*, 20 February.

Feffer, Andrew. 2003. "The Land Belongs to the People: Reframing Urban Protest in Post-Sixties Philadelphia." In *The World the Sixties Made*, edited by Van Gosse and Richard Moser, 67–97. Philadelphia: Temple University Press.

Feldberg, Michael. 1973. "Urbanization as a Cause of Violence: Philadelphia as a Test Case." In *The Peoples of Philadelphia*, edited by Allen F. Davis and Mark H. Haller, 53–69. Philadelphia: Temple University Press.

Fielding, Steve. 1988. "Irish Politics in Manchester, 1890–1914." *International Review of Social History* 33:261–284.

———. 1992. "A Separate Culture? Irish Catholics in Working-Class Manchester and Salford, c. 1890–1939." In *Workers' Worlds*, edited by Andrew Davies and Steven Fielding, 23–48. Manchester: Manchester University Press.

Finke, Ulrich. 1985. "The Art-Treasures Exhibition." In *Art and Architecture in Victorian Manchester*, edited by John H. G. Archer, 102–126. Manchester: Manchester University Press.

Fischer, Claude S. 1975. "Toward a Subcultural Theory of Urbanism." *American Journal of Sociology* 80:1319–1341.

Fisher, Sidney George. 1967. *A Philadelphia Perspective: The Diary of Sidney George Fisher Covering the Years 1834–1871*. Philadelphia: Historical Society of Pennsylvania.

Fletcher, A. Woodruffe. 1897. "The Economic Results of the Ship Canal in Manchester and the Surrounding Districts." *Transactions of the Manchester Statistical Society* 1896–1897:83–108.

———. 1899. "The Economic Results of the Ship Canal on Manchester and Surrounding Districts, II." *Transactions of the Manchester Statistical Society* 1898–1899:156–169.

Fletcher, David E. 1992. *England's North West*. Manchester: Civic Trust in the North West.

Fogg, William. 1893. "Workers in Cotton Factories and the Eight Hours' Day." *Transactions of the Manchester Statistical Society* 1892–1893:1–24.

Foner, Eric. 1970. *Free Soil, Free Labor, Free Men*. New York: Oxford University Press.

Foner, Nancy. 2005. *In a New Land*. New York: New York University Press.

Fowler, Alan. 2003. *Lancashire Cotton Operatives and Work, 1900–1950*. Burlington, VT: Ashgate.

Fowler, Alan, and Terry Wyke. 1993. *Many Arts, Many Skills*. Manchester: Manchester Metropolitan University Press.

Frangopulo, N. J. 1965. "Foreign Communities in Victorian Manchester." *Manchester Review* 10:189–207.

Franklin, Benjamin. 1986. *The Autobiography and Other Writings*. New York: Penguin.

Freedley, Edwin T. 1859. *Philadelphia and Its Manufactures*. Philadelphia: Edward Young.

———. 1867. *Philadelphia and Its Manufactures*. Philadelphia: Edward Young.

Friedman, Thomas L. 2007. *The World Is Flat*. New York: Farrar, Straus and Giroux.

Friedmann, John. 1986. "The World City Hypothesis." *Development and Change* 17:69–84.

———. 1995. "Where We Stand: A Decade of World City Research." In *World Cities in a World-System*, edited by Paul L. Knox and Peter J. Taylor, 21–47. New York: Cambridge University Press.

Friedmann, John, and Goetz Wolff. 1982. "World City Formation: An Agenda for Research and Action." *International Journal of Urban and Regional Research* 6:309–343.

Frobel, F., J. Heinrichs, and Otto Kreye. 1980. *The New International Division of Labour*. Cambridge: Cambridge University Press.

Gadian, D. S. 1993. "Class Consciousness in Oldham and Other North-West Industrial Towns, 1830–50." In *The Victorian City*, edited by R. J. Morris and Richard Rodger, 243–257. London: Longman.

Gamble, Kenny, and Leon Huff. 1997. "The Philly Sound." New York: Sony Music Entertainment.

Gammage, Jeff. 2004. "Chinatown Is Choking." *Philadelphia Inquirer*, 15 February, p. M1.

Garrard, John. 1983. *Leadership and Power in Victorian Industrial Towns*. Manchester: Manchester University Press.

Gartner, Michael, ed. 1971. *Riding the Pennsy to Ruin*. Princeton, NJ: Dow Jones Books.

Garvan, Anthony N. B. 1963. "Proprietary Philadelphia as an Artifact." In *The Historian and the City*, edited by Oscar Handlin and John Burchard, 177–201. Cambridge, MA: MIT Press.

Gatell, Frank O. 1966. "Sober Second Thoughts on Van Buren, the Albany Regency, and the Wall Street Conspiracy." *Journal of American History* 53:19–40.

Gatrell, V.A.C. 1982. "Incorporation and the Pursuit of Liberal Hegemony in Manchester, 1790–1839." In *Municipal Reform and the Industrial City*, edited by Derek Fraser, 15–60. New York: St. Martin's Press.

Geffen, Elizabeth M. 1982. "Industrial Development and Social Crisis, 1841–1854." In *Philadelphia: A 300-Year History*, edited by Russell F. Weigley, 307–362. New York: W. W. Norton.

Gelbart, Marcia. 2001. "Airport Seeking Money—and Fast." *Philadelphia Inquirer*, 8 May, p. E1.

George, John. 1997. "Foreign Patients Focus of Hospitals." *Philadelphia Business Journal*, 14 November, p. 1.

Gibbons, Herbert A. 1926. *John Wanamaker*. Port Washington, NY: Kennikat Press.

Giddens, Anthony. 1981. *A Contemporary Critique of Historical Materialism*. London: Macmillan.

———. 1984. *The Constitution of Society*. Berkeley: University of California Press.

———. 1990. *The Consequences of Modernity*. Stanford, CA: Stanford University Press.

Gillette, Howard, Jr. 1970. "Corrupt and Contented: Philadelphia's Political Machine, 1865–1887." Ph.D. thesis, Yale University.

————. 1980. "The Emergence of the Modern Metropolis: Philadelphia in the Age of Its Consolidation." In *The Divided Metropolis*, edited by William W. Cutler III and Howard Gillette Jr., 3–26. Westport, CT: Greenwood Press.

Giordano, Benito, and Laura Twomey. 2002. "Economic Transitions: Restructuring Local Labour Markets." In *City of Revolution*, edited by Jamie Peck and Kevin Ward, 50–75. Manchester: Manchester University Press.

Glaab, Charles N., and A. Theodore Brown. 1983. *A History of Urban America*. New York: Macmillan.

Glassberg, David. 1983. "Public Ritual and Cultural Hierarchy: Philadelphia's Civic Celebrations at the Turn of the Century." *Pennsylvania Magazine of History and Biography* 107:421–448.

Golab, Caroline. 1973. "The Immigrant and the City: Poles, Italians, and Jews in Philadelphia, 1870–1920." In *The Peoples of Philadelphia*, edited by Allen F. Davis and Mark H. Haller, 203–230. Philadelphia: Temple University Press.

————. 1977. *Immigrant Destinations*. Philadelphia: Temple University Press.

González, Sara. 2006. "Scalar Narratives in Bilbao: A Cultural Politics of Scales Approach to the Study of Urban Policy." *International Journal of Urban and Regional Research* 30:836–857.

Goode, Judith, and Jo Anne Schneider. 1994. *Reshaping Ethnic and Racial Relations in Philadelphia: Immigrants in a Divided City*. Philadelphia: Temple University Press.

Goodrich, Carter. 1960. *Government Promotion of American Canals and Railroads, 1800–1890*. New York: Columbia University Press.

Gorenstein, Nathan. 1997. "Pact to Reopen Shipyard Is Signed." *Philadelphia Inquirer*, 22 October, p. A1.

Graham, Edward M., and Paul R. Krugman. 1993. "The Surge in Foreign Direct Investment in the 1980s." In *Foreign Direct Investment*, edited by Kenneth A. Froot, 13–36. Chicago: University of Chicago Press.

————. 1995. *Foreign Direct Investment in the United States*. Washington, DC: Institute for International Economics.

Great Britain. 1854. *Census of Great Britain in 1851*. London: Longman, Brown, Green, and Longmans.

————. 1891. *Census of England and Wales, 1891*. London: HMSO.

————. 1913. *Census of England and Wales, 1911*. London: HMSO.

————. 1953. *Census of England and Wales*. London: HMSO.

————. 1973. *Census of England and Wales*. London: HMSO.

————. 1982. *Census of England and Wales*. London: HMSO.

————. 1991. *Census of England and Wales*. London: HMSO.

Great Britain, Office for National Statistics. 2001. *Census of England and Wales*. London: HMSO.

————. 2004. *Census 2001: Key Statistics for Urban Areas in the South East*. London: TSO.

Great Britain, Office of Population Censuses and Surveys. 1982. *Census 1981: County Reports*. London: HMSO.

Greater Manchester Council. 1975. "Employment and the Economy." Manchester: Greater Manchester Council.

Greater Philadelphia First. 1999. "Our People, Our Region." Philadelphia: GPF.

Greater Philadelphia First Corporation. 1986. "Making Greater Philadelphia First." Philadelphia: GPFC.

Green, Arnold W. 1951. *Henry Charles Carey*. Philadelphia: University of Pennsylvania Press.

Gunn, Simon. 1992. "The Manchester Middle Class, 1850–1880." Ph.D. thesis, University of Manchester.

———. 2000. *The Public Culture of the Victorian Middle Class*. Manchester: Manchester University Press.

Guthrie, Jonathan. 2007. "Internet Age to Revive Forum Where Victorians Traded Rail Shares." *Financial Times*, 30 March, p. A5.

Haber, Samuel. 1964. *Efficiency and Uplift: Scientific Management in the Progressive Era, 1890–1920*. Chicago: University of Chicago Press.

Haines, Michael R. 1981. "Poverty, Economic Stress, and the Family in a Late-Nineteenth-Century American City: Whites in Philadelphia, 1880." In *Philadelphia: Work, Space, Family, and Group Experience in the 19th Century*, edited by Theodore Hershberg, 240–276. New York: Oxford University Press.

Hall, Jessica. 1991. "Master of the Arts." *Philadelphia* (October): 49–51.

Hall, Peter. 2001. "Global City-Regions in the Twenty-first Century." In *Global City-Regions*, edited by Allen J. Scott, 59–77. New York: Oxford University Press.

Hambleton, Robin, Hank V. Savitch, and Murray Stewart, eds. 2003. *Globalism and Local Democracy*. New York: Palgrave Macmillan.

Hammond, Bray. 1957. *Banks and Politics in America from the Revolution to the Civil War*. Princeton, NJ: Princeton University Press.

Hammond, J. L. 1934. *C. P. Scott of the* Manchester Guardian. London: G. Bell and Sons.

Hannerz, Ulf. 1997. "Scenarios for Peripheral Cultures." In *Culture, Globalization, and the World-System*, edited by Anthony D. King, 107–128. Minneapolis: University of Minnesota Press.

Hannigan, John. 1998. *Fantasy City*. London: Routledge.

Harford, Ian. 1994. *Manchester and Its Ship Canal Movement*. Staffordshire, UK: Keele University Press.

Harnetty, Peter. 1972. *Imperialism and Free Trade: Lancashire and India in the Mid-Nineteenth Century*. Vancouver: University of British Columbia Press.

Harris, Linda K. 2000. "Philadelphia Seeks to Attract More Immigrants." *Philadelphia Inquirer*, 18 October, pp. B1–B5.

———. 2001. "Over a Decade, Downtown Finds New Life." *Philadelphia Inquirer*, 20 March.

Hartz, Louis. 1948. *Economic Policy and Democratic Thought: Pennsylvania, 1776–1860*. Chicago: Quadrangle Books.

Haslam, Dave. 1999. *Manchester England: The Story of the Pop Cult City*. London: Fourth Estate.

Haughton, Graham, and Aidan While. 1999. "From Corporate City to Citizens City? Urban Leadership *After* Local Entrepreneurialism in the United Kingdom." *Urban Affairs Review* 35:3–23.

Häussermann, Hartmut, and Anne Haila. 2004. "The European City: A Conceptual Framework and Normative Project." In *Cities of Europe*, edited by Yuri Kazepov, 43–64. Malden, MA: Blackwell.

Heitzman, James. 2004. *Network City*. New York: Oxford University Press.

Henderson, W. O. 1934. *The Lancashire Cotton Famine, 1861–1865*. Manchester: Manchester University Press.

Henry, Ian P., and Juan Luis Paramio-Salcines. 1999. "Sport and the Analysis of Symbolic Regimes: A Case Study of the City of Sheffield." *Urban Affairs Review* 34:641–666.

Herd, Dean, and Terry Patterson. 2002. "Poor Manchester: Old Problems and New Deals." In *City of Revolution*, edited by Jamie Peck and Kevin Ward, 190–213. Manchester: Manchester University Press.

Hershberg, Theodore. 1981. "Free Blacks in Antebellum Philadelphia: A Study of Ex-Slaves, Freeborn, and Socioeconomic Decline." In *Philadelphia: Work, Space, Family, and Group Experience in the 19th Century*, edited by Theodore Hershberg, 368–391. New York: Oxford University Press.

———. 1994. "Regionalism." *Philadelphia Inquirer*, 11 September, p. E5.

Hershberg, Theodore, Stephanie W. Greenberg, Alan N. Burstein, William L. Yancey, and Eugene P. Ericksen. 1981. "A Tale of Three Cities: Blacks, Immigrants, and Opportunity in Philadelphia, 1850–1880, 1930, 1970." In *Philadelphia: Work, Space, Family, and Group Experience in the 19th Century*, edited by Theodore Hershberg, 461–491. New York: Oxford University Press.

Hertz, Gerald B. 1912. *The Manchester Politician, 1750–1912.* London: Sherratt and Hughes.

Hetherington, Peter. 1984. "Test of Left Strength." *Manchester Guardian*, 17 May, p. 17.

———. 1993. "Readiness Is All." *Manchester Guardian*, 14 June (Special Supplement on the Olympics 2000 bid).

Hewitt, Martin. 1996. *The Emergence of Stability in the Industrial City: Manchester, 1832–67.* Aldershot, UK: Scolar Press.

Heyck, T. W. 1982. *The Transformation of Intellectual Life in Victorian England.* New York: St. Martin's Press.

Hill, Christopher R. 1996. *Olympic Politics.* Manchester: Manchester University Press.

Hilton, J. A. 1994. *Catholic Lancashire.* Chichester, UK: Philimore.

Hine, Thomas. 1992. "The Arts as an Avenue to Restore South Broad Street's Leading Role." *Philadelphia Inquirer*, 13 September, p. N1.

Hobbs, Heidi. 1994. *City Hall Goes Abroad.* Newbury Park, CA: Sage.

Hobsbawm, Eric J. 1968. *Industry and Empire.* London: Weidenfeld and Nicolson.

———. 1984. *Worlds of Labour.* London: Weidenfeld and Nicolson.

Hobson, J. A. 1919. *Richard Cobden: The International Man.* New York: Henry Holt.

Hochheiser, Sheldon. 1986. *Rohm and Haas: History of a Chemical Company.* Philadelphia: University of Pennsylvania Press.

Hodos, Jerome. 2001. "Second Cities: Globalist Development Strategies and Local Political Culture." *Jahrbuch fur Wirtschaftsgeschichte* 2001:27–45.

———. 2002. "Globalization, Regionalism, and Urban Restructuring: The Case of Philadelphia." *Urban Affairs Review* 37:358–379.

———. 2006. "The 1876 Centennial in Philadelphia: Elite Networks and Political Culture." In *Social Capital in the City*, edited by Richardson Dilworth, 19–39. Philadelphia: Temple University Press.

———. 2007. "Globalization and the Concept of the Second City." *City and Community* 6, no. 4 (December 2007): 315–333.

Hoge, Warren. 2001. "Rioting in Britain Gives Voice to Silent Minorities." *New York Times*, 29 May, p. A1.

Holden, Adam. 2002. "Bomb Sites: The Politics of Opportunity." In *City of Revolution*, edited by Jamie Peck and Kevin Ward, 133–154. Manchester: Manchester University Press.

Holston, James, and Arjun Appadurai. 1996. "Cities and Citizenship." *Public Culture* 8:187–204.

Howe, Anthony. 1984. *The Cotton Masters, 1830–1860*. Oxford: Clarendon Press.

———. 1997. *Free Trade and Liberal England, 1846–1946*. Oxford: Clarendon Press.

Huler, Scott. 1989. "Why Can't We Be Like Cleveland?" *Philadelphia* (October): 99–107.

Hymer, Stephen. 1979. *The Multinational Corporation*. Cambridge: Cambridge University Press.

Hytner Commission. 1981. "Report of the Moss Side Enquiry Panel to the Leader of the Greater Manchester Council." Manchester: Greater Manchester Council.

Infield, Tom. 1986. "Russians among Us." *Philadelphia Inquirer*, 12 October, p. 14.

International Directory of Corporate Affiliations. 1981. *International Directory of Corporate Affiliations 1981/82*. Skokie, IL: National Register Publishing.

———. 1991. *International Directory of Corporate Affiliations*. Wilmette, IL: National Register Publishing.

Itzkoff, Donald M. 1985. *Off the Track*. Westport, CT: Greenwood Press.

Jessop, Bob. 1996. "A Neo-Gramscian Approach to the Regulation of Urban Regimes." In *Reconstructing Urban Regime Theory*, edited by Mickey Lauria, 51–73. Thousand Oaks, CA: Sage.

Johnson, David R. 1973. "Crime Patterns in Philadelphia, 1840–70." In *The Peoples of Philadelphia*, edited by Allen F. Davis and Mark H. Haller, 89–110. Philadelphia: Temple University Press.

Jonas, Andrew E. G., and David Wilson, eds. 1999. *The Urban Growth Machine*. Albany: State University of New York Press.

Joyce, Patrick. 1980. *Work, Society and Politics*. London: Methuen.

Judd, Dennis, and Michael Parkinson, eds. 1990. *Leadership and Urban Regeneration*. Newbury Park, CA: Sage.

Juliani, Richard N. 1980. *The Social Organization of Immigration*. New York: Arno Press.

———. 1998. *Building Little Italy*. University Park: Pennsylvania State University Press.

Kadaba, Lini S. 1998. "They Find Niche, and Fuel Economy." *Philadelphia Inquirer*, 22 November, p. B1.

Kaiser, Carl W., Jr. 1939. "History of the Academic Protectionist-Free Trade Controversy in America Before 1860." Ph.D. thesis, University of Pennsylvania.

Kanter, Rosabeth Moss. 1995. *World Class: Thriving Locally in the Global Economy*. New York: Simon and Schuster.

Kaplan, Herbert H. 2006. *Nathan Mayer Rothschild and the Creation of a Dynasty*. Stanford, CA: Stanford University Press.

Kargon, Robert H. 1977. *Science in Victorian Manchester*. Baltimore: Johns Hopkins University Press.

Katznelson, Ira. 1973. *Black Men, White Cities*. London: Oxford University Press.

———. 1981. *City Trenches*. Chicago: University of Chicago Press.

Kay, James Phillips. 1832. *The Moral and Physical Condition of the Working Classes*. London: James Ridgway.

Kazal, Russell A. 1998. "Becoming 'Old Stock': The Waning of German-American Identity in Philadelphia, 1900–1930." Ph.D. thesis, University of Pennsylvania.

Keeling, David J. 1995. "Transport and the World City Paradigm." In *World Cities in a World-System*, edited by Paul L. Knox and Peter J. Taylor, 115–131. New York: Cambridge University Press.

Kelly, Elinor. 1990. "Transcontinental Families, Gujarat and Lancashire: A Comparative Study." In *South Asians Overseas*, edited by Colin Clarke, Ceri Peach, and Steven Vertovec, 251–268. Cambridge: Cambridge University Press.

Kennedy, Michael. 1970. *Portrait of Manchester*. London: Robert Hale.

Kidd, Alan J. 1985. "Introduction: The Middle Class in Nineteenth-Century Manchester." In *City, Class, and Culture*, edited by Alan J. Kidd and K. W. Roberts, 1–24. Manchester: Manchester University Press.

Kidd, Alan J., and K. W. Roberts, eds. 1985. *City, Class, and Culture: Studies of Social Policy and Cultural Production in Victorian Manchester*. Manchester: Manchester University Press.

Kindleberger, Charles P. 2000. *Comparative Political Economy*. Cambridge, MA: MIT Press.

King, Anthony. 1998. *The End of the Terraces*. London: Leicester University Press.

King, Anthony D. 1990a. *Global Cities*. London: Routledge.

———. 1990b. *Urbanism, Colonialism and the World-Economy*. New York: Routledge.

———, ed. 1997. *Culture, Globalization and the World-System*. Minneapolis: University of Minnesota Press.

———. 2004. *Spaces of Global Cultures*. New York: Routledge.

Kirby, Andrew, Sallie Marston, and Kenneth Seasholes. 1995. "World Cities and Global Communities: The Municipal Foreign Policy Movement and New Roles for Cities." In *World Cities in a World-System*, edited by Paul L. Knox and Peter J. Taylor, 267–279. New York: Cambridge University Press.

Kirk, Neville. 1985. *The Growth of Working-Class Reformism in Mid-Victorian England*. London: Croom Helm.

Kleniewski, Nancy. 1984. "From Industrial to Corporate City: The Role of Urban Renewal." In *Marxism and the Metropolis*, edited by William K. Tabb and Larry Sawers, 205–222. New York: Oxford University Press.

Knox, Paul L. 1995. "World Cities in a World-System." In *World Cities in a World-System*, edited by Paul L. Knox and Peter J. Taylor, 3–20. New York: Cambridge University Press.

Koss, Joan Dee. 1965. "Puerto Ricans in Philadelphia: Migration and Accommodation." Ph.D. thesis, University of Pennsylvania.

Koval, John P., Larry Bennett, Michael I. J. Bennett, Fassil Demissie, Roberta Garner, and Kiljoong Kim, eds. 2006. *The New Chicago*. Philadelphia: Temple University Press.

Kresl, Peter Karl. 1992. *The Urban Economy and Regional Trade Liberalization*. New York: Praeger.

Kresl, Peter Karl, and Gary Gappert, eds. 1995. *North American Cities and the Global Economy*. Thousand Oaks, CA: Sage.

"Labour Rebellion." 1983. *Manchester Guardian*, 17 March, p. 6.

Lane, Roger. 1986. *Roots of Violence in Black Philadelphia, 1860–1900*. Cambridge, MA: Harvard University Press.

Large, Peter. 1982. "Where the Computer Industry Started." *Manchester Guardian*, 15 February, p. 13.

Larson, Magali Sarfatti. 1977. *The Rise of Professionalism*. Berkeley: University of California Press.

Lauria, Mickey, ed. 1996. *Reconstructing Urban Regime Theory*. Thousand Oaks, CA: Sage.

Laurie, Bruce, Theodore Hershberg, and George Alter. 1981. "Immigrants and Industry: The Philadelphia Experience, 1850–1880." In *Philadelphia: Work, Space, Family, and Group Experience in the 19th Century*, edited by Theodore Hershberg, 93–119. New York: Oxford University Press.

Laurie, Bruce, and Mark Schmitz. 1981. "Manufacture and Productivity: The Making of an Industrial Base, Philadelphia, 1850–1880." In *Philadelphia: Work, Space, Family, and Group Experience in the 19th Century*, edited by Theodore Hershberg, 43–92. New York: Oxford University Press.

Law, C. M., and E. K. Grime. 1993. "Salford Quays 1: The Context." In *Urban Waterside Regeneration*, edited by K. N. White, E. G. Bellinger, A. J. Saul, M. Symes, and K. Hendry, 72–81. London: Ellis Harwood.

Layton-Henry, Zig. 1994. "Britain: The Would-Be Zero-Immigration Country." In *Controlling Immigration*, edited by Wayne A. Cornelius, Philip L. Martin, and James F. Hollifield, 273–296. Stanford, CA: Stanford University Press.

Lee, Jennifer. 2002. *Civility in the City*. Cambridge, MA: Harvard University Press.

Leech, Bosdin. 1907. *History of the Manchester Ship Canal from Its Inception to Its Completion*. Manchester: Sherratt and Hughes.

Lemon, James T. 1967. "Urbanization and the Development of Eighteenth-Century Southeastern Pennsylvania and Adjacent Delaware." *William and Mary Quarterly* 24:501–542.

Lever, W. F. 1997. "Delinking Urban Economies: The European Experience." *Journal of Urban Affairs* 19:227–238.

Levine, Marc V. 1989a. "The Politics of Partnership: Urban Redevelopment since 1945." In *Unequal Partnerships: The Political Economy of Urban Redevelopment in Postwar America*, edited by Gregory D. Squires, 12–34. New Brunswick, NJ: Rutgers University Press.

———. 1989b. "Urban Redevelopment in a Global Economy: The Cases of Montreal and Baltimore." In *Cities in a Global Society*, edited by Richard V. Knight and Gary Gappert, 141–152. Newbury Park, CA: Sage.

Lewis, Brian. 2001. *The Middlemost and the Milltowns*. Stanford, CA: Stanford University Press.

Lewis, James. 1981. "Mistrust Deepens between Police and Inner-City Blacks." *Manchester Guardian*, 8 June, p. 3.

———. 1982a. "Labour Council's Savage Cuts Anger Party." *Manchester Guardian*, 28 January, p. 2.

———. 1982b. "Labour Right Wins Top Jobs on Council." *Manchester Guardian*, 15 May, p. 3.

———. 1982c. "Revolt Looms on Heseltine's Cuts Demand." *Manchester Guardian*, 25 January, p. 2.

———. 1982d. "Roots of a Conflict." *Manchester Guardian*, 29 March, p. 13.

———. 1983. "Labour Council Members Defy Party Line." *Manchester Guardian*, p. 26.

Licht, Walter. 1992. *Getting Work*. Philadelphia: University of Pennsylvania Press.

Lieberson, Stanley. 1980. *A Piece of the Pie: Blacks and White Immigrants since 1880*. Berkeley: University of California Press.

Light, Ivan, and Edna Bonacich. 1988. *Immigrant Entrepreneurs: Koreans in Los Angeles, 1965–1982*. Berkeley: University of California Press.

Lim, Nelson. 2001. "On the Backs of Blacks? Immigrants and the Fortunes of African Americans." In *Strangers at the Gates*, edited by Roger Waldinger, 186–227. Berkeley: University of California Press.

Lin, Jan. 1998. "Globalization and the Revalorizing of Ethnic Places in Immigration Gateway Cities." *Urban Affairs Review* 34:313–339.

Lin, Jennifer. 1993. "In Kensington, Two Groups Live So Close, Yet So Far Away." *Philadelphia Inquirer*, 8 August, p. A1.

———. 2000a. "Chinatown Fears It Will Lose Its Way." *Philadelphia Inquirer*, 14 June, p. A1.

———. 2000b. "Chinatown Triumphant." *Philadelphia Inquirer*, 26 November, p. 12.

Lindstrom, Diane. 1978. *Economic Development in the Philadelphia Region, 1810–1850*. New York: Columbia University Press.

Lippincott, Joanna Wharton. 1909. *Biographical Memoranda Concerning Joseph Wharton*. Philadelphia: J. B. Lippincott.

Livingood, James W. 1947. *The Philadelphia-Baltimore Trade Rivalry, 1780–1860*. Harrisburg: Pennsylvania Historical and Museum Commission.

Lloyd, Richard. 2004. "The Neighborhood in Cultural Production: Material and Symbolic Resources in the New Bohemia." *City and Community* 3:343–372.

Lloyd-Jones, Roger, and M. J. Lewis. 1988. *Manchester and the Age of the Factory*. London: Croom Helm.

Logan, John R., and Harvey L. Molotch. 1987. *Urban Fortunes*. Berkeley: University of California Press.

London Stock Exchange. 2010. http://www.londonstockexchange.com/about-the-exchange/company-overview/our-history/our-history.htm.

Lounsberry, Emilie. 1998. "Made (Poor) in America." *Philadelphia Inquirer*, 3 May, p. A1.

Lowe, Benjamin. 2001. "US Airways Cuts 1,100 Jobs at City Airport." *Philadelphia Inquirer*, 28 September, p. C1.

Lubetkin, M. John. 2006. *Jay Cooke's Gamble*. Norman: University of Oklahoma Press.

Luce, Thomas F., and Anita A. Summers. 1987. *Local Fiscal Issues in the Philadelphia Metropolitan Area*. Philadelphia: University of Pennsylvania Press.

Lyall, Sarah. 2001a. "In Ravaged English City, Racial Mix Was Volatile." *New York Times*, 31 May. Available at http://www.nytimes.com/2001/05/31/world/in-ravaged-english-city-racial-mix-was-volatile.html?scp=1&sq=sarah+lyall&st=nyt (accessed 12 November 2010).

———. 2001b. "Shadowy Party Heats Up British Racial Tensions." *New York Times*, 4 July. Available at http://www.nytimes.com/2001/07/04/world/shadowy-party-heats-up-british-racial-tensions.html?scp=1&sq=sarah+lyall&st=nyt (accessed 12 November 2010).

Lyons, Donald, and Scott Salmon. 1995. "World Cities, Multinational Corporations, and Urban Hierarchy: The Case of the United States." In *World Cities in a World-System*, edited by Paul L. Knox and Peter J. Taylor, 98–114. New York: Cambridge University Press.

MacDonald, Stuart. 1985. "The Royal Manchester Institution." In *Art and Architecture in Victorian Manchester*, edited by John H. G. Archer, 28–45. Manchester: Manchester University Press.

Madden, Janice Fanning, and William J. Stull. 1991. *Work, Wages, and Poverty: Income Distribution in Postindustrial Philadelphia*. Philadelphia: University of Pennsylvania Press.

Madigan, Charles, ed. 2004. *Global Chicago*. Urbana: University of Illinois Press.

Manchester Airport. 1991. "Annual Report 1990/91." Manchester: Manchester Airport.

———. 2007. "About Our Airport and Our Group." Manchester Airport. Available at http://www.manchesterairport.co.uk/manweb.nsf/Content/AboutUsAndOurGroup (accessed 28 November 2010).

———. n.d. "Monthly Passenger Statistics for December 2005." Manchester Airport. Available at http://www.manchesterairport.co.uk/manweb.nsf/Content/TrafficStatisticsArchive (accessed 30 January 2007).

Manchester and Salford Inner Area Partnership Research Group. 1978. "Subject Papers." Manchester: Manchester and Salford Inner Area Study.

Manchester Chamber of Commerce. 1839 (1996). "Report in the Manchester Chamber of Commerce on the Destructive Effects of the Corn Laws." In *The Corn Laws: The Formation of Popular Economics in Britain*, edited by Alon Kadish, 157–272. London: William Pickering.

———. 1883. "Sixty-Second Annual Report of the Directors." Manchester: Manchester Chamber of Commerce.

Manchester City Council. 1993. "Economic Development Strategy." Manchester: Manchester City Council.

———. 1994. "City Pride: Prospectus for Consultation." Manchester: Manchester City Council.

———. 1995a. "All Set for the Golden Games." Manchester: Manchester City Council.

———. 1995b. *Manchester: 50 Years of Change*. London: HMSO.

Manchester City Planning Department. 1981a. *Planning and Economic Bulletin #2*. Manchester: City Planning Department.

———. 1981b. *Planning and Economic Bulletin #4*. Manchester: City Planning Department.

———. 1982. *Planning and Economic Bulletin #5*. Manchester: City Planning Department.

———. 1986. "Castlefield Urban Heritage Park." *Planning and Economic Bulletin* #13: 34–39.

———. 1987. "Manchester Airport: Recent Developments and Future Expansion." *Planning and Economic Bulletin* #14: 42–46.

Manchester City Pride. 1997. "City Pride 2: Partnerships for a Successful Future." Manchester: Manchester City Pride.

Manchester Guardian. 1857a. "The Art Treasures Exhibition." *Manchester Guardian*, 5 May, p. 3.

———. 1857b. *A Handbook to the Manchester Art Treasures Exhibition*. London: Bradbury and Evans.

———. 1857c. "Handbook to the Gallery of British Paintings." In *A Handbook to the Manchester Art Treasures Exhibition*, 4–5. London: Bradbury and Evans.

———. 1857d. "Handbook to the Museum of Ornamental Art." In *A Handbook to the Manchester Art Treasures Exhibition*, 4–5. London: Bradbury and Evans.

———. 1857e. "Opening of the Art Treasures Exhibition." *Manchester Guardian*, 6 May, p. 3.

———. 1882. "The Proposed Manchester Ship Canal." *Manchester Guardian*, 28 June, p. 6.

———. 1894a. "Manchester in 1894." *Manchester Guardian*, 1 January, pp. 3–5.

———. 1894b. "Opening of Manchester Ship Canal." *Manchester Guardian*, 2 January, p. 5.

———. 1894c. "Summary of News—Yesterday Morning." *Manchester Guardian*, 2 January, p. 4.

———. 1894d. "Summary of News: The Queen's Visit." *Manchester Guardian*, 22 May, p. 7.

Manchester International Airport Authority. 1982. "Annual Report 1981/82." Manchester: Manchester International Airport Authority.

Manchester Literary and Philosophical Society. 1852. "Memoirs of the Literary and Philosophical Society of Manchester." Manchester: Manchester Literary and Philosophical Society.

Manchester Millennium. 1997. "Rebuilding Manchester." Manchester: Manchester Millennium.

Markusen, Ann R. 1999. "Four Structures for Second Tier Cities." In *Second Tier Cities*, edited by Ann R. Markusen, Yong-Sook Lee, and Sean DiGiovanna, 21–41. Minneapolis: University of Minnesota Press.

Markusen, Ann R., Yong-Sook Lee, and Sean DiGiovanna, eds. 1999. *Second-Tier Cities*. Minneapolis: University of Minnesota Press.

Mason, Tony. 1980. *Association Football and English Society, 1863–1915*. Brighton, UK: Harvester Press.

Massey, Douglas S., Joaquin Arango, Graeme Hugo, Ali Kouaouci, Adela Pellegrino, and J. Edward Taylor. 1998. *Worlds in Motion*. New York: Oxford University Press.

Massey, Douglas S., and Nancy A. Denton. 1993. *American Apartheid: Segregation and the Making of the Underclass*. Cambridge, MA: Harvard University Press.

Maynard, Micheline. 2005. "U.S. Air Picks Its Path; Two Airlines Still Looking." *New York Times*, 28 September. Available at http://www.nytimes.com/2005/09/28/business/28bankrupt.html?sq=micheline%20maynard&st=nyt&adxnnl=1&scp=1&adxnnlx=1289761400-fT3K9xkiXlQqws5UIN3r1Q (accessed 12 November 2010).

McCaffery, Peter. 1993. *When Bosses Ruled Philadelphia*. University Park: Pennsylvania State University Press.

McClure, Alexander K. 1905. *Old Time Notes of Pennsylvania*. Philadelphia: John C. Winston.

McCord, Norman. 1958. *The Anti–Corn Law League, 1838–1846*. London: George Allen and Unwin.

McFaul, John M. 1972. *The Politics of Jacksonian Finance*. Ithaca, NY: Cornell University Press.

McGrane, Reginald C. 1965. *The Panic of 1837*. New York: Russell and Russell.

McGurty, Frank. 1994. "New Authority Spans the River." *Financial Times*, 4 May (Special Supplement).

McNeill, Donald. 1999. *Urban Change and the European Left*. London: Routledge.

Medcalf, William. 1854. "On the Municipal Institutions of the City of Manchester." *Transactions of the Manchester Statistical Society* 1853–1854:17–32.

Mellor, Rosemary. 1989. "Transitions in Urbanization: Twentieth-Century Britain." *International Journal of Urban and Regional Research* 13:573–595.

———. 1997. "Cool Times for a Changing City." In *Transforming Cities*, edited by Nick Jewson and Susanne MacGregor, 56–69. London: Routledge.

Merttens, F. 1901. "The Growth of Foreign Competition." *Transactions of the Manchester Statistical Society* 1900–1901:107–141.

Messinger, Gary S. 1985. *Manchester in the Victorian Age*. Manchester: Manchester University Press.

Meyer, David R. 1986. "The World System of Cities: Relations between International Financial Metropolises and South American Cities." *Social Forces* 64:553–581.

———. 1991. "Change in the World System of Metropolises: The Role of Business Intermediaries." *Urban Geography* 12:393–416.

Meyer, John. 1980. "The World Polity and the Authority of the Nation-State." In *Studies of the Modern World-System*, edited by Albert Bergesen, 109–13. New York: Academic Press.

Meyers, Marvin. 1957. *The Jacksonian Persuasion*. Stanford, CA: Stanford University Press.

Milestone, Katie. 1996. "Regional Variations: Northernness and New Urban Economies of Hedonism." In *From the Margins to the Centre*, edited by Justin O'Connor and Derek Wynne, 91–116. Aldershot, UK: Arena.

Miller, Richard G. 1982. "The Federal City, 1783–1800." In *Philadelphia: A 300-Year History*, edited by Russell F. Weigley, 155–207. New York: W. W. Norton.

Mills, William Haslam. 1921. *The* Manchester Guardian*: A Century of History*. London: Chatto and Windus.

———. 1922. *The Manchester Reform Club, 1871–1921*. Manchester: Charles Hobson.

Millward, Pauline. 1985. "The Stockport Riots of 1852: A Study of Anti-Catholic and Anti-Irish Sentiment." In *The Irish in the Victorian City*, edited by Roger Swift and Sheridan Gilley, 207–224. London: Croom Helm.

Mole, Phil. 1996. "Fordism, Post-Fordism, and the Contemporary City." In *From the Margins to the Centre*, edited by Justin O'Connor and Derek Wynne, 15–48. Aldershot, UK: Arena.

Mollenkopf, John H. 1978. "The Postwar Politics of Urban Development." In *Marxism and the Metropolis*, edited by William K. Tabb and Larry Sawers, 117–152. New York: Oxford University Press.

Mollenkopf, John H., and Manuel Castells, eds. 1991. *Dual City: Restructuring New York*. New York: Russell Sage Foundation.

Molotch, Harvey. 1976. "The City as a Growth Machine: Toward a Political Economy of Place." *American Journal of Sociology* 82:309–332.

Moon, Tom. 2000. "The Philadelphia Story." *Vibe* (October): 122–128.

Morais, Henry Samuel. 1894. *The Jews of Philadelphia*. Philadelphia: Levytpe.

Morley, John. 1890. *Life of Richard Cobden*. Boston: Roberts Brothers.

Morris, Michael. 1981. "Anderton Orders Inquiry into Riot Police 'Brutality.'" *Manchester Guardian*, 22 July, p. 26.

———. 1984. "Following the Boys in the Halle Band." *Manchester Guardian*, 19 March, p. 19.

Morris, Michael, Malcolm Pithers, Robin Thornber, and Nikki Knewstub. 1981. "1,000 on Rampage in Moss Side." *Manchester Guardian*, 9 July, p. 1.

Morrison, Steven A., and Clifford Winston. 1995. *The Evolution of the Airline Industry*. Washington, DC: Brookings Institution.

Muller, Thomas. 1993. *Immigrants and the American City*. New York: New York University Press.

Mumford, Lewis. 1938. *The Culture of Cities*. New York: Harcourt Brace Jovanovich.

———. 1961. *The City in History*. New York: Harcourt Brace Jovanovich.

Nasdaq OMX. 2010. "PHLX." http://www.phlx.com.

Nash, Gary B. 1979. *The Urban Crucible*. Cambridge, MA: Harvard University Press.

———. 1988. *Forging Freedom*. Cambridge, MA: Harvard University Press.

Neal, Frank. 1990. "Manchester Origins of the English Orange Order." *Manchester Region History Review* 4:12–24.

Nelson, Daniel. 1980. *Frederick W. Taylor and the Rise of Scientific Management*. Madison: University of Wisconsin Press.

Nicholls, Robert. 1996. *Trafford Park: The First Hundred Years*. Chichester, UK: Philimore.

Nisenson, Eric. 1993. *Ascension: John Coltrane and His Quest*. New York: Da Capo.

———. 1997. *Blue: The Murder of Jazz*. New York: Da Capo.

NOMIS (National Online Manpower Information System). 2007. "2001 Census Standard Tables." NOMIS. Available at http://www.nomisweb.co.uk (accessed 28 February 2007).

Noyelle, Thierry J., and Anna B. Dutka. 1988. *International Trade in Business Services*. Cambridge, MA: Ballinger.

Noyelle, Thierry, and Thomas M. Stanback Jr. 1984. *The Economic Transformation of American Cities*. Totowa, NJ: Rowman and Allanheld.

Oberholtzer, Ellis P. 1907. *Jay Cooke: Financier of the Civil War*. New York: Burt Franklin.

O'Connor, Justin, and Derek Wynne. 1996. "Left Loafing: City Cultures and Postmodern Lifestyles." In *From the Margins to the Centre*, edited by Justin O'Connor and Derek Wynne, 49–90. Aldershot, UK: Arena.

Oestreich, James R. 2001. "Philadelphia Gets a New Concert Hall a Century Aborning." *New York Times*, 9 December, pp. AE35–AE36.

O'Hearn, Denis. 1994. "Innovation and the World-System Hierarchy: British Subjugation of the Irish Cotton Industry, 1780–1830." *American Journal of Sociology* 100:587–621.

"Or Should It Be Avenue? Learning Something from the French." 1993. *Philadelphia Inquirer*, 22 November, p. A14.

Orr, Marion E., and Gerry Stoker. 1994. "Urban Regimes and Leadership in Detroit." *Urban Affairs Quarterly* 30:48–73.

Owen, David. 1983. *The Manchester Ship Canal*. Manchester: Manchester University Press.

———. 1996. "Size, Structure and Growth of the Ethnic Minority Populations." In *Ethnicity in the 1991 Census*, edited by David Coleman and John Salt, 80–123. London: HMSO.

Parkinson-Bailey, John J. 2000. *Manchester: An Architectural History*. Manchester: Manchester University Press.

Parsons, J.C.G. 1904. *The Centenary of the Manchester Royal Exchange, 1804–1904*. Manchester: George Falkner and Sons/Manchester Royal Exchange.

Patten, Simon. 1890. *The Economic Basis of Protection*. Philadelphia: J. B. Lippincott.

Patterson, Elizabeth C. 1970. *John Dalton and the Atomic Theory*. Garden City, NY: Doubleday.

Peck, Jamie, and Adam Tickell. 1994. "Searching for a New Institutional Fix: The *After*-Fordist Crisis and the Global-Local Disorder." In *Post-Fordism: A Reader*, edited by Ash Amin, 280–315. Cambridge, MA: Blackwell.

———. 1995. "Business Goes Local: Dissecting the 'Business Agenda' in Manchester." *International Journal of Urban and Regional Research* 19:55–78.

Peck, Jamie, and Kevin Ward, eds. 2002. *City of Revolution*. Manchester: Manchester University Press.

Peirce, Neal R. 1993. *Citistates*. Washington, DC: Seven Locks Press.

Peirce, Neal R., and Curtis W. Johnson. 1995. "Reinventing the Region: The Peirce Report." *Philadelphia Inquirer*, 26 March (Special Supplement).

Petshek, Kirk R. 1973. *The Challenge of Urban Reform*. Philadelphia: Temple University Press.

Petzinger, Thomas, Jr. 1995. *Hard Landing*. New York: Random House/Times Business.

Philadelphia City Planning Commission. 1988. *The Plan for Center City*. Philadelphia: Philadelphia City Planning Commission.

Philadelphia International Airport. 2007. "About Philadelphia International Airport." Philadelphia International Airport. Available at http://www.phl.org/about.html (accessed 28 November 2010).

Philadelphia Orchestra Association. 1992. *Riccardo Muti: Twenty Years in Philadelphia*. Philadelphia: Philadelphia Orchestra Association.

Philadelphia Stock Exchange. 1992. "Annual Report." Philadelphia: Philadelphia Stock Exchange.

Pickering, Paul A. 1995. *Chartism and the Chartists in Manchester and Salford*. New York: St. Martin's Press.

Pieda plc. 1993. "Regional Economic Strategy for North West England." Manchester: North West Business Leadership Team.

Platt, Harold L. 2005. *Shock Cities*. Chicago: University of Chicago Press.

Pooley, Colin G., and Shani D'Cruze. 1994. "Migration and Urbanization in North-West England circa 1760–1830." *Social History* 19:339–358.

Portes, Alejandro. 1998. "Economic Sociology and the Sociology of Immigration: A Conceptual Overview." In *The Economic Sociology of Immigration*, edited by Alejandro Portes, 1–41. New York: Russell Sage Foundation.

Portes, Alejandro, and Robert D. Manning. 1986. "The Immigrant Enclave: Theory and Empirical Examples." In *Competitive Ethnic Relations*, edited by Susan Olzak and Joane Nagel, 47–68. Orlando, FL: Academic Press.

Port of Manchester. 1901. "Official Sailing List." Manchester: Port of Manchester.

———. 1902. "Official Sailing List." Manchester: Port of Manchester.

Potter, John E. 1876. *Hand-Book to the Centennial Grounds and Fairmount Park*. Philadelphia: John E. Potter.

Power, Edward. 1988. "Asian Immigrants Lend New Life to City's Sewing Industry." *Philadelphia Inquirer*, 28 February, p. A1.

Quilley, Stephen. 1995. "Economic Transformations and Local Strategy in Manchester." Ph.D. thesis, University of Manchester.

———. 1999. "Entrepreneurial Manchester: The Genesis of Elite Consensus." *Antipode* 31:185–211.

———. 2000. "Manchester First: From Municipal Socialism to the Entrepreneurial City." *International Journal of Urban and Regional Research* 24:601–615.

———. 2002. "Entrepreneurial Turns: Municipal Socialism and After." In *City of Revolution*, edited by Jamie Peck and Kevin Ward, 76–94. Manchester: Manchester University Press.

Radakrishnan, Smitha. 2008. "Examining the 'Global' Indian Middle Class: Gender and Culture in the Silicon Valley/Bangalore Circuit." *Journal of Intercultural Studies* 29:7–20.

Randel, William Peirce. 1969. *Centennial: American Life in 1876*. Philadelphia: Chilton Book.

Ravenscroft, Richard S. 1994. "Don't Turn the Academy of Music into a Sort of Halfway House." *Philadelphia Inquirer*, 10 July, p. C7.

Read, Donald. 1958. *Peterloo: The "Massacre" and Its Background*. Manchester: Manchester University Press.

———. 1959. "Chartism in Manchester." In *Chartist Studies*, edited by Asa Briggs, 29–64. London: Macmillan.

Redfield, Robert, and Milton Singer. 1969. "The Cultural Role of Cities." In *Classic Essays on the Culture of Cities*, edited by Richard Sennett, 206–233. Englewood Cliffs, NJ: Prentice-Hall.

Redford, Arthur. 1934. *Manchester Merchants and Foreign Trade, 1794–1858*. Manchester: Manchester University Press.

———. 1940. *The History of Local Government in Manchester*. London: Longmans, Green.

———. 1956. *Manchester Merchants and Foreign Trade*. Vol. 2, *1850–1939*. Manchester: Manchester University Press.

———. 1964. *Labour Migration in England, 1800–1850*. Manchester: Manchester University Press.

Reed, Howard C. 1981. *The Preeminence of International Financial Centers*. New York: Praeger.

Rees, Philip, and Deborah Phillips. 1996. "Geographical Patterns in a Cluster of Pennine Cities." In *Ethnicity in the 1991 Census*, edited by Peter Ratcliffe, 271–293. London: HMSO.

Reeves, Hope. 2001. "A Trail of Refuse." *New York Times Magazine*, 18 February, p. 14.

Rhodes, Martin. 1996. "Globalization, the State and the Restructuring of Regional Economies." In *Globalization and Public Policy*, edited by Philip Gummett, 161–180. Cheltenham, UK: Edward Elgar.

Rhor, Monica. 2001. "Chinatown Celebrates Victory without a Stadium." *Philadelphia Inquirer*, 15 January, p. B1.

Richardson, Edgar P. 1982. "The Athens of America, 1800–1825." In *Philadelphia: A 300-Year History*, edited by Russell F. Weigley, 208–257. New York: W. W. Norton.

Robbins, Keith. 1979. *John Bright*. London: Routledge and Kegan Paul.

Roberts, Bryan. 1978a. "Agrarian Organization and Urban Development." In *Manchester and Sao Paulo*, edited by John D. Wirth and Robert L. Jones, 77–105. Stanford, CA: Stanford University Press.

———. 1978b. "Migration, the Industrial Economy and Collective Consumption." Paper presented at the UNESCO Conference on Migration in Mexico.

Roberts, Jeffrey P. 1980. "Railroads and the Downtown: Philadelphia, 1830–1900." In *The Divided Metropolis*, edited by William W. Cutler III and Howard Gillette Jr., 27–55. Westport, CT: Greenwood Press.

Roberts, Robert. 1971. *The Classic Slum*. London: Penguin.

Robertson, Roland. 1992. *Globalization: Social Theory and Global Culture*. Newbury Park, CA: Sage.

———. 1997. "Social Theory, Cultural Relativity, and the Problem of Globality." In *Culture, Globalization and the World-System*, edited by Anthony D. King, 69–90. Minneapolis: University of Minnesota Press.

Robson, Brian. 2002. "Mancunian Ways: The Politics of Regeneration." In *City of Revolution*, edited by Jamie Peck and Kevin Ward, 34–49. Manchester: Manchester University Press.

Rodgers, Brian. 1986. "Manchester: Metropolitan Planning by Collaboration and Consent; or Civic Hope Frustrated." In *Regional Cities in the UK, 1890–1980*, edited by George Gordon, 41–58. London: Harper and Row.

Rodgers, H. B. 1980. "Manchester Revisited: A Profile of Urban Change." In *The Continuing Conurbation*, edited by H. P. White, 26–36. Westmead, UK: Gower.

Roscoe, Henry E. 1895. *John Dalton and the Rise of Modern Chemistry*. New York: Macmillan.

Rose, Mary B. 2000. *Firms, Networks, and Business Values*. New York: Cambridge University Press.

Ross, Christopher. 1992. *The Urban System and Networks of Corporate Control*. Greenwich, CT: JAI Press.

Roth, Silke, and Susanne Frank. 2000. "Festivalization and the Media: Weimar, Cultural Capital of Europe 1999." *Cultural Policy* 6:219–241.

Rottenberg, Dan. 2001. *The Man Who Made Wall Street*. Philadelphia: University of Pennsylvania Press.

Rowe, Kenneth W. 1933. *Mathew Carey: A Study in American Economic Development*. Baltimore: Johns Hopkins University Press.

Roy, William G. 1997. *Socializing Capital*. Princeton, NJ: Princeton University Press.

Ruggie, John G. 1982. "International Regimes, Transactions, and Change: Embedded Liberalism in the Postwar Economic Order." *International Organization* 36:379–415.

Russell, Dave. 2000. "Musicians in the English Provincial City: Manchester, c. 1860–1914." In *Music and British Culture, 1785–1914*, edited by Christina Bashford and Leanne Langley, 233–253. New York: Oxford University Press.

Rutheiser, Charles. 1996. *Imagineering Atlanta*. New York: Verso.

Ryan, Rachel. 1937. *A Biography of Manchester*. London: Methuen.

Rydell, Robert W. 1984. *All the World's a Fair*. Chicago: University of Chicago Press.

Saffron, Inga. 1992. "Cultivating Culture." *Philadelphia Inquirer*, 13 September, p. N1.

———. 1993. "Le Grand Philly." *Philadelphia Inquirer*, 12 November, p. E1.

Salisbury, Stephan. 1992a. "Annenberg Donates to Arts Avenue." *Philadelphia Inquirer*, 12 December, p. A1.

———. 1992b. "Avenue of the Arts: A $60.6 Million Step." *Philadelphia Inquirer*, 2 December, p. A1.

———. 1993a. "Advocate for Arts." *Philadelphia Inquirer*, 17 June, p. G1.

———. 1993b. "Financial Support for the Arts Plunges." *Philadelphia Inquirer*, 6 December, p. A1.

———. 1994. "Millions Given to City Arts Corridor." *Philadelphia Inquirer*, 19 January, p. B1.

———. 1995. "Avenue of the Arts Is Sputtering." *Philadelphia Inquirer*, 12 May, p. A1.

Sallez, Alain, and Pierre Verot. 1991. "Strategies for Cities to Face Competition in the Framework of European Integration." *Ekistics* 58:292–298.

Salsbury, Stephen. 1982. *No Way to Run a Railroad*. New York: McGraw-Hill.

Sanderson, Michael. 1972. *The Universities and British Industry, 1850–1970*. London: Routledge and Kegan Paul.

Saragoza, Alex M. 1988. *The Monterrey Elite and the Mexican State, 1880–1940*. Austin: University of Texas Press.

Sass, Steven A. 1982. *The Pragmatic Imagination*. Philadelphia: University of Pennsylvania Press.

Sassen, Saskia. 1991. *The Global City: New York, London, Tokyo*. Princeton, NJ: Princeton University Press.

———. 1994. *Cities in a World Economy*. Thousand Oaks, CA: Sage.

———. 1996. "Whose City Is It? Globalization and the Formation of New Claims." *Public Culture* 8:205–223.

———. 1998. "Immigration and Local Labor Markets." In *The Economic Sociology of Immigration*, edited by Alejandro Portes, 87–127. New York: Russell Sage Foundation.

———. 2001a. "Global Cities and Global City-Regions: A Comparison." In *Global City-Regions*, edited by Allen J. Scott, 78–95. New York: Oxford University Press.

———. 2001b. *The Global City*. Princeton, NJ: Princeton University Press.

Saunders, Richard. 1978. *The Railroad Mergers and the Coming of Conrail*. Westport, CT: Greenwood Press.

———. 2003. *Main Lines*. DeKalb: Northern Illinois University Press.

Savitch, Hank V., and Paul Kantor. 2002. *Cities in the International Marketplace*. Princeton, NJ: Princeton University Press.

Scharf, J. Thomas, and Thompson Westcott. 1884. *History of Philadelphia, 1609–1884*. Philadelphia: L. H. Everts.

Schlegel, Marvin W. 1947. *Ruler of the Reading: The Life of Franklin B. Gowen, 1836–1889*. Harrisburg, PA: Archives Publishing Company of Pennsylvania.

Schlesinger, Arthur M., Jr. 1945. *The Age of Jackson*. New York: Book Find Club.

Schlosser, Eric. 1998. "Saturday Night at the Hacienda." *Atlantic Monthly* (October): 22–34.

Scholes, John. 1871. "Manchester Foreign Merchants." Manchester: Manchester Central Library.

Schopmeyer, Kim. 2000. "A Demographic Portrait of Arab Detroit." In *Arab Detroit*, edited by Nabeel Abraham and Andrew Shryock, 61–92. Detroit: Wayne State University Press.

Schotter, H. W. 1927. *The Growth and Development of the Pennsylvania Railroad Company*. Philadelphia: Allen Lane and Scott.

Scott, E. L. 1968. "Dalton and William Henry." In *John Dalton and the Progress of Science*, edited by D.S.L. Cardwell, 220–239. Manchester: Manchester University Press.

Scranton, Philip. 1983. *Proprietary Capitalism*. New York: Cambridge University Press.

———. 1989. *Figured Tapestry*. New York: Cambridge University Press.

Semmel, Bernard. 1970. *The Rise of Free Trade Imperialism*. Cambridge: Cambridge University Press.

Shaffer, Gwen. 2000. "Foreign Aid." *Philadelphia City Paper*, 23 November, pp. 23–29.

Shapiro, Howard. 1997. "Overseas Travel to Get a Big Boost." *Philadelphia Inquirer*, 4 November, p. A10.

Sharp, James R. 1970. *The Jacksonians versus the Banks*. New York: Columbia University Press.

Sharpless, John B. 1978. "Intercity Development and Dependency: Liverpool and Manchester." In *Manchester and Sao Paulo*, edited by John D. Wirth and Robert L. Jones, 131–156. Stanford, CA: Stanford University Press.

Sharratt, Tom. 1984. "'Rebels' Become Labour Leaders in Manchester." *Manchester Guardian*, 16 May, p. 3.

Shaw, Gareth. 1989. "Industrialization, Urban Growth, and the City Economy." In *The Rise and Fall of Great Cities*, edited by Richard Lawton, 55–79. London: Belhaven Press.

Shaw, William A. 1912. *Manchester Old and New*. London: Cassell.

Short, J. R., Y. Kim, M. Kuus, and H. Wells. 1996. "The Dirty Little Secret of World Cities Research: Data Problems in Comparative Analysis." *International Journal of Urban and Regional Research* 20:697–717.

Silver, Arthur W. 1966. *Manchester Men and Indian Cotton, 1847–72*. Manchester: Manchester University Press.

Silver, Vernon. 1998. "Regional Markets at Home on Computers." *Philadelphia Inquirer*, 22 February, p. D3.

Singer, Audrey, Domenic Vitiello, Michael Katz, and David Park. 2008. "Recent Immigration to Philadephia: Regional Change in an Emerging Gateway." Washington, DC: Brookings Institution.

Singleton, John. 1991. *Lancashire on the Scrapheap*. New York: Oxford University Press.

Sklair, Leslie. 1998. "Globalization and the Corporations: The Case of the California *Fortune* Global 500." *International Journal of Urban and Regional Research* 22:195–215.

Smelser, Neil J. 1959. *Social Change in the Industrial Revolution*. London: Routledge and Kegan Paul.

Smith, David. 1989. *North and South*. London: Penguin.

Smith, David, and Michael Timberlake. 2002. "Hierarchies of Dominance among World Cities: A Network Approach." In *Global Networks, Linked Cities*, edited by Saskia Sassen, 117–143. New York: Routledge.

Smith, J. B., and Jason Chapman. 1838. "Address of the Manchester Anti–Corn Law Association." *Manchester Guardian*, 12 December, p. 3.

Smith, Suzanne E. 1999. *Dancing in the Street*. Cambridge, MA: Harvard University Press.

Smith, Walter B. 1953. *Economic Aspects of the Second Bank of the United States*. Cambridge, MA: Harvard University Press.

Sokolove, Michael, and Peter Dobrin. 1994. "Powerful Foes Resist Moving Orchestra." *Philadelphia Inquirer*, 20 March, p. A1.

Spencer, Joseph. 1877. "The Growth of the Cotton Trade in Great Britain, America, and the Continent of Europe, during the Half Century Ending with the Year 1875." *Transactions of the Manchester Statistical Society* 1876–1877:231–240.

Spruyt, Hendrik. 1994. *The Sovereign State and Its Competitors*. Princeton, NJ: Princeton University Press.

Srinivas, Smriti. 2001. *Landscapes of Urban Memory*. Minneapolis: University of Minnesota Press.

Stanback, Thomas M., Jr., and Thierry Noyelle. 1982. *Cities in Transition*. Totowa, NJ: Allanheld, Osmun.

Steffens, Henry John. 1979. *James Prescott Joule and the Concept of Energy*. New York: Science History Publications/Neale Watson.

Steffens, Lincoln. 1904. *The Shame of the Cities*. New York: Peter Smith.

Stone, Clarence N. 1989. *Regime Politics*. Lawrence: University Press of Kansas.

Storper, Michael. 1997. *The Regional World*. New York: Guilford Press.

Strange, John Hadley. 1973. "Blacks and Philadelphia Politics: 1963–66." In *Black Politics in Philadelphia*, edited by Miriam Ershkowitz and Joseph Zikmund, 109–144. New York: Basic Books.

Stull, William J., and Janice Fanning Madden. 1990. *Post-Industrial Philadelphia*. Philadelphia: University of Pennsylvania Press.

Sugrue, Thomas J. 1996. *The Origins of the Urban Crisis*. Princeton, NJ: Princeton University Press.

Summers, Anita, and Thomas Luce. 1985. *Economic Report on the Philadelphia Metropolitan Region 1985*. Philadelphia: University of Pennsylvania Press.

Sumner, William G. 1896. *A History of Banking in the United States*. New York: Journal of Commerce and Commercial Bulletin.

Swenson, Deborah. 1993. "Foreign Mergers and Acquisitions in the United States." In *Foreign Direct Investment*, edited by Kenneth A. Froot, 255–283. Chicago: University of Chicago Press.

Taylor, Frank H., and Wilfred H. Schoff. 1912. *The Port and City of Philadelphia*. Philadelphia: International Congress of Navigation.

Taylor, Frederick W. 1911. *The Principles of Scientific Management*. New York: Harper and Brothers.

Taylor, George R. 1951. *The Transportation Revolution*. New York: Rinehart.

Taylor, Ian, Karen Evans, and Penny Fraser. 1996. *A Tale of Two Cities*. London: Routledge.

Taylor, Matthew. 1997. "Little Englanders: Tradition, Identity and Professional Football in Lancashire, 1880–1930." In *Football and Regional Identity in Europe*, edited by Siegfried Gehrmann, 33–48. Munster: Lit Verlag.

Taylor, Peter J. 1995. "World Cities and Territorial States: The Rise and Fall of Their Mutuality." In *World Cities in a World-System*, edited by Paul L. Knox and Peter J. Taylor, 48–62. New York: Cambridge University Press.

———. 2004. *World City Network*. New York: Routledge.

Taylor, Peter J., D.R.F. Walker, and J. V. Beaverstock. 2002. "Firms and Their Global Service Networks." In *Global Networks, Linked Cities*, edited by Saskia Sassen, 93–116. New York: Routledge.

Temple University. 2010. Office of International Services. Temple University. http://www.temple.edu/ois.

Thackray, Arnold. 1972. *John Dalton*. Cambridge, MA: Harvard University Press.
———. 1974. "Natural Knowledge in Cultural Context: The Manchester Model." *American Historical Review* 79:672–709.
Thomas, George, John Meyer, John Boli, and Francisco Ramirez. 1987. *Institutional Structure*. Newbury Park, CA: Sage.
Thompson, E. P. 1963. *The Making of the English Working Class*. New York: Vintage.
Thompson, Heather Ann. 2001. *Whose Detroit?* Ithaca, NY: Cornell University Press.
Thompson, Robert Ellis. 1875. *Social Science and National Economy*. Philadelphia: Porter and Coates.
Thornber, Robin. 1981. "Half-Time, Waiting for the Action." *Manchester Guardian*, 10 July, p. 4.
Tickell, Adam, and Jamie Peck. 1996. "The Return of the Manchester Men: Men's Words and Men's Deeds in the Remaking of the Local State." *Transactions of the Institute of British Geographers* 21:595–616.
Tickell, Adam, Jamie Peck, and Peter Dicken. 1995. "The Fragmented Region: Business, the State, and Economic Development in North West England." In *The Regions and the New Europe*, edited by Martin Rhodes, 247–272. Manchester: Manchester University Press.
Tilly, Charles. 1990. *Coercion, Capital, and European States*. Cambridge, MA: Basil Blackwell.
Tolles, Frederick B. 1948. *Meeting House and Counting House*. Chapel Hill: University of North Carolina Press.
———. 1960. *Quakers and the Atlantic Culture*. New York: Macmillan.
Trafford Park Development Corporation. 1997. "Company Census of the Trafford Park Urban Development Area." Manchester: Trafford Park Development Corporation.
Treuherz, Julian. 1985. "Ford Madox Brown and the Manchester Murals." In *Art and Architecture in Victorian Manchester*, edited by John H. G. Archer, 162–208. Manchester: Manchester University Press.
Tweedale, Geoffrey. 1986. "Transatlantic Specialty Steels: Sheffield High-Grade Steel Firms and the USA, 1860–1940." In *British Multinationals*, edited by Geoffrey Jones, 75–95. Aldershot, UK: Gower.
———. 1995. *Steel City*. Oxford: Clarendon Press.
Ung, Elisa, and Laura J. Bruch. 2000. "A Battle Cry beyond Chinatown." *Philadelphia Inquirer*, 8 June, p. A1.
Ung, Elisa, and Linda K. Harris. 2000. "In Chinatown, 1,500 Protest Stadium Plans." *Philadelphia Inquirer*, 9 June, p. B1.
Union League of Philadelphia. 1866. *Names of the Officers and Members of the Union League of Philadelphia*. Philadelphia: Sherman.
———. 1876. "Thirteenth Annual Report of the Board of Directors." Philadelphia: Union League.
University of Manchester. 2010. Office of Student Records. University of Manchester. http://www.manchester.ac.uk.
University of Salford. 2010. International Office. University of Salford. http://www.salford.ac.uk/international.
Update Manchester. 1997. "Focus on Wuhan." *Update Manchester* 2:19.
U.S. Army Corps of Engineers. 1990. "Waterborne Commerce of the United States." Fort Belvoir, VA: U.S. Army Corps of Engineers.

———. 2006. "Tonnage for Selected U.S. Ports in 2001." New Orleans, LA: Waterborne Commerce Statistics Center.

U.S. Bureau of the Census. 1854. *Compendium of the Seventh Census*. Washington: AOP Nicholson.

U.S. Census Office 1872. *Ninth Census of the United States, 1870*. Washington: Government Printing Office.

———. 1883. *Tenth Census of the United States, 1880*. Washington: Government Printing Office.

U.S. Department of Commerce. 1953. *County Business Patterns*. Washington, DC: Government Printing Office.

———. 2003. *County Business Patterns*. Washington, DC: Government Printing Office.

U.S. Department of Commerce, Bureau of the Census. 1892. *Eleventh Census of the United States, 1890*. Washington, DC: Government Printing Office.

———. 1914. *Census of Population and Housing*, vol. 4, Occupation Statistics. Washington, DC: Government Printing Office.

———. 1952. *Census of Population and Housing*. Washington, DC: Government Printing Office.

———. 1972. *Census of Population and Housing*. Washington, DC: Government Printing Office.

———. 1984a. *Census of Population and Housing*. Washington, DC: Government Printing Office.

———. 1984b. *Geographical Mobility for Metropolitan Areas*. Washington, DC: Government Printing Office.

———. 1992. *Census of Population and Housing*. Washington, DC: Government Printing Office.

———. 2000a. *Census 2000*. Table P159, "Poverty Status in 1999." Washington, DC: Government Printing Office. Available at http://factfinder.census.gov (accessed 25 November 2010).

———. 2000b. *Census 2000*. Table PCT049, "Residence in 1995 for the Population 5 Years and Over." Washington, DC: Government Printing Office. Available at http://factfinder.census.gov (accessed 25 November 2010).

———. 2000c. *Census 2000*. Table PCT075, "Sex by Age by Go-Outside-Home Disability by Employment for the Civilian Noninstitutionalized Population 16 years and Over." Washington, DC: Government Printing Office. Available at http://factfinder.census.gov (accessed 25 November 2010).

U.S. Department of Transportation. 1973. "Northeastern Railroad Problem: A Report to the Congress." Washington, DC: U.S. Department of Transportation.

U.S. Treasury Department. 1862. *Report of the Commerce and Navigation of the United States*. Washington, DC: Government Printing Office.

———. 1892. *Report of the Commerce and Navigation of the United States*. Washington, DC: Government Printing Office.

———. 1895. *Immigration and Passenger Movement at Ports of the United States During the Year Ending June 30, 1894*. Washington, DC: Government Printing Office.

———. 1912. *Report of the Commerce and Navigation of the United States*. Washington, DC: Government Printing Office.

Valdes, Lesley, and Thomas Hine. 1991. "New Plan for a New Concert Hall." *Philadelphia Inquirer*, 25 August, p. B1.

Vigier, Francois. 1970. *Change and Apathy*. Cambridge, MA: MIT Press.

Vitiello, Domenic, and George E. Thomas. 2010. *The Philadelphia Stock Exchange and the City It Made*. Philadelphia: University of Pennsylvania Press.

Wadsworth, Alfred P., and Julia de Lacy Mann. 1931. *The Cotton Trade and Industrial Lancashire, 1600–1780*. Manchester: Manchester University Press.

Wahl, William N. 1895. *The Franklin Institute of the State of Pennsylvania for the Promotion of the Mechanic Arts: A Sketch of Its Organization and History*. Philadelphia: Franklin Institute.

Wahrman, Drohr. 1995. *Imagining the Middle Class*. New York: Cambridge University Press.

Wainwright, Nicholas B. 1953. *History of the Philadelphia National Bank*. Philadelphia: Philadelphia National Bank.

———. 1982. "The Age of Nicholas Biddle, 1825–1841." In *Philadelphia: A 300-Year History*, edited by Russell F. Weigley, 258–306. New York: W. W. Norton.

Waldinger, Roger. 1996. *Still the Promised City?* Cambridge, MA: Harvard University Press.

———. 2001a. "Strangers at the Gates." In *Strangers at the Gates*, edited by Roger Waldinger, 1–29. Berkeley: University of California Press.

———, ed. 2001b. *Strangers at the Gates*. Berkeley: University of California Press.

Waldinger, Roger, and Jennifer Lee. 2001. "New Immigrants in Urban America." In *Strangers at the Gates*, edited by Roger Waldinger, 30–79. Berkeley: University of California Press.

Wallerstein, Immanuel. 1974. *The Modern World System*. London: Academic Press.

Walls, Nina de Angeli. 1993. "Art and Industry in Philadelphia: Origins of the Philadelphia School of Design for Women, 1848 to 1876." *Pennsylvania Magazine of History and Biography* 117:177–199.

Walter, E. V. 1976. "Manchester Town Hall: The City as a Work of Art." Manuscript, University of Manchester, Department of Sociology.

Wanamaker, John. 1911. *Golden Book of the Wanamaker Stores*. Philadelphia: John Wanamaker.

Ward, Robin H. 1975. "Residential Succession and Race Relations in Moss Side, Manchester." Ph.D. thesis, University of Manchester.

Warner, John H. 1999. "The 1880s Rebellion against the AMA Code of Ethics: 'Scientific Democracy' and the Dissolution of Orthodoxy." In *The American Medical Ethics Revolution*, edited by Robert B. Baker, Arthur L. Caplan, Linda L. Emanuel, and Stephen R. Latham, 52–69. Baltimore: Johns Hopkins University Press.

Warner, Sam Bass, Jr. 1963. "Innovation and the Industrialization of Philadelphia, 1800–1850." In *The Historian and the City*, edited by Oscar Handlin and John Burchard, 63–69. Cambridge, MA: MIT Press.

———. 1968. *The Private City: Philadelphia in Three Periods of Its Growth*. Philadelphia: University of Pennsylvania Press.

Warner, Susan. 2000. "Now to Make a Drug Merger Work." *Philadelphia Inquirer*, 24 December, pp. E1–E5.

Warner, Susan, and Neill A. Borowski. 1994. "Factories Back in Business." *Philadelphia Inquirer*, 4 December, pp. A1–A14.

Warner, Susan, and Ken Dilanian. 1999. "Shipbuilder Plans to Sell; Yard at Risk." *Philadelphia Inquirer*, 14 April, pp. A1–A21.

Watts, John. 1866. *The Facts of the Cotton Famine*. London: Frank Cass.

Webb, Beatrice Potter. 1891. *The Co-operative Movement in Great Britain*. London: Swan Sonnenschein.

Weber, Max. 1958. *The City*. New York: Free Press.

Weigley, Russell F. 1982. "The Border City in Civil War, 1854–1865." In *Philadelphia: A 300-Year History*, edited by Russell F. Weigley, 363–416. New York: W. W. Norton.

Wendt, Henry. 1993. *Global Embrace*. New York: Harper Collins.

Werbner, Pnina. 1990. *The Migration Process*. New York: Berg.

Werly, John M. 1973. "The Irish in Manchester, 1832–49." *Irish Historical Studies* 18:345–358.

Whalen, Carmen Teresa. 2001. *From Puerto Rico to Philadelphia*. Philadelphia: Temple University Press.

Wharton, Joseph. 1875. "National Self-Protection." *Atlantic Monthly* (September): 298–315.

Whiffen, Marcus. 1985. "The Architecture of Sir Charles Barry in Manchester and Neighbourhood." In *Art and Architecture in Victorian Manchester*, edited by John H. G. Archer, 46–64. Manchester: Manchester University Press.

Whiteman, Maxwell. 1975. *Gentlemen in Crisis*. Philadelphia: Union League.

Whitfield, Roy. 1988. "The Double Life of Friedrich Engels." *Manchester Region History Review* 2:13–19.

Who Owns Whom. 1973. *Who Owns Whom: North American Edition*. London: O. W. Roskill.

———. 1974. *Who Owns Whom 1974*. London: O. W. Roskill.

———. 1980. *Who Owns Whom 1980*. London: Dun and Bradstreet.

———. 1991. *Who Owns Whom 1991*. High Wycombe, UK: Dun and Bradstreet.

———. 1998. *Who Owns Whom 1998*. High Wycombe, UK: Dun and Bradstreet.

Wiener, Martin J. 1981. *English Culture and the Decline of the Industrial Spirit, 1850–1980*. Cambridge: Cambridge University Press.

Wilburn, Jean A. 1967. *Biddle's Bank*. New York: Columbia University Press.

Williams, Bill. 1976. *The Making of Manchester Jewry, 1740–1875*. Manchester: Manchester University Press.

———. 1985. "The Anti-Semitism of Tolerance: Middle-Class Manchester and the Jews, 1870–1900." In *City, Class, and Culture*, edited by Alan J. Kidd and K. W. Roberts, 74–102. Manchester: Manchester University Press.

Williams, George. 1994. *The Airline Industry and the Impact of Deregulation*. Brookfield, VT: Ashgate.

Williams, Raymond. 1973. *The Country and the City*. New York: Oxford University Press.

Wilson, Kenneth L., and Alejandro Portes. 1980. "Immigrant Enclaves: An Analysis of the Labor Market Experiences of Cubans in Miami." *American Journal of Sociology* 86:295–319.

Winant, Howard. 2001. *The World Is a Ghetto*. New York: Basic.

Winch, Julie. 2000. "Introduction." In *The Elite of Our People*, edited by Julie Winch, 1–73. University Park: Pennsylvania State University Press.

Wolf, Stephanie Grauman. 1976. *Urban Village: Population, Community, and Family Structure in Germantown, Pennsylvania, 1683–1800*. Princeton, NJ: Princeton University Press.

Wornom, Douglas. 1974. *History, Passenger Train, and Through Car Service: Pennsylvania Railroad, 1849–1947*. Chicago: Owen Davies.

Wright, Esmond. 1986. *Franklin of Philadelphia*. Cambridge, MA: Harvard University Press.

Wynne, Derek, and Justin O'Connor. 1998. "Consumption and the Postmodern City." *Urban Studies* 35:841–864.

Yates, W. Ross. 1987. *Joseph Wharton: Quaker Industrial Pioneer*. Bethlehem, PA: Lehigh University Press.

Zachary, Alan M. 1974. "Social Thought in the Philadelphia Leadership Community, 1800–1840." Ph.D. thesis, Northwestern University.

Zecker, Robert M. 1998. "All Our Own Kind Here": The Creation of a Slovak-American Community in Philadelphia, 1890–1945." Ph.D. thesis, University of Pennsylvania.

Zeitlin, Jonathan. 1983. "The Labour Strategies of British Engineering Employers, 1890–1922." In *Managerial Strategies and Industrial Relations*, edited by Howard F. Gospel and Craig R. Littler, 25–54. London: Heineman.

Zeitlin, Jonathan, and Peter Totterdill. 1989. "Markets, Technology, and Local Intervention: The Case of Clothing." In *Reversing Industrial Decline?* edited by Paul Hirst and Jonathan Zeitlin, 155–190. Oxford: Berg.

Zhou, Min. 1992. *Chinatown*. Philadelphia: Temple University Press.

Zukin, Sharon. 1989. *Loft Living*. New Brunswick, NJ: Rutgers University Press.

———. 1991. *Landscapes of Power*. Berkeley: University of California Press.

———. 1995. *The Cultures of Cities*. Cambridge, MA: Blackwell.

Zunz, Olivier. 1982. *The Changing Face of Inequality*. Chicago: University of Chicago Press.

Index

Jerome I. **Hodos** is Associate Professor of Sociology at Franklin & Marshall College. He is a contributor to *Social Capital in the City* (Temple) and *The City in American Political Development.*